POCKET WORLD ATLAS

IN ASSOCIATION WITH
THE ROYAL GEOGRAPHICAL SOCIETY
WITH THE INSTITUTE OF BRITISH GEOGRAPHERS

CONTENTS

WORLD MAPS

EUROPE

ASIA

Published in Great Britain in 2006 by Philip's,
a division of Octopus Publishing Group Limited,
2–4 Heron Quays, London E14 4JP

Cartography by Philip's

ISBN-13 978-0-540-09074-7
ISBN-10 0-540-09074-3

A CIP catalogue record for this book is available from the British Library.

Printed in Hong Kong

Details of other Philip's titles and services can be found on our website at: www.philips-maps.co.uk

Philip's World Atlases are published in association with The Royal Geographical Society (with The Institute of British Geographers).

The Society was founded in 1830 and given a Royal Charter in 1859 for 'the advancement of geographical science'. Today it is a leading world centre for geographical learning – supporting education, teaching, research and expeditions, and promoting public understanding of the subject.

Further information about the Society and how to join may be found on its website at: www.rgs.org

FLIGHT PATHS

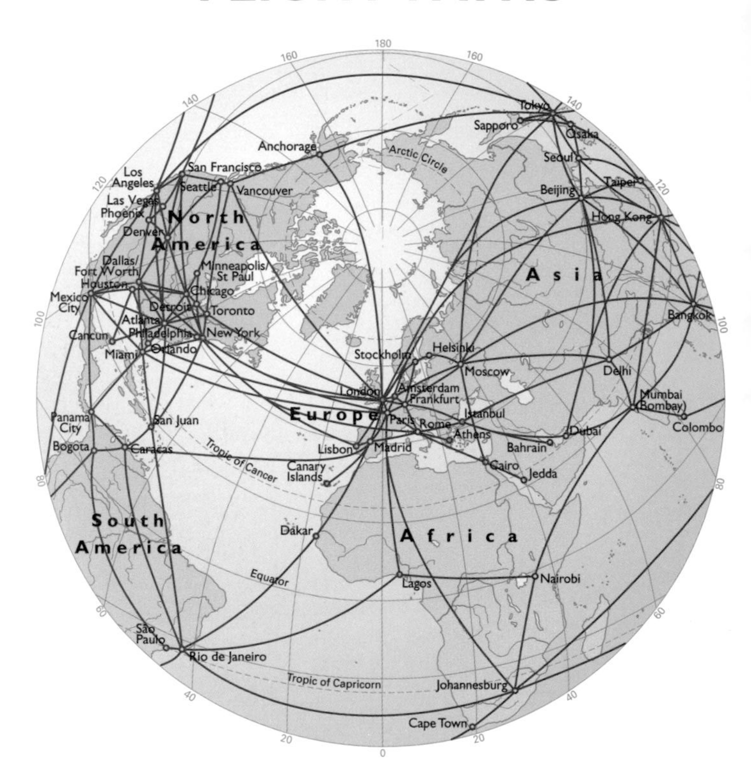

The flight paths shown on the maps above usually follow the shortest, most direct route from A to B, known as the *great-circle route*. A great circle is any circle that divides the globe into equal halves. Aircraft do not always fly along great-circle routes, however. Lack of search and rescue and emergency landing provisions, together with limits on fuel consumption and minimum flying altitudes, mean that commercial aircraft do not usually fly across Antarctica.

WORLD'S BUSIEST AIRPORTS

TOTAL NUMBER OF PASSENGERS IN MILLIONS (2005)

Airport	Passengers
ATLANTA HARTSFIELD INTL. (ATL)	85.9
CHICAGO O'HARE INTL. (ORD)	76.5
LONDON HEATHROW (LHR)	67.9
TOKYO HANEDA (HND)	63.3
LOS ANGELES INTL. (LAX)	61.5
DALLAS FORT WORTH INTL. (DFW)	59.9
PARIS CHARLES DE GAULLE (CDG)	53.8
FRANKFURT INTL. (FRA)	52.2
AMSTERDAM SCHIPHOL (AMS)	39.5

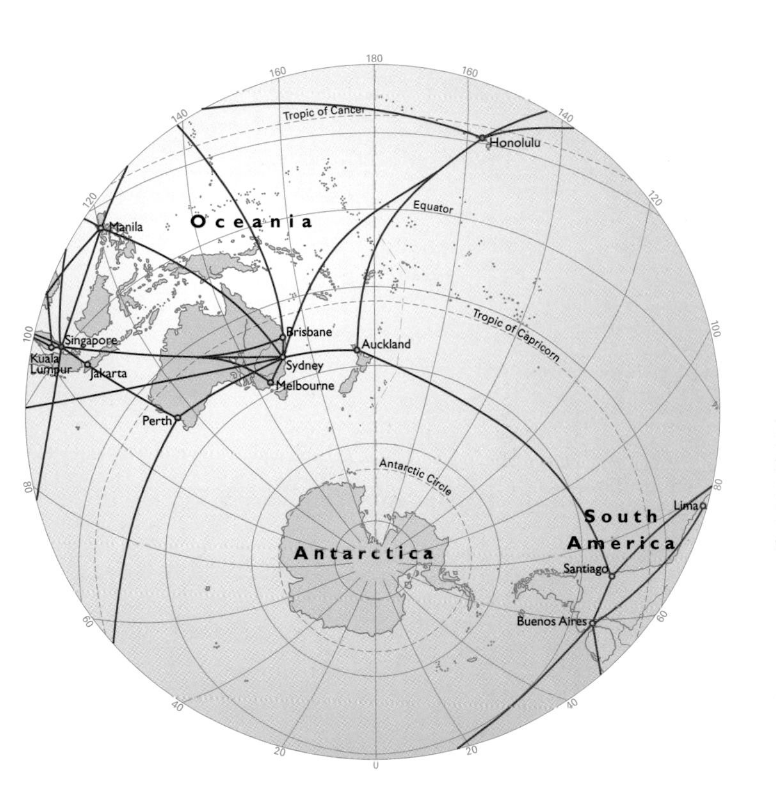

FLIGHT TIMES FROM LONDON

ATHENS	*4hrs*	*05mins*
AUCKLAND	*24hrs*	*20mins*
BANGKOK	*14hrs*	*30mins*
BUENOS AIRES	*14hrs*	*20mins*
HONG KONG	*14hrs*	*10mins*
LOS ANGELES	*12hrs*	*00mins*
MOSCOW	*3hrs*	*50mins*
MUMBAI (BOMBAY)	*11hrs*	*15mins*
NEW YORK	*6hrs*	*50mins*

FLIGHT TIMES FROM NEW YORK

FRANKFURT	*8hrs*	*35mins*
JOHANNESBURG	*17hrs*	*45mins*
MEXICO CITY	*5hrs*	*45mins*
PARIS	*8hrs*	*15mins*
ROME	*9hrs*	*35mins*
SANTIAGO	*12hrs*	*55mins*
SINGAPORE	*23hrs*	*10mins*
TOKYO	*14hrs*	*35mins*
VANCOUVER	*7hrs*	*25mins*

INTERNATIONAL ORGANIZATIONS

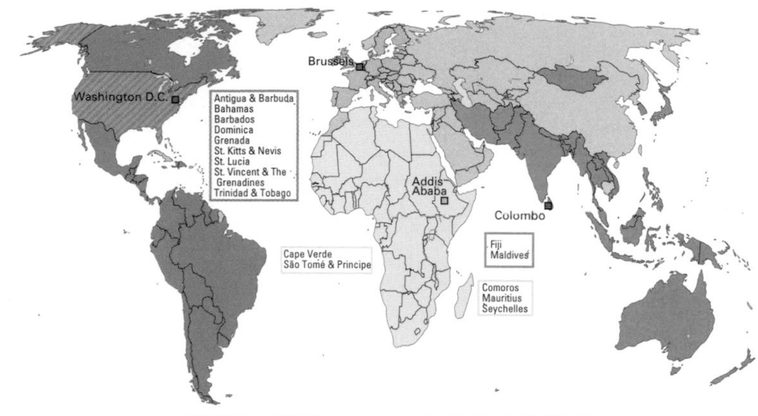

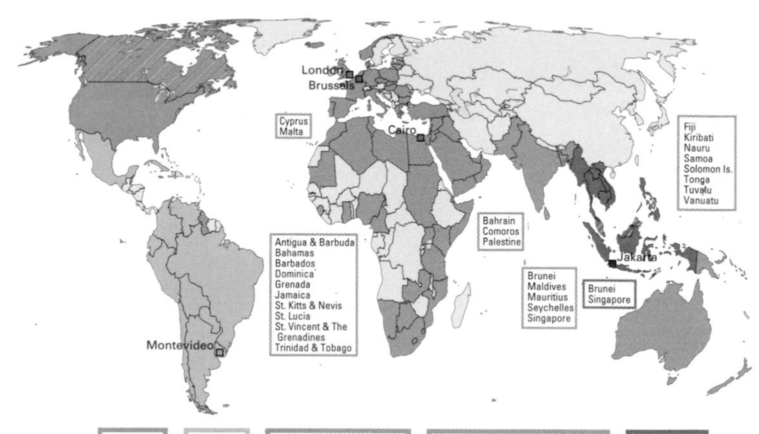

GLOSSARY OF ACRONYMS

ACP African-Caribbean-Pacific
APEC Asia-Pacific Economic Co-operation
ASEAN Association of South-east Asian Nations
AU African Union
EU European Union
G8 Group of 'Eight'
LAIA Latin American Integration Association
NATO North Atlantic Treaty Organization
OAS Organization of American States
OECD Organization for Economic Co-operation and Development
OPEC Oganization for Petroleum Exporting Countries

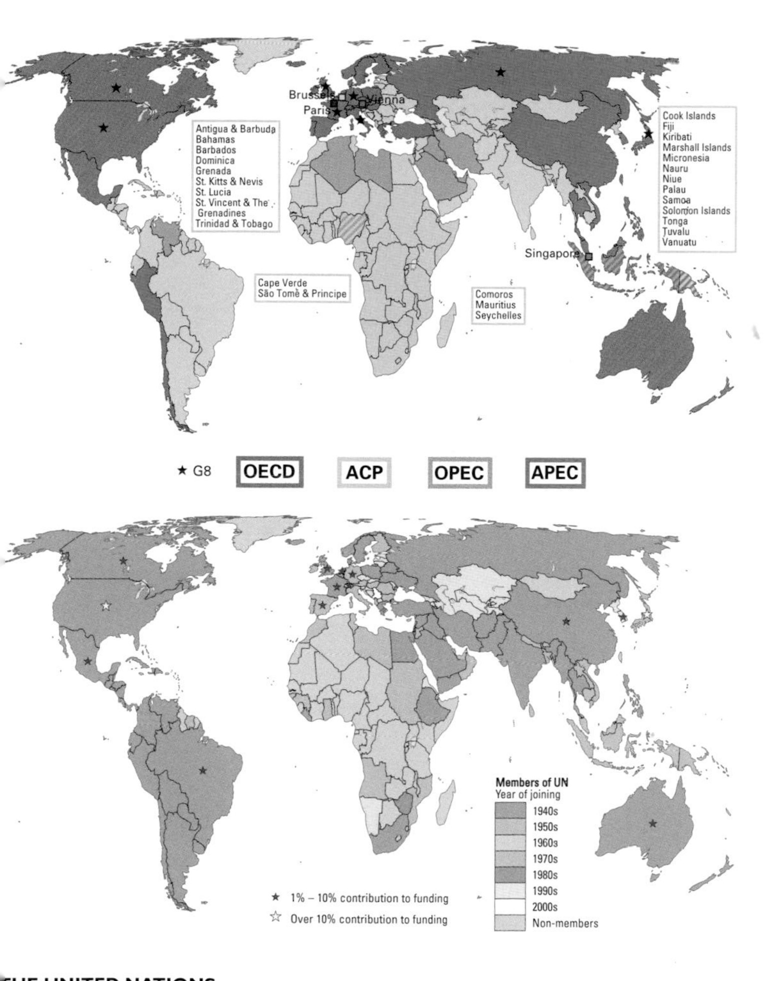

THE UNITED NATIONS

Created in 1945 to promote peace and co-operation and based in New York, the UN is the world's largest international organization. The UN annual budget for 2005 was US$1.8 billion. Contributions are assessed by the members' ability to pay, with the maximum 22% of the total (USA's share), and the minimum 0.01 %. The European Union pays over 37% of the budget. From the original 51, membership of the UN has now grown to 192. Recent additions include East Timor, Switzerland and Montenegro. There are only two independent states which are not members – Taiwan and the Vatican City.

GAZETTEER OF NATIONS

Listed below are the principal countries and territories of the world. The area figures give the total area of land, inland water and ice. The population figures are 2005 estimates where available. The annual income is the Gross Domestic Product per capita in US dollars. Gross Domestic Product per capita has been measured using the purchasing power parity method; this enables comparisons to be made between countries through their purchasing power (in US dollars), showing real price levels of goods and services rather than using currency exchange rates. The figures are the latest available, usually 2005 estimates.

AFGHANISTAN

AREA 652,090 sq km [251,772 sq mi]
POPULATION 29,929,000
CAPITAL Kabul
GOVERNMENT Transitional
ANNUAL INCOME US$800
CURRENCY Afghani = 100 puls

ALBANIA

AREA 28,748 sq km [11,100 sq mi]
POPULATION 3,563,000
CAPITAL Tirana
GOVERNMENT Multiparty republic
ANNUAL INCOME US$4,900
CURRENCY Lek = 100 qindars

ALGERIA

AREA 2,381,741 sq km [919,590 sq mi]
POPULATION 32,532,000
CAPITAL Algiers
GOVERNMENT Socialist republic
ANNUAL INCOME US$7,300
CURRENCY Algerian dinar = 100 centimes

ANDORRA

AREA 468 sq km [181 sq mi]
POPULATION 71,000
CAPITAL Andorra La Vella
GOVERNMENT Parliamentary co-princedom
ANNUAL INCOME US$26,800
CURRENCY Euro = 100 cents

ANGOLA

AREA 1,246,700 sq km [481,351 sq mi]
POPULATION 11,191,000
CAPITAL Luanda
GOVERNMENT Multiparty republic
ANNUAL INCOME US$2,500
CURRENCY Kwanza = 100 lwei

ANTIGUA & BARBUDA

AREA 442 sq km [171 sq mi]
POPULATION 69,000
CAPITAL St John's
GOVERNMENT Constitutional monarchy
ANNUAL INCOME US$11,000
CURRENCY East Caribbean dollar = 100 cents

ARGENTINA

AREA 2,780,400 sq km [1,073,512 sq mi]
POPULATION 39,538,000
CAPITAL Buenos Aires
GOVERNMENT Federal republic
ANNUAL INCOME US$13,600
CURRENCY Argentine peso = 10,000 australs

ARMENIA

AREA 29,800 sq km [11,506 sq mi]
POPULATION 2,983,000
CAPITAL Yerevan
GOVERNMENT Multiparty republic
ANNUAL INCOME US$5,100
CURRENCY Dram = 100 couma

AUSTRALIA

AREA 7,741,220 sq km [2,988,885 sq mi]
POPULATION 20,090,000
CAPITAL Canberra
GOVERNMENT Federal constitutional monarchy
ANNUAL INCOME US$32,000
CURRENCY Australian dollar = 100 cents

AUSTRIA

AREA 83,859 sq km [32,378 sq mi]
POPULATION 8,185,000
CAPITAL Vienna
GOVERNMENT Federal republic
ANNUAL INCOME US$32,900
CURRENCY Euro = 100 cents

AZERBAIJAN

AREA 86,600 sq km [33,436 sq mi]
POPULATION 7,912,000
CAPITAL Baku
GOVERNMENT Federal multiparty republic
ANNUAL INCOME US$4,600
CURRENCY Azerbaijani manat = 100 gopik

BAHAMAS

AREA 13,878 sq km [5,358 sq mi]
POPULATION 302,000 **CAPITAL** Nassau
GOVERNMENT Constitutional parliamentary democracy
ANNUAL INCOME US$18,800
CURRENCY Bahamian dollar = 100 cents

BAHRAIN

AREA 694 sq km [268 sq mi]
POPULATION 688,000 **CAPITAL** Manama
GOVERNMENT Monarchy (emirate) with a cabinet appointed by the Emir
ANNUAL INCOME US$20,500
CURRENCY Bahrain dinar = 1,000 fils

BANGLADESH

AREA 143,998 sq km [55,598 sq mi]
POPULATION 144,320,000
CAPITAL Dhaka
GOVERNMENT Multiparty republic
ANNUAL INCOME US$2,100
CURRENCY Taka = 100 paisas

BARBADOS

AREA 430 sq km [166 sq mi]
POPULATION 279,000
CAPITAL Bridgetown
GOVERNMENT Parliamentary democracy
ANNUAL INCOME US$17,300
CURRENCY Barbados dollar = 100 cents

BELARUS

AREA 207,600 sq km [80,154 sq mi]
POPULATION 10,300,000
CAPITAL Minsk
GOVERNMENT Multiparty republic
ANNUAL INCOME US$7,600
CURRENCY Belarusian rouble = 100 kopecks

BELGIUM

AREA 30,528 sq km [11,787 sq mi]
POPULATION 10,364,000
CAPITAL Brussels
GOVERNMENT Federal constitutional monarchy
ANNUAL INCOME US$31,800
CURRENCY Euro = 100 cents

BELIZE

AREA 22,966 sq km [8,867 sq mi]
POPULATION 279,000
CAPITAL Belmopan
GOVERNMENT Constitutional monarchy
ANNUAL INCOME US$6,800
CURRENCY Belizean dollar = 100 cents

BENIN

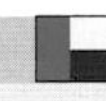

AREA 112,622 sq km [43,483 sq mi]
POPULATION 7,460,000
CAPITAL Porto-Novo
GOVERNMENT Multiparty republic
ANNUAL INCOME US$1,200
CURRENCY CFA franc = 100 centimes

BHUTAN

AREA 47,000 sq km [18,147 sq mi]
POPULATION 2,232,000
CAPITAL Thimphu
GOVERNMENT Constitutional monarchy
ANNUAL INCOME US$1,400
CURRENCY Ngultrum = 100 chetrum

BOLIVIA

AREA 1,098,581 sq km [424,162 sq mi]
POPULATION 8,858,000 **CAPITAL** La Paz (seat of government); Sucre (legal capital/seat of judiciary)
GOVERNMENT Multiparty republic
ANNUAL INCOME US$2,700
CURRENCY Boliviano = 100 centavos

BOSNIA-HERZEGOVINA

AREA 51,197 sq km [19,767 sq mi]
POPULATION 4,025,000 **CAPITAL** Sarajevo
GOVERNMENT Federal republic
ANNUAL INCOME US$6,800
CURRENCY Convertible marka = 100 convertible pfenniga

BOTSWANA

AREA 581,730 sq km [224,606 sq mi]
POPULATION 1,640,000
CAPITAL Gaborone
GOVERNMENT Multiparty republic
ANNUAL INCOME US$10,100
CURRENCY Pula = 100 thebe

BRAZIL

AREA 8,514,215 sq km [3,287,338 sq mi]
POPULATION 186,113,000
CAPITAL Brasília
GOVERNMENT Federal republic
ANNUAL INCOME US$8,500
CURRENCY Real = 100 centavos

BRUNEI

AREA 5,765 sq km [2,226 sq mi]
POPULATION 372,000
CAPITAL Bandar Seri Begawan
GOVERNMENT Constitutional sultanate
ANNUAL INCOME US$23,600
CURRENCY Bruneian dollar = 100 cents

BULGARIA

AREA 110,912 sq km [42,823 sq mi]
POPULATION 7,450,000
CAPITAL Sofia
GOVERNMENT Multiparty republic
ANNUAL INCOME US$9,000
CURRENCY Lev = 100 stotinki

BURKINA FASO

AREA 274,200 sq km [105,791 sq mi]
POPULATION 13,925,000
CAPITAL Ouagadougou
GOVERNMENT Multiparty republic
ANNUAL INCOME US$1,200
CURRENCY CFA franc = 100 centimes

BURMA (MYANMAR)

AREA 676,578 sq km [261,227 sq mi]
POPULATION 42,909,000 **CAPITAL** Rangoon (Yangon); Pyinmana (administrative capital)
GOVERNMENT Military regime
ANNUAL INCOME US$1,800
CURRENCY Kyat = 100 pyas

BURUNDI

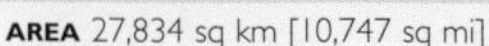

AREA 27,834 sq km [10,747 sq mi]
POPULATION 6,371,000
CAPITAL Bujumbura
GOVERNMENT Republic
ANNUAL INCOME US$700
CURRENCY Burundi franc = 100 centimes

CAMBODIA

AREA 181,035 sq km [69,898 sq mi]
POPULATION 13,607,000
CAPITAL Phnom Penh
GOVERNMENT Constitutional monarchy
ANNUAL INCOME US$2,100
CURRENCY Riel = 100 sen

CAMEROON

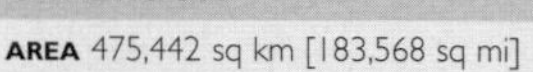

AREA 475,442 sq km [183,568 sq mi]
POPULATION 16,380,000
CAPITAL Yaoundé
GOVERNMENT Multiparty republic
ANNUAL INCOME US$2,000
CURRENCY CFA franc = 100 centimes

CANADA

AREA 9,970,610 sq km [3,849,653 sq mi]
POPULATION 32,805,000 **CAPITAL** Ottawa
GOVERNMENT Federal multiparty constitutional monarchy
ANNUAL INCOME US$32,800
CURRENCY Canadian dollar = 100 cents

CAPE VERDE

AREA 4,033 sq km [1,557 sq mi]
POPULATION 418,000
CAPITAL Praia
GOVERNMENT Multiparty republic
ANNUAL INCOME US$6,200
CURRENCY Cape Verde escudo = 100 centavos

CENTRAL AFRICAN REPUBLIC

AREA 622,984 sq km [240,534 sq mi]
POPULATION 3,800,000
CAPITAL Bangui
GOVERNMENT Multiparty republic
ANNUAL INCOME US$1,200
CURRENCY CFA franc = 100 centimes

CHAD

AREA 1,284,000 sq km [495,752 sq mi]
POPULATION 9,826,000
CAPITAL Ndjamena
GOVERNMENT Multiparty republic
ANNUAL INCOME US$1,900
CURRENCY CFA franc = 100 centimes

CHILE

AREA 756,626 sq km [292,133 sq mi]
POPULATION 15,981,000
CAPITAL Santiago
GOVERNMENT Multiparty republic
ANNUAL INCOME US$11,300
CURRENCY Chilean peso = 100 centavos

CHINA

AREA 9,596,961 sq km [3,705,387 sq mi]
POPULATION 1,306,314,000
CAPITAL Beijing
GOVERNMENT Single-party Communist republic
ANNUAL INCOME US$6,200
CURRENCY Renminbi yuan = 10 jiao = 100 fen

COLOMBIA

AREA 1,138,914 sq km [439,735 sq mi]
POPULATION 42,954,000
CAPITAL Bogotá
GOVERNMENT Multiparty republic
ANNUAL INCOME US$7,100
CURRENCY Colombian peso = 100 centavos

COMOROS

AREA 2,235 sq km [863 sq mi]
POPULATION 671,000
CAPITAL Moroni
GOVERNMENT Multiparty republic
ANNUAL INCOME US$600
CURRENCY CFA franc = 100 centimes

CONGO

AREA 342,000 sq km [132,046 sq mi]
POPULATION 3,039,000
CAPITAL Brazzaville
GOVERNMENT Military regime
ANNUAL INCOME US$800
CURRENCY CFA franc = 100 centimes

CONGO (DEM. REP. OF THE)

AREA 2,344,858 sq km [905,350 sq mi]
POPULATION 60,086,000
CAPITAL Kinshasa
GOVERNMENT Single-party republic
ANNUAL INCOME US$800
CURRENCY Congolese franc = 100 centimes

COSTA RICA

AREA 51,100 sq km [19,730 sq mi]
POPULATION 4,016,000
CAPITAL San José
GOVERNMENT Multiparty republic
ANNUAL INCOME US$10,000
CURRENCY Costa Rican colón = 100 céntimos

CROATIA

AREA 56,538 sq km [21,829 sq mi]
POPULATION 4,496,000
CAPITAL Zagreb
GOVERNMENT Multiparty republic
ANNUAL INCOME US$11,600
CURRENCY Kuna = 100 lipas

CUBA

AREA 110,861 sq km [42,803 sq mi]
POPULATION 11,347,000
CAPITAL Havana
GOVERNMENT Socialist republic
ANNUAL INCOME US$3,300
CURRENCY Cuban peso = 100 centavos

CYPRUS

AREA 9,251 sq km [3,572 sq mi]
POPULATION 780,000
CAPITAL Nicosia
GOVERNMENT Multiparty republic
ANNUAL INCOME US$21,600
CURRENCY Cypriot pound = 100 cents

CZECH REPUBLIC

AREA 78,866 sq km [30,450 sq mi]
POPULATION 10,241,000
CAPITAL Prague
GOVERNMENT Multiparty republic
ANNUAL INCOME US$18,100
CURRENCY Czech koruna = 100 haler

DENMARK

AREA 43,094 sq km [16,639 sq mi]
POPULATION 5,432,000
CAPITAL Copenhagen
GOVERNMENT Parliamentary monarchy
ANNUAL INCOME US$33,500
CURRENCY Danish krone = 100 øre

DJIBOUTI

AREA 23,200 sq km [8,958 sq mi]
POPULATION 477,000
CAPITAL Djibouti
GOVERNMENT Multiparty republic
ANNUAL INCOME US$1,300
CURRENCY Djiboutian franc = 100 centimes

DOMINICA

AREA 751 sq km [290 sq mi]
POPULATION 69,000
CAPITAL Roseau
GOVERNMENT Parliamentary democracy
ANNUAL INCOME US$5,500
CURRENCY East Caribbean dollar = 100 cents

DOMINICAN REPUBLIC

AREA 48,511 sq km [18,730 sq mi]
POPULATION 8,950,000
CAPITAL Santo Domingo
GOVERNMENT Multiparty republic
ANNUAL INCOME US$6,500
CURRENCY Dominican peso = 100 centavos

EAST TIMOR

AREA 14,874 sq km [5,743 sq mi]
POPULATION 1,041,000
CAPITAL Dili
GOVERNMENT Republic
ANNUAL INCOME US$400
CURRENCY US dollar = 100 cents

ECUADOR

AREA 283,561 sq km [109,483 sq mi]
POPULATION 13,364,000
CAPITAL Quito
GOVERNMENT Multiparty republic
ANNUAL INCOME US$3,900
CURRENCY US dollar = 100 cents

EGYPT

AREA 1,001,449 sq km [386,659 sq mi]
POPULATION 77,506,000
CAPITAL Cairo
GOVERNMENT Republic
ANNUAL INCOME US$4,400
CURRENCY Egyptian pound = 100 piastres

EL SALVADOR

AREA 21,041 sq km [8,124 sq mi]
POPULATION 6,705,000
CAPITAL San Salvador
GOVERNMENT Republic
ANNUAL INCOME US$5,100
CURRENCY US dollar = 100 cents

EQUATORIAL GUINEA

AREA 28,051 sq km [10,830 sq mi]
POPULATION 536,000
CAPITAL Malabo
GOVERNMENT Multiparty republic (transitional)
ANNUAL INCOME US$2,700
CURRENCY CFA franc = 100 centimes

ERITREA

AREA 117,600 sq km [45,405 sq mi]
POPULATION 4,562,000
CAPITAL Asmara
GOVERNMENT Transitional government
ANNUAL INCOME US$1,000
CURRENCY Nakfa = 100 cents

ESTONIA

AREA 45,100 sq km [17,413 sq mi]
POPULATION 1,333,000
CAPITAL Tallinn
GOVERNMENT Multiparty republic
ANNUAL INCOME US$16,400
CURRENCY Estonian kroon = 100 senti

ETHIOPIA

AREA 1,104,300 sq km [426,370 sq mi]
POPULATION 73,053,000
CAPITAL Addis Ababa
GOVERNMENT Federation of nine provinces
ANNUAL INCOME US$800
CURRENCY Birr = 100 cents

FIJI ISLANDS

AREA 18,274 sq km [7,056 sq mi]
POPULATION 893,000
CAPITAL Suva
GOVERNMENT Transitional
ANNUAL INCOME US$6,000
CURRENCY Fijian dollar = 100 cents

FINLAND

AREA 338,145 sq km [130,558 sq mi]
POPULATION 5,223,000
CAPITAL Helsinki
GOVERNMENT Multiparty republic
ANNUAL INCOME US$30,300
CURRENCY Euro = 100 cents

FRANCE

AREA 551,500 sq km [212,934 sq mi]
POPULATION 60,656,000
CAPITAL Paris
GOVERNMENT Multiparty republic
ANNUAL INCOME US$29,900
CURRENCY Euro = 100 cents

FRENCH GUIANA

AREA 91,000 sq km [34,749 sq mi]
POPULATION 196,000
CAPITAL Cayenne
GOVERNMENT Overseas department of France
ANNUAL INCOME US$8,300
CURRENCY Euro = 100 cents

FRENCH POLYNESIA

AREA 4,167 sq km [1,544 sq mi]
POPULATION 270,000
CAPITAL Papeete
GOVERNMENT French overseas territory
ANNUAL INCOME US$17,500
CURRENCY French Pacific franc = 100 cents

GABON

AREA 267,668 sq km [103,347 sq mi]
POPULATION 1,389,000
CAPITAL Libreville
GOVERNMENT Multiparty republic
ANNUAL INCOME US$5,800
CURRENCY CFA franc = 100 centimes

GAMBIA, THE

AREA 11,295 sq km [4,361 sq mi]
POPULATION 1,593,000
CAPITAL Banjul
GOVERNMENT Military regime
ANNUAL INCOME US$1,900
CURRENCY Dalasi = 100 butut

GEORGIA

AREA 69,700 sq km [26,911 sq mi]
POPULATION 4,677,000
CAPITAL Tbilisi
GOVERNMENT Multiparty republic
ANNUAL INCOME US$3,400
CURRENCY Lari = 100 tetri

GERMANY

AREA 357,022 sq km [137,846 sq mi]
POPULATION 82,431,000
CAPITAL Berlin
GOVERNMENT Federal multiparty republic
ANNUAL INCOME US$29,700
CURRENCY Euro = 100 cents

GHANA

AREA 238,533 sq km [92,098 sq mi]
POPULATION 21,030,000
CAPITAL Accra
GOVERNMENT Republic
ANNUAL INCOME US$2,500
CURRENCY Cedi = 100 pesewas

GREECE

AREA 131,957 sq km [50,949 sq mi]
POPULATION 10,668,000
CAPITAL Athens
GOVERNMENT Multiparty republic
ANNUAL INCOME US$22,800
CURRENCY Euro = 100 cents

GREENLAND

AREA 2,175,600 sq km [838,999 sq mi]
POPULATION 56,000 **CAPITAL** Nuuk (Godthåb)
GOVERNMENT Self-governing overseas administrative division of Denmark
ANNUAL INCOME US$20,000
CURRENCY Danish krone = 100 øre

GRENADA

AREA 344 sq km [133 sq mi]
POPULATION 90,000
CAPITAL St George's
GOVERNMENT Constitutional monarchy
ANNUAL INCOME US$5,000
CURRENCY East Caribbean dollar = 100 cents

GUADELOUPE

AREA 1,705 sq km [658 sq mi]
POPULATION 449,000
CAPITAL Basse-Terre
GOVERNMENT French overseas territory
ANNUAL INCOME US$7,900
CURRENCY Euro = 100 cents

GUATEMALA

AREA 108,889 sq km [42,042 sq mi]
POPULATION 14,655,000
CAPITAL Guatemala City
GOVERNMENT Republic
ANNUAL INCOME US$4,300
CURRENCY US dollar; Quetzal = 100 centavos

GUINEA

AREA 245,857 sq km [94,925 sq mi]
POPULATION 9,468,000
CAPITAL Conakry
GOVERNMENT Multiparty republic
ANNUAL INCOME US$2,200
CURRENCY Guinean franc = 100 cauris

GUINEA-BISSAU

AREA 36,125 sq km [13,948 sq mi]
POPULATION 1,416,000
CAPITAL Bissau
GOVERNMENT 'Interim' government
ANNUAL INCOME US$800
CURRENCY CFA franc = 100 centimes

GUYANA

AREA 214,969 sq km [83,000 sq mi]
POPULATION 765,000
CAPITAL Georgetown
GOVERNMENT Multiparty republic
ANNUAL INCOME US$3,900
CURRENCY Guyanese dollar = 100 cents

HAITI

AREA 27,750 sq km [10,714 sq mi]
POPULATION 8,122,000
CAPITAL Port-au-Prince
GOVERNMENT Multiparty republic
ANNUAL INCOME US$1,600
CURRENCY Gourde = 100 centimes

HONDURAS

AREA 112,088 sq km [43,277 sq mi]
POPULATION 6,975,000
CAPITAL Tegucigalpa
GOVERNMENT Republic
ANNUAL INCOME US$2,900
CURRENCY Honduran lempira = 100 centavos

HUNGARY

AREA 93,032 sq km [35,920 sq mi]
POPULATION 10,007,000
CAPITAL Budapest
GOVERNMENT Multiparty republic
ANNUAL INCOME US$15,900
CURRENCY Forint = 100 fillér

ICELAND

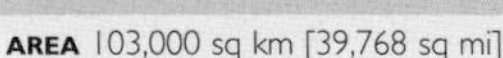

AREA 103,000 sq km [39,768 sq mi]
POPULATION 297,000
CAPITAL Reykjavik
GOVERNMENT Multiparty republic
ANNUAL INCOME US$34,600
CURRENCY Icelandic króna = 100 aurar

INDIA

AREA 3,287,263 sq km [1,269,212 sq mi]
POPULATION 1,080,264,000
CAPITAL New Delhi
GOVERNMENT Multiparty federal republic
ANNUAL INCOME US$3,400
CURRENCY Indian rupee = 100 paisa

INDONESIA

AREA 1,904,569 sq km [735,354 sq mi]
POPULATION 241,974,000
CAPITAL Jakarta
GOVERNMENT Multiparty republic
ANNUAL INCOME US$3,700
CURRENCY Indonesian rupiah = 100 sen

IRAN

AREA 1,648,195 sq km [636,368 sq mi]
POPULATION 68,018,000
CAPITAL Tehran
GOVERNMENT Islamic republic
ANNUAL INCOME US$8,100
CURRENCY Iranian rial = 100 dinars

IRAQ

AREA 438,317 sq km [169,234 sq mi]
POPULATION 26,075,000
CAPITAL Baghdad
GOVERNMENT Republic
ANNUAL INCOME US$3,400
CURRENCY New Iraqi dinar

IRELAND

AREA 70,273 sq km [27,132 sq mi]
POPULATION 4,016,000
CAPITAL Dublin
GOVERNMENT Multiparty republic
ANNUAL INCOME US$34,100
CURRENCY Euro = 100 cents

ISRAEL

AREA 20,600 sq km [7,954 sq mi]
POPULATION 6,277,000
CAPITAL Jerusalem
GOVERNMENT Multiparty republic
ANNUAL INCOME US$22,200
CURRENCY New Israeli shekel = 100 agorat

ITALY

AREA 301,318 sq km [116,339 sq mi]
POPULATION 58,103,000
CAPITAL Rome
GOVERNMENT Multiparty republic
ANNUAL INCOME US$28,300
CURRENCY Euro = 100 cents

IVORY COAST (CÔTE D'IVOIRE)

AREA 322,463 sq km [124,503 sq mi]
POPULATION 17,298,000
CAPITAL Yamoussoukro
GOVERNMENT Multiparty republic
ANNUAL INCOME US$1,400
CURRENCY CFA franc = 100 centimes

JAMAICA

AREA 10,991 sq km [4,244 sq mi]
POPULATION 2,732,000
CAPITAL Kingston
GOVERNMENT Constitutional monarchy
ANNUAL INCOME US$4,300
CURRENCY Jamaican dollar = 100 cents

JAPAN

AREA 377,829 sq km [145,880 sq mi]
POPULATION 127,417,000
CAPITAL Tokyo
GOVERNMENT Constitutional monarchy
ANNUAL INCOME US$30,400
CURRENCY Yen = 100 sen

JORDAN

AREA 89,342 sq km [34,495 sq mi]
POPULATION 5,760,000
CAPITAL Amman
GOVERNMENT Constitutional monarchy
ANNUAL INCOME US$4,800
CURRENCY Jordanian dinar = 1,000 fils

KAZAKHSTAN

AREA 2,724,900 sq km [1,052,084 sq mi]
POPULATION 15,186,000
CAPITAL Astana
GOVERNMENT Multiparty republic
ANNUAL INCOME US$8,700
CURRENCY Tenge = 100 tiyn

KENYA

AREA 580,367 sq km [224,080 sq mi]
POPULATION 33,830,000
CAPITAL Nairobi
GOVERNMENT Multiparty republic
ANNUAL INCOME US$1,200
CURRENCY Kenyan shilling = 100 cents

KIRIBATI

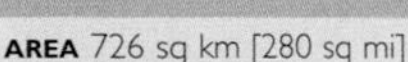

AREA 726 sq km [280 sq mi]
POPULATION 103,000
CAPITAL Tarawa
GOVERNMENT Republic
ANNUAL INCOME US$800
CURRENCY Australian dollar = 100 cents

KOREA, NORTH

AREA 120,538 sq km [46,540 sq mi]
POPULATION 22,912,000
CAPITAL Pyŏngyang
GOVERNMENT Single-party people's republic
ANNUAL INCOME US$1,800
CURRENCY North Korean won = 100 chon

KOREA, SOUTH

AREA 99,268 sq km [38,327 sq mi]
POPULATION 48,423,000
CAPITAL Seoul
GOVERNMENT Multiparty republic
ANNUAL INCOME US$20,300
CURRENCY South Korean won = 100 chon

KUWAIT

AREA 17,818 sq km [6,880 sq mi]
POPULATION 2,336,000
CAPITAL Kuwait City
GOVERNMENT Constitutional monarchy
ANNUAL INCOME US$22,100
CURRENCY Kuwaiti dinar = 1,000 fils

KYRGYZSTAN

AREA 199,900 sq km [77,181 sq mi]
POPULATION 5,146,000
CAPITAL Bishkek
GOVERNMENT Multiparty republic
ANNUAL INCOME US$1,800
CURRENCY Kyrgyzstani som = 100 tyiyn

LAOS

AREA 236,800 sq km [91,428 sq mi]
POPULATION 6,217,000
CAPITAL Vientiane
GOVERNMENT Single-party republic
ANNUAL INCOME US$1,900
CURRENCY Kip = 100 at

LATVIA

AREA 64,600 sq km [24,942 sq mi]
POPULATION 2,290,000
CAPITAL Riga
GOVERNMENT Multiparty republic
ANNUAL INCOME US$12,800
CURRENCY Latvian lat = 10 santimi

LEBANON

AREA 10,400 sq km [4,015 sq mi]
POPULATION 3,826,000
CAPITAL Beirut
GOVERNMENT Multiparty republic
ANNUAL INCOME US$5,100
CURRENCY Lebanese pound = 100 piastres

LESOTHO

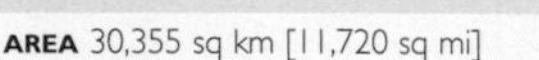

AREA 30,355 sq km [11,720 sq mi]
POPULATION 1,867,000
CAPITAL Maseru
GOVERNMENT Constitutional monarchy
ANNUAL INCOME US$3,300
CURRENCY Loti = 100 lisente

LIBERIA

AREA 111,369 sq km [43,000 sq mi]
POPULATION 3,482,000
CAPITAL Monrovia
GOVERNMENT Multiparty republic
ANNUAL INCOME US$700
CURRENCY Liberian dollar = 100 cents

LIBYA

AREA 1,759,540 sq km [679,358 sq mi]
POPULATION 5,766,000
CAPITAL Tripoli
GOVERNMENT Single-party socialist state
ANNUAL INCOME US$8,400
CURRENCY Libyan dinar = 1,000 dirhams

LIECHTENSTEIN

AREA 160 sq km [62 sq mi]
POPULATION 34,000 **CAPITAL** Vaduz
GOVERNMENT Hereditary constitutional monarchy
ANNUAL INCOME US$25,000
CURRENCY Swiss franc = 100 centimes

LITHUANIA

AREA 65,200 sq km [25,174 sq mi]
POPULATION 3,597,000
CAPITAL Vilnius
GOVERNMENT Multiparty republic
ANNUAL INCOME US$13,700
CURRENCY Litas = 100 centai

LUXEMBOURG

AREA 2,586 sq km [998 sq mi]
POPULATION 469,000 **CAPITAL** Luxembourg
GOVERNMENT Constitutional monarchy (Grand Duchy)
ANNUAL INCOME US$62,700
CURRENCY Euro = 100 cents

MACEDONIA (FYROM)

AREA 25,713 sq km [9,928 sq mi]
POPULATION 2,045,000
CAPITAL Skopje
GOVERNMENT Multiparty republic
ANNUAL INCOME US$7,400
CURRENCY Macedonian denar = 100 paras

MADAGASCAR

AREA 587,041 sq km [226,657 sq mi]
POPULATION 18,040,000
CAPITAL Antananarivo
GOVERNMENT Republic
ANNUAL INCOME US$900
CURRENCY Malagasy franc = 100 centimes

MALAWI

AREA 118,484 sq km [45,747 sq mi]
POPULATION 12,159,000
CAPITAL Lilongwe
GOVERNMENT Multiparty republic
ANNUAL INCOME US$600
CURRENCY Malawian kwacha = 100 tambala

MALAYSIA

AREA 329,758 sq km [127,320 sq mi]
POPULATION 23,953,000 **CAPITAL** Kuala Lumpur; Putrajaya (administrative capital awaiting completion)
GOVERNMENT Federal constitutional monarchy
ANNUAL INCOME US$10,400
CURRENCY Ringgit = 100 cents

MALDIVES

AREA 298 sq km [115 sq mi]
POPULATION 349,000
CAPITAL Malé
GOVERNMENT Republic
ANNUAL INCOME US$3,900
CURRENCY Rufiyaa = 100 laari

MALI

AREA 1,240,192 sq km [478,838 sq mi]
POPULATION 12,292,000
CAPITAL Bamako
GOVERNMENT Multiparty republic
ANNUAL INCOME US$1,000
CURRENCY CFA franc = 100 centimes

MALTA

AREA 316 sq km [122 sq mi]
POPULATION 399,000
CAPITAL Valletta
GOVERNMENT Multiparty republic
ANNUAL INCOME US$18,800
CURRENCY Maltese lira = 100 cents

MARSHALL ISLANDS

AREA 181 sq km [70 sq mi]
POPULATION 59,000 **CAPITAL** Majuro
GOVERNMENT Constitutional government in free association with the US
ANNUAL INCOME US$1,600
CURRENCY US dollar = 100 cents

MARTINIQUE

AREA 1,102 sq km [425 sq mi]
POPULATION 433,000
CAPITAL Fort-de-France
GOVERNMENT Overseas department of France
ANNUAL INCOME US$14,400
CURRENCY Euro = 100 cents

MAURITANIA

AREA 1,025,520 sq km [395,953 sq mi]
POPULATION 3,087,000
CAPITAL Nouakchott
GOVERNMENT Multiparty Islamic republic
ANNUAL INCOME US$2,000
CURRENCY Ouguiya = 5 khoums

MAURITIUS

AREA 2,040 sq km [788 sq mi]
POPULATION 1,231,000
CAPITAL Port Louis
GOVERNMENT Multiparty democracy
ANNUAL INCOME US$13,300
CURRENCY Mauritian rupee = 100 cents

MEXICO

AREA 1,958,201 sq km [756,061 sq mi]
POPULATION 106,203,000
CAPITAL Mexico City
GOVERNMENT Federal republic
ANNUAL INCOME US$10,000
CURRENCY Mexican peso = 100 centavos

MICRONESIA, FED. STATES OF

AREA 702 sq km [271 sq mi]
POPULATION 108,000 **CAPITAL** Palikir
GOVERNMENT Constitutional government in free association with the US
ANNUAL INCOME US$2,000
CURRENCY US dollar = 100 cents

MOLDOVA

AREA 33,851 sq km [13,070 sq mi]
POPULATION 4,455,000
CAPITAL Chişinău
GOVERNMENT Multiparty republic
ANNUAL INCOME US$2,100
CURRENCY Moldovan leu = 100 bani

MONACO

AREA 1 sq km [0.4 sq mi]
POPULATION 32,000
CAPITAL Monaco
GOVERNMENT Constitutional monarchy
ANNUAL INCOME US$27,000
CURRENCY Euro = 100 cents

MONGOLIA

AREA 1,566,500 sq km [604,826 sq mi]
POPULATION 2,791,000
CAPITAL Ulan Bator
GOVERNMENT Multiparty republic
ANNUAL INCOME US$2,200
CURRENCY Tugrik = 100 möngös

MONTENEGRO

AREA 14,026 sq km [5,415 sq mi]
POPULATION 630,548
CAPITAL Podgorica
GOVERNMENT Republic
ANNUAL INCOME US$3,800
CURRENCY Euro = 100 cents

MOROCCO

AREA 446,550 sq km [172,413 sq mi]
POPULATION 32,726,000
CAPITAL Rabat
GOVERNMENT Constitutional monarchy
ANNUAL INCOME US$4,300
CURRENCY Moroccan dirham = 100 centimes

MOZAMBIQUE

AREA 801,590 sq km [309,494 sq mi]
POPULATION 19,407,000
CAPITAL Maputo
GOVERNMENT Multiparty republic
ANNUAL INCOME US$1,300
CURRENCY Metical = 100 centavos

NAMIBIA

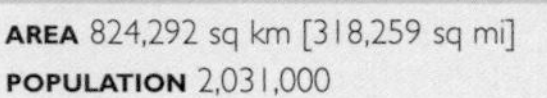

AREA 824,292 sq km [318,259 sq mi]
POPULATION 2,031,000
CAPITAL Windhoek
GOVERNMENT Multiparty republic
ANNUAL INCOME US$7,800
CURRENCY Namibian dollar = 100 cents

NAURU

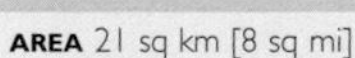

AREA 21 sq km [8 sq mi]
POPULATION 13,000
CAPITAL Yaren
GOVERNMENT Republic
ANNUAL INCOME US$5,000
CURRENCY Australian dollar = 100 cents

NEPAL

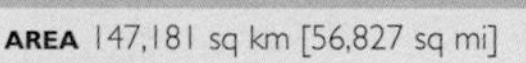

AREA 147,181 sq km [56,827 sq mi]
POPULATION 27,677,000
CAPITAL Katmandu
GOVERNMENT Constitutional monarchy
ANNUAL INCOME US$1,500
CURRENCY Nepalese rupee = 100 paisa

NETHERLANDS

AREA 41,526 sq km [16,033 sq mi]
POPULATION 16,407,000 **CAPITAL** Amsterdam; The Hague (seat of government)
GOVERNMENT Constitutional monarchy
ANNUAL INCOME US$30,500
CURRENCY Euro = 100 cents

NETHERLANDS ANTILLES

AREA 800 sq km [309 sq mi]
POPULATION 220,000 **CAPITAL** Willemstad
GOVERNMENT Parliamentary democracy
ANNUAL INCOME US$11,400
CURRENCY Netherlands Antillean gilder = 100 cents

NEW CALEDONIA

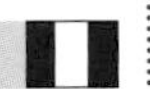

AREA 18,575 sq km [7,172 sq mi]
POPULATION 216,000
CAPITAL Nouméa
GOVERNMENT French overseas territory
ANNUAL INCOME US$15,000
CURRENCY French Pacific franc = 100 cents

NEW ZEALAND

AREA 270,534 sq km [104,453 sq mi]
POPULATION 4,035,000
CAPITAL Wellington
GOVERNMENT Constitutional monarchy
ANNUAL INCOME US$24,100
CURRENCY New Zealand dollar = 100 cents

NICARAGUA

AREA 129,494 sq km [50,193 sq mi]
POPULATION 5,465,000 **CAPITAL** Managua
GOVERNMENT Multiparty republic
ANNUAL INCOME US$2,800
CURRENCY Córdoba oro (gold córdoba) = 100 centavos

NIGER

AREA 1,267,000 sq km [489,189 sq mi]
POPULATION 11,666,000
CAPITAL Niamey
GOVERNMENT Multiparty republic
ANNUAL INCOME US$900
CURRENCY CFA franc = 100 centimes

NIGERIA

AREA 923,768 sq km [356,667 sq mi]
POPULATION 128,772,000
CAPITAL Abuja
GOVERNMENT Federal multiparty republic
ANNUAL INCOME US$1,000
CURRENCY Naira = 100 kobo

NORWAY

AREA 323,877 sq km [125,049 sq mi]
POPULATION 4,593,000
CAPITAL Oslo
GOVERNMENT Constitutional monarchy
ANNUAL INCOME US$42,400
CURRENCY Norwegian krone = 100 ore

OMAN

AREA 309,500 sq km [119,498 sq mi]
POPULATION 3,002,000 **CAPITAL** Muscat
GOVERNMENT Monarchy with consultative council
ANNUAL INCOME US$13,400
CURRENCY Omani rial = 100 baizas

PAKISTAN

AREA 796,095 sq km [307,372 sq mi]
POPULATION 162,420,000
CAPITAL Islamabad
GOVERNMENT Military regime
ANNUAL INCOME US$2,400
CURRENCY Pakistani rupee = 100 paisa

PALAU

AREA 459 sq km [177 sq mi]
POPULATION 20,000 **CAPITAL** Koror
GOVERNMENT Constitutional government in free association with the US
ANNUAL INCOME US$9,000
CURRENCY US dollar = 100 cents

PANAMA

AREA 75,517 sq km [29,157 sq mi]
POPULATION 3,039,000
CAPITAL Panamá
GOVERNMENT Multiparty republic
ANNUAL INCOME US$7,300
CURRENCY US dollar; Balboa = 100 centésimos

PAPUA NEW GUINEA

AREA 462,840 sq km [178,703 sq mi]
POPULATION 5,545,000
CAPITAL Port Moresby
GOVERNMENT Constitutional monarchy
ANNUAL INCOME US$2,400
CURRENCY Kina = 100 toea

PARAGUAY

AREA 406,752 sq km [157,047 sq mi]
POPULATION 6,348,000
CAPITAL Asunción
GOVERNMENT Multiparty republic
ANNUAL INCOME US$4,900
CURRENCY Guaraní = 100 céntimos

PERU

AREA 1,285,216 sq km [496,222 sq mi]
POPULATION 27,926,000
CAPITAL Lima
GOVERNMENT Transitional republic
ANNUAL INCOME US$6,000
CURRENCY New sol = 100 centavos

PHILIPPINES

AREA 300,000 sq km [115,830 sq mi]
POPULATION 87,857,000
CAPITAL Manila
GOVERNMENT Multiparty republic
ANNUAL INCOME US$5,100
CURRENCY Philippine peso = 100 centavos

POLAND

AREA 323,250 sq km [124,807 sq mi]
POPULATION 38,635,000
CAPITAL Warsaw
GOVERNMENT Multiparty republic
ANNUAL INCOME US$12,700
CURRENCY Zloty = 100 groszy

PORTUGAL

AREA 88,797 sq km [34,285 sq mi]
POPULATION 10,566,000
CAPITAL Lisbon
GOVERNMENT Multiparty republic
ANNUAL INCOME US$18,400
CURRENCY Euro = 100 cents

PUERTO RICO

AREA 8,875 sq km [3,427 sq mi]
POPULATION 3,917,000
CAPITAL San Juan
GOVERNMENT Commonwealth of the US
ANNUAL INCOME US$18,500
CURRENCY US dollar = 100 cents

QATAR

AREA 11,437 sq km [4,247 sq mi]
POPULATION 863,000
CAPITAL Doha
GOVERNMENT Constitutional absolute monarchy
ANNUAL INCOME US$26,000
CURRENCY Qatari riyal = 100 dirhams

RÉUNION

AREA 2,510 sq km [969 sq mi]
POPULATION 777,000
CAPITAL St-Denis
GOVERNMENT Overseas department of France
ANNUAL INCOME US$6,200
CURRENCY Euro = 100 cents

ROMANIA

AREA 238,391 sq km [92,043 sq mi]
POPULATION 22,330,000
CAPITAL Bucharest
GOVERNMENT Multiparty republic
ANNUAL INCOME US$8,300
CURRENCY Leu = 100 bani

RUSSIA

AREA 17,075,400 sq km [6,592,812 sq mi]
POPULATION 143,420,000
CAPITAL Moscow
GOVERNMENT Federal multiparty republic
ANNUAL INCOME US$10,700
CURRENCY Russian ruble = 100 kopeks

RWANDA

AREA 26,338 sq km [10,169 sq mi]
POPULATION 8,441,000
CAPITAL Kigali
GOVERNMENT Republic
ANNUAL INCOME US$1,300
CURRENCY Rwandan franc = 100 centimes

ST KITTS & NEVIS

AREA 261 sq km [101 sq mi]
POPULATION 39,000
CAPITAL Basseterre
GOVERNMENT Constitutional monarchy
ANNUAL INCOME US$8,800
CURRENCY East Caribbean dollar = 100 cents

ST LUCIA

AREA 539 sq km [208 sq mi]
POPULATION 166,000
CAPITAL Castries
GOVERNMENT Parliamentary democracy
ANNUAL INCOME US$5,400
CURRENCY East Caribbean dollar = 100 cents

ST VINCENT & THE GRENADINES

AREA 388 sq km [150 sq mi]
POPULATION 118,000
CAPITAL Kingstown
GOVERNMENT Parliamentary democracy
ANNUAL INCOME US$2,900
CURRENCY East Caribbean dollar = 100 cents

SAMOA

AREA 2,831 sq km [1,093 sq mi]
POPULATION 177,000 **CAPITAL** Apia
GOVERNMENT Mix of parliamentary democracy and constitutional monarchy
ANNUAL INCOME US$5,600
CURRENCY Samoan dollar = 100 sene

SAN MARINO

AREA 61 sq km [24 sq mi]
POPULATION 29,000
CAPITAL San Marino
GOVERNMENT Independent republic
ANNUAL INCOME US$34,600
CURRENCY Euro = 100 cents

SÃO TOMÉ & PRÍNCIPE

AREA 964 sq km [372 sq mi]
POPULATION 187,000
CAPITAL São Tomé
GOVERNMENT Republic
ANNUAL INCOME US$1,200
CURRENCY Dobra = 100 cêntimos

SAUDI ARABIA

AREA 2,149,690 sq km [829,995 sq mi]
POPULATION 26,418,000 **CAPITAL** Riyadh
GOVERNMENT Absolute monarchy with consultative assembly
ANNUAL INCOME US$12,900
CURRENCY Saudi riyal = 100 halalas

SENEGAL

AREA 196,722 sq km [75,954 sq mi]
POPULATION 11,127,000
CAPITAL Dakar
GOVERNMENT Multiparty republic
ANNUAL INCOME US$1,800
CURRENCY CFA franc = 100 centimes

SERBIA

AREA 88,361 sq km [34,116 sq mi]
POPULATION 9,396,411
CAPITAL Belgrade
GOVERNMENT Republic
ANNUAL INCOME US$4,400
CURRENCY New dinar = 100 paras

SEYCHELLES

AREA 455 sq km [176 sq mi]
POPULATION 81,000
CAPITAL Victoria
GOVERNMENT Democratic republic
ANNUAL INCOME US$7,800
CURRENCY Seychelles rupee = 100 cents

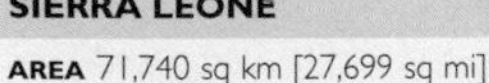

SIERRA LEONE

AREA 71,740 sq km [27,699 sq mi]
POPULATION 6,018,000
CAPITAL Freetown
GOVERNMENT Single party republic
ANNUAL INCOME US$800
CURRENCY Leone = 100 cents

SINGAPORE

AREA 683 sq km [264 sq mi]
POPULATION 4,426,000
CAPITAL Singapore City
GOVERNMENT Multiparty republic
ANNUAL INCOME US$29,700
CURRENCY Singapore dollar = 100 cents

SLOVAK REPUBLIC

AREA 49,012 sq km [18,924 sq mi]
POPULATION 5,431,000
CAPITAL Bratislava
GOVERNMENT Multiparty republic
ANNUAL INCOME US$15,700
CURRENCY Slovak koruna = 100 halierov

SLOVENIA

AREA 20,256 sq km [7,821 sq mi]
POPULATION 2,011,000
CAPITAL Ljubljana
GOVERNMENT Multiparty republic
ANNUAL INCOME US$20,900
CURRENCY Tolar = 100 stotin

SOLOMON ISLANDS

AREA 28,896 sq km [11,157 sq mi]
POPULATION 538,000
CAPITAL Honiara
GOVERNMENT Parliamentary democracy
ANNUAL INCOME US$1,700
CURRENCY Solomon Islands dollar = 100 cents

SOMALIA

AREA 637,657 sq km [246,199 sq mi]
POPULATION 8,592,000 **CAPITAL** Mogadishu
GOVERNMENT Single-party republic, military dominated
ANNUAL INCOME US$600
CURRENCY Somali shilling = 100 cents

SOUTH AFRICA

AREA 1,221,037 sq km [471,442 sq mi]
POPULATION 44,344,000 **CAPITAL** Cape Town (legislative); Tshwane/Pretoria (administrative); Bloemfontein (judiciary) **GOVERNMENT** Multiparty republic **ANNUAL INCOME** US$11,900
CURRENCY Rand = 100 cents

SPAIN

AREA 497,548 sq km [192,103 sq mi]
POPULATION 40,341,000
CAPITAL Madrid
GOVERNMENT Constitutional monarchy
ANNUAL INCOME US$25,100
CURRENCY Euro = 100 cents

SRI LANKA

AREA 65,610 sq km [25,332 sq mi]
POPULATION 20,065,000
CAPITAL Colombo
GOVERNMENT Multiparty republic
ANNUAL INCOME US$4,300
CURRENCY Sri Lankan rupee = 100 cents

SUDAN

AREA 2,505,813 sq km [967,494 sq mi]
POPULATION 40,187,000
CAPITAL Khartoum
GOVERNMENT Military regime
ANNUAL INCOME US$2,100
CURRENCY Sudanese dinar = 10 Sudanese pounds

SURINAME

AREA 163,265 sq km [63,037 sq mi]
POPULATION 438,000
CAPITAL Paramaribo
GOVERNMENT Multiparty republic
ANNUAL INCOME US$4,700
CURRENCY Surinamese dollar = 100 cents

SWAZILAND

AREA 17,364 sq km [6,704 sq mi]
POPULATION 1,174,000
CAPITAL Mbabane
GOVERNMENT Monarchy
ANNUAL INCOME US$5,300
CURRENCY Lilangeni = 100 cents

SWEDEN

AREA 449,964 sq km [173,731 sq mi]
POPULATION 9,002,000
CAPITAL Stockholm
GOVERNMENT Constitutional monarchy
ANNUAL INCOME US$29,600
CURRENCY Swedish krona = 100 öre

SWITZERLAND

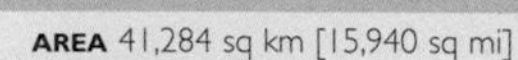

AREA 41,284 sq km [15,940 sq mi]
POPULATION 7,489,000
CAPITAL Bern
GOVERNMENT Federal republic
ANNUAL INCOME US$35,000
CURRENCY Swiss franc = 100 centimes

SYRIA

AREA 185,180 sq km [71,498 sq mi]
POPULATION 18,449,000
CAPITAL Damascus
GOVERNMENT Multiparty republic
ANNUAL INCOME US$3,500
CURRENCY Syrian pound = 100 piastres

TAIWAN

AREA 35,980 sq km [13,900 sq mi]
POPULATION 22,894,000
CAPITAL Taipei
GOVERNMENT Unitary multiparty republic
ANNUAL INCOME US$26,700
CURRENCY New Taiwan dollar = 100 cents

TAJIKISTAN

AREA 143,100 sq km [55,521 sq mi]
POPULATION 7,164,000
CAPITAL Dushanbe
GOVERNMENT Transitional democracy
ANNUAL INCOME US$1,200
CURRENCY Somoni = 100 dirams

TANZANIA

AREA 945,090 sq km [364,899 sq mi]
POPULATION 36,766,000
CAPITAL Dodoma
GOVERNMENT Multiparty republic
ANNUAL INCOME US$700
CURRENCY Tanzanian shilling = 100 cents

THAILAND

AREA 513,115 sq km [198,114 sq mi]
POPULATION 65,444,000
CAPITAL Bangkok
GOVERNMENT Constitutional monarchy
ANNUAL INCOME US$8,300
CURRENCY Baht = 100 satang

TOGO

AREA 56,785 sq km [21,925 sq mi]
POPULATION 5,682,000
CAPITAL Lomé
GOVERNMENT Multiparty republic
ANNUAL INCOME US$1,600
CURRENCY CFA franc = 100 centimes

TONGA

AREA 650 sq km [251 sq mi]
POPULATION 112,000
CAPITAL Nuku'alofa
GOVERNMENT Hereditary constitutional monarchy
ANNUAL INCOME US$2,300
CURRENCY Pa'anga = 100 seniti

TRINIDAD & TOBAGO

AREA 5,130 sq km [1,981 sq mi]
POPULATION 1,089,000
CAPITAL Port of Spain
GOVERNMENT Parliamentary democracy
ANNUAL INCOME US$12,700
CURRENCY Trinidad & Tobago dollar = 100 cents

TUNISIA

AREA 163,610 sq km [63,170 sq mi]
POPULATION 10,075,000
CAPITAL Tunis
GOVERNMENT Multiparty republic
ANNUAL INCOME US$7,600
CURRENCY Tunisian dinar = 1,000 millimes

TURKEY

AREA 774,815 sq km [299,156 sq mi]
POPULATION 69,661,000
CAPITAL Ankara
GOVERNMENT Multiparty republic
ANNUAL INCOME US$7,900
CURRENCY New Turkish lira = 100 kurus

TURKMENISTAN

AREA 488,100 sq km [188,455 sq mi]
POPULATION 4,952,000
CAPITAL Ashkhabad
GOVERNMENT Single party republic
ANNUAL INCOME US$5,900
CURRENCY Turkmen manat = 100 tenesi

TUVALU

AREA 26 sq km [10 sq mi]
POPULATION 12,000 **CAPITAL** Fongafale
GOVERNMENT Constitutional monarchy with parliamentary democracy
ANNUAL INCOME US$1,100
CURRENCY Australian dollar; Tuvaluan dollar

UGANDA

AREA 241,038 sq km [93,065 sq mi]
POPULATION 27,269,000
CAPITAL Kampala
GOVERNMENT Republic in transition
ANNUAL INCOME US$1,700
CURRENCY Ugandan shilling = 100 cents

UKRAINE

AREA 603,700 sq km [233,089 sq mi]
POPULATION 47,425,000
CAPITAL Kiev
GOVERNMENT Multiparty republic
ANNUAL INCOME US$6,800
CURRENCY Hryvnia = 100 kopiykas

UNITED ARAB EMIRATES

AREA 83,600 sq km [32,278 sq mi]
POPULATION 2,563,000 **CAPITAL** Abu Dhabi
GOVERNMENT Federation of seven emirates, each with its own government
ANNUAL INCOME US$29,100
CURRENCY Dirham = 100 fils

UNITED KINGDOM

AREA 241,857 sq km [93,381 sq mi]
POPULATION 60,441,000
CAPITAL London
GOVERNMENT Constitutional monarchy
ANNUAL INCOME US$30,900
CURRENCY Pound sterling = 100 pence

UNITED STATES OF AMERICA

AREA 9,629,091 sq km [3,717,792 sq mi]
POPULATION 295,734,000
CAPITAL Washington, DC
GOVERNMENT Federal republic
ANNUAL INCOME US$41,800
CURRENCY US dollar = 100 cents

URUGUAY

AREA 175,016 sq km [67,574 sq mi]
POPULATION 3,416,000
CAPITAL Montevideo
GOVERNMENT Multiparty republic
ANNUAL INCOME US$10,000
CURRENCY Uruguayan peso = 100 centésimos

UZBEKISTAN

AREA 447,400 sq km [172,741 sq mi]
POPULATION 26,851,000
CAPITAL Tashkent
GOVERNMENT Socialist republic
ANNUAL INCOME US$1,900
CURRENCY Uzbekistani sum = 100 tyiyn

VANUATU

AREA 12,189 sq km [4,706 sq mi]
POPULATION 206,000
CAPITAL Port-Vila
GOVERNMENT Parliamentary republic
ANNUAL INCOME US$2,900
CURRENCY Vatu

VENEZUELA

AREA 912,050 sq km [352,143 sq mi]
POPULATION 25,375,000
CAPITAL Caracas
GOVERNMENT Federal republic
ANNUAL INCOME US$6,400
CURRENCY Bolívar = 100 céntimos

VIETNAM

AREA 331,689 sq km [128,065 sq mi]
POPULATION 83,536,000
CAPITAL Hanoi
GOVERNMENT Socialist republic
ANNUAL INCOME US$3,000
CURRENCY Dong = 10 hao = 100 xu

YEMEN

AREA 527,968 sq km [203,848 sq mi]
POPULATION 20,727,000
CAPITAL Sana'
GOVERNMENT Multiparty republic
ANNUAL INCOME US$800
CURRENCY Yemeni rial = 100 fils

ZAMBIA

AREA 752,618 sq km [290,586 sq mi]
POPULATION 11,262,000
CAPITAL Lusaka
GOVERNMENT Multiparty republic
ANNUAL INCOME US$900
CURRENCY Zambian kwacha = 100 ngwee

ZIMBABWE

AREA 390,757 sq km [150,871 sq mi]
POPULATION 12,747,000
CAPITAL Harare
GOVERNMENT Multiparty republic
ANNUAL INCOME US$1,900
CURRENCY Zimbabwean dollar = 100 cents

WORLD MAPS – GENERAL REFERENCE

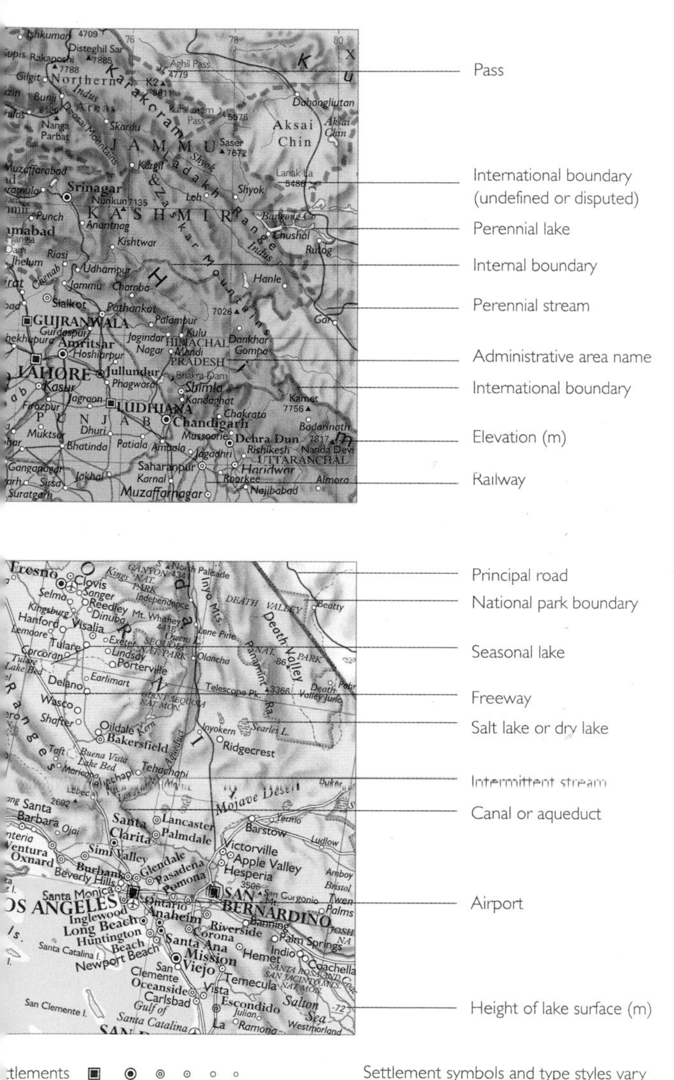

Capital cities have red infills

Settlement symbols and type styles vary according to the scale of each map and indicate the importance of towns rather than specific population figures.

PACIFIC OCEAN
ARCTIC OCEAN
NORTH ATLANTIC OCEAN
North America
Asia
Europe
North Pole
Magnetic Pole
Arctic Circle
International Dateline
PROJECTION CENTRED ON LONDON
CANADA
UNITED STATES
MEXICO
RUSSIA
CHINA
INDIA
MONGOLIA
JAPAN
KAZAKHSTAN
IRAN
AFGHANISTAN
PAKISTAN
GREENLAND (Denmark)
ICELAND
NORWAY
SWEDEN
FINLAND
UNITED KINGDOM
IRELAND
FRANCE
SPAIN
PORTUGAL
GERMANY
POLAND
UKRAINE
BELARUS
TURKEY
ITALY
GREECE
Alaska (U.S.A.)
Anchorage
Aleutian Is. (U.S.A.)
Kuril Is.
Sakhalin
Svalbard (Norw.)
Baffin I.
Newfoundland
Bermuda (U.K.)
Azores (Port.)
Tokyo
Osaka
Seoul
Pyongyang
Shenyang
Beijing
Tianjin
Shanghai
Wuhan
Hong Kong
Xi'an
Chongqing
Hanoi
Bangkok
Rangoon
Dacca
Kolkata (Calcutta)
Chennai (Madras)
Colombo
Bangalore
Hyderabad
Mumbai (Bombay)
New Delhi
Delhi
Lahore
Islamabad
Katmandu
Karachi
Kabul
Tashkent
Astana
Ulan Bator
Tehran
Bagdad
Riyadh
Muscat
Baku
Ashkhabad
Moscow
St. Petersburg
Helsinki
Stockholm
Oslo
Copenhagen
Warsaw
Berlin
Bonn
Vienna
Budapest
Istanbul
Ankara
Athens
Beirut
Jerusalem
Rome
Tunis
Paris
London
Amsterdam
Madrid
Lisbon
Gibraltar
Reykjavik
Nuuk
Vancouver
Seattle
San Francisco
Los Angeles
San Diego
Phoenix
Dallas
Houston
Chicago
Detroit
Toronto
Ottawa
Montréal
Boston
New York
Philadelphia
Washington
Atlanta
Miami
Havana
Kingston
Santo Domingo
Monterrey
Guadalajara
Mexico City
Medellín
Bogota
Caracas
Quito
CUBA
BAHAMAS
HAITI
DOM. REP.
JAMAICA
PUERTO RICO (U.S.A.)
BELIZE
HONDURAS
GUATEMALA
EL SALVADOR
NICARAGUA
COSTA RICA
PANAMA
ECUADOR
Turks & Caicos (U.K.)
Virgin Is.
Guadeloupe (Fr.)
DOMINICA
ST. LUCIA
ST. VINC.
ANT. & BAR.
ST. KITTS-NEVIS
SRI LANKA
MALDIVES
Andaman Is. (India)
Lakshadweep Is. (India)
BURMA
THAILAND
CAMBODIA
LAOS
VIETNAM
TAIWAN
BANGLADESH
BHUTAN
NEPAL
SOUTH KOREA
NORTH KOREA
OMAN
QATAR
BAHRAIN
KUWAIT
SYRIA
IRAQ
JORDAN
ISRAEL
GEORGIA
TURKMENISTAN
UZBEKISTAN
KYRG.
TAJ.
MALTA
100
120
140
160
180

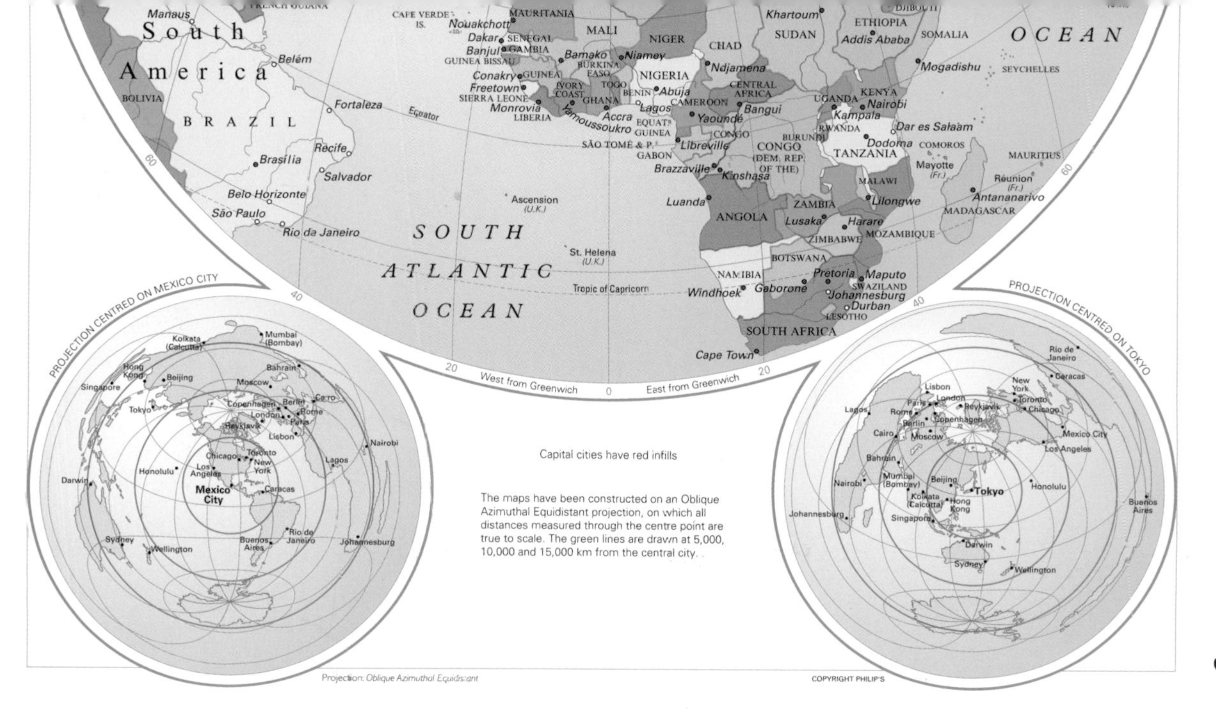

Capital cities have red infills

The maps have been constructed on an Oblique Azimuthal Equidistant projection, on which all distances measured through the centre point are true to scale. The green lines are drawn at 5,000, 10,000 and 15,000 km from the central city.

Projection: Oblique Azimuthal Equidistant

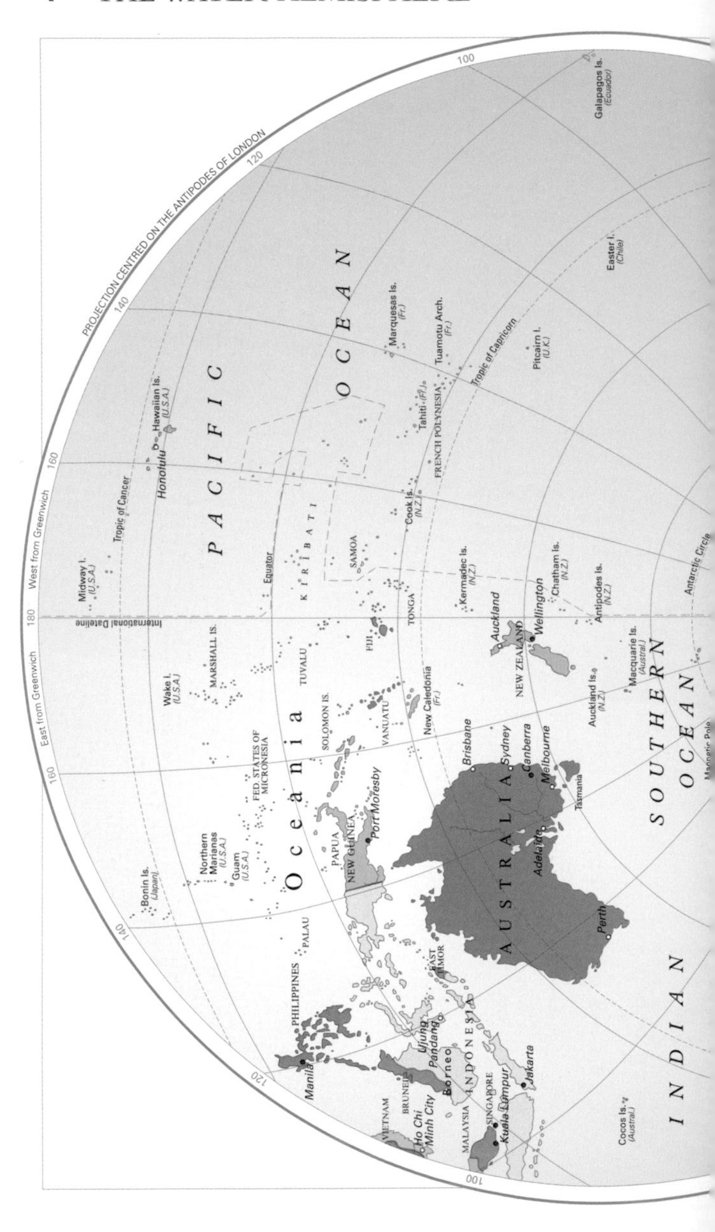
PROJECTION CENTRED ON THE ANTIPODES OF LONDON
East from Greenwich
West from Greenwich
International Dateline
PACIFIC OCEAN
SOUTHERN OCEAN
INDIAN
Oceania
Tropic of Cancer
Tropic of Capricorn
Equator
Antarctic Circle
Galapagos Is. (Ecuador)
Easter I. (Chile)
Pitcairn I. (U.K.)
Marquesas Is. (Fr.)
Tuamotu Arch. (Fr.)
Tahiti (Fr.)
FRENCH POLYNESIA
Hawaiian Is. (U.S.A.)
Honolulu
Midway I. (U.S.A.)
Cook Is. (N.Z.)
KIRIBATI
SAMOA
TONGA
FIJI
TUVALU
Kermadec Is. (N.Z.)
Chatham Is. (N.Z.)
Antipodes Is. (N.Z.)
Auckland Is. (N.Z.)
Macquarie Is. (Austral.)
Auckland
Wellington
NEW ZEALAND
Wake I. (U.S.A.)
MARSHALL IS.
SOLOMON IS.
VANUATU
New Caledonia (Fr.)
FED. STATES OF MICRONESIA
Northern Marianas (U.S.A.)
Guam (U.S.A.)
Bonin Is. (Japan)
PALAU
PAPUA NEW GUINEA
Port Moresby
AUSTRALIA
Brisbane
Sydney
Canberra
Melbourne
Adelaide
Perth
Tasmania
EAST TIMOR
PHILIPPINES
Manila
Ujung Pandang
Borneo
BRUNEI
INDONESIA
Jakarta
MALAYSIA
SINGAPORE
Kuala Lumpur
VIETNAM
Ho Chi Minh City
Cocos Is. (Austral.)
100
120
140
160
180

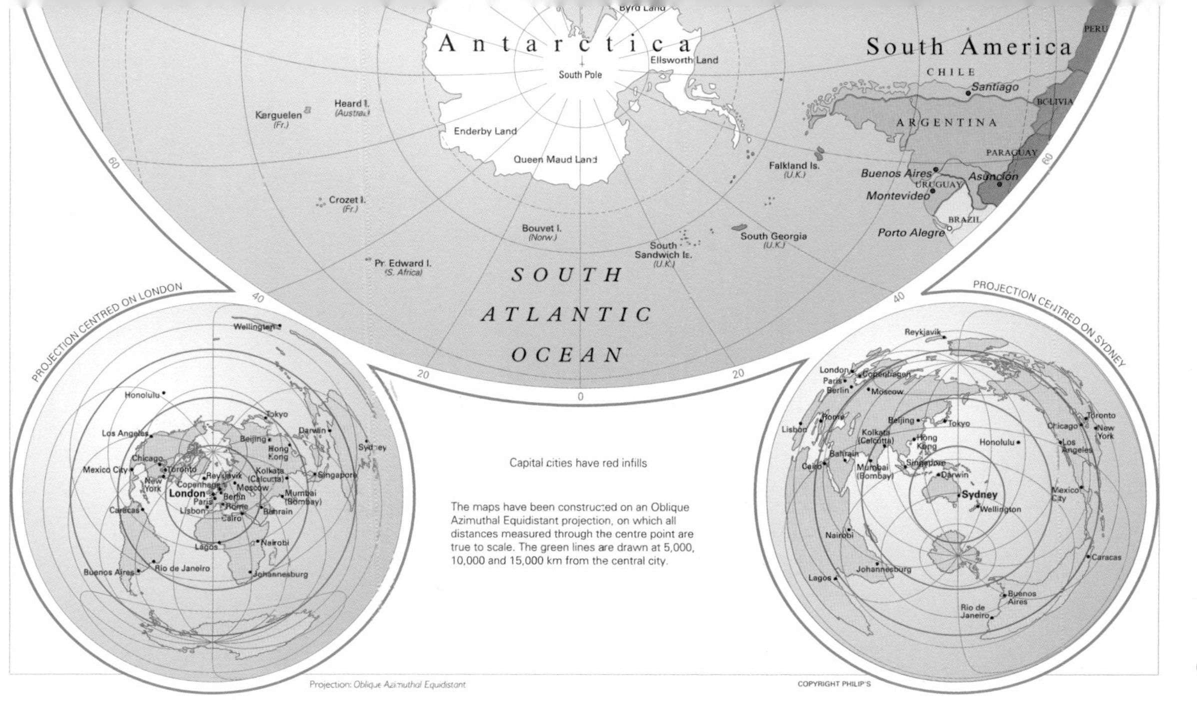
Antarctica
South America
South Pole
Ellsworth Land
Byrd Land
CHILE
Santiago
BOLIVIA
PERU
ARGENTINA
PARAGUAY
Asunción
URUGUAY
Buenos Aires
Montevideo
BRAZIL
Porto Alegre
Kerguelen (Fr.)
Heard I. (Austral.)
Enderby Land
Queen Maud Land
Falkland Is. (U.K.)
Crozet I. (Fr.)
Bouvet I. (Norw.)
South Sandwich Is. (U.K.)
South Georgia (U.K.)
Pr. Edward I. (S. Africa)
SOUTH
ATLANTIC
OCEAN
60
40
20
0
PROJECTION CENTRED ON LONDON
Wellington
Honolulu
Tokyo
Darwin
Sydney
Los Angeles
Beijing
Hong Kong
Chicago
Toronto
Mexico City
Reykjavik
Kolkata (Calcutta)
Singapore
New York
Copenhagen
Moscow
London
Berlin
Mumbai (Bombay)
Paris
Rome
Caracas
Lisbon
Bahrain
Cairo
Lagos
Nairobi
Rio de Janeiro
Buenos Aires
Johannesburg
PROJECTION CENTRED ON SYDNEY
Reykjavik
London
Copenhagen
Paris
Berlin
Moscow
Rome
Beijing
Tokyo
Toronto
Lisbon
Chicago
New York
Kolkata (Calcutta)
Hong Kong
Honolulu
Los Angeles
Bahrain
Cairo
Mumbai (Bombay)
Singapore
Darwin
Mexico City
Sydney
Wellington
Nairobi
Caracas
Johannesburg
Lagos
Buenos Aires
Rio de Janeiro
Capital cities have red infills
The maps have been constructed on an Oblique Azimuthal Equidistant projection, on which all distances measured through the centre point are true to scale. The green lines are drawn at 5,000, 10,000 and 15,000 km from the central city.
Projection: Oblique Azimuthal Equidistant
COPYRIGHT PHILIP'S

1 2 3 4 5 6 7 8

30 25 20 15 10 5 0 5 10 15

C
D
E
F
G
H
J

60
55
50
45
40
35

Arctic Circle
ICELAND
Reykjavík
Norwegian Sea
Faroe Is. (Den.)
Shetland Is.
Orkney Is.
Hebrides
ATLANTIC OCEAN
UNITED KINGDOM
SCOTLAND
Aberdeen
Dundee
Glasgow
Edinburgh
N. IRELAND
Belfast
IRELAND
Dublin
Cork
Newcastle-upon-Tyne
Manchester
Leeds
Liverpool
Sheffield
WALES
ENGLAND
Birmingham
Cardiff
Bristol
Plymouth
Southampton
LONDON
North Sea
English Channel
Channel Is. (U.K.)
Brest
Le Havre
Rouen
Seine
PARIS
FRANCE
Nantes
Loire
Bay of Biscay
Gironde
Limoges
Bordeaux
Garonne
Toulouse
Dijon
Lyons
St-Étienne
Rhône
Grenoble
Marseilles
Toulon
Nice
MONACO
Lille
Luxembourg
BELGIUM
Brussels
Antwerp
Amsterdam
The Hague
Rotterdam
NETHERLANDS
LUX.
Meuse
Bergen
Stavanger
Oslo
Trondheim
NORWAY
SWEDEN
Uppsala
Örebro
Vänern
Vättern
Jönköping
Gothenburg
Skagerrak
Kattegat
Aalborg
Århus
DENMARK
Copenhagen
Malmö
Kiel
Hamburg
Bremen
Elbe
Hannover
Berlin
Magdeburg
GERMANY
Essen
Dortmund
Cologne
Bonn
Halle
Leipzig
Chemnitz
Dresden
Frankfurt am Main
Nuremberg
Rhine
Strasbourg
Stuttgart
Munich
Zürich
LIECH.
Vaduz
Bern
SWITZERLAND
Geneva
Innsbruck
Salzburg
AUSTRIA
Linz
Vienna
Graz
Prague
CZECH REP.
Ostrava
Gdańsk
Szczecin
Bydgoszcz
Poznań
Oder
POLAND
Wrocław
Katowice
Baltic
Bratislava
Budapest
HUNGARY
SLOVENIA
Ljubljana
Zagreb
CROATIA
Trieste
Venice
Milan
Turin
Genoa
Bologna
SAN MARINO
Florence
Tiber
ITALY
Rome
Adriatic Sea
Split
BOSNIA-HERZEGOVINA
MONTENEGRO
Podgorica
Naples
Bari
Taranto
Tyrrhenian Sea
Corsica
Ajaccio
Sardinia
Cagliari
Palermo
Messina
Sicily
Catania
Ionian Sea
Pantelleria (Italy)
MALTA
Valletta
Tunis
TUNISIA
Constantine
Annaba
Algiers
ALGERIA
Mediterranean Sea
Africa
MOROCCO
Melilla (Sp.)
Tangier
Ceuta
Str. of Gibraltar
Gibraltar (U.K.)
Málaga
Granada
Cádiz
Seville
Córdoba
Guadalquivir
Murcia
Alicante
Valencia
Balearic Is.
Palma
Majorca
Minorca
Ibiza
Barcelona
Andorra-la-Vella
ANDORRA
Zaragoza
Ebro
Bilbao
Valladolid
Madrid
SPAIN
Tagus
Guadiana
Douro
La Coruña
Vigo
Porto
PORTUGAL
Lisbon

m	ft
0	
200	600
1000	3000
2000	6000
4000	12 000

Projection: Bonne
West from Greenwich 0 East from Greenwich 5 10 15

4 5 6 7 9

■ LONDON Capital Cities

100 0 100 200 300 400 500 600 700 800 km
100 0 100 200 300 400 500 miles
11 12 13 14 15 16 17 18 19
C
D
E
F
G
H
J
10 11 12 13 14 15
Hammerfest
Murmansk
KARELIA
White Sea
Arkhangelsk
N. Dvina
KOMI
Ob
Luleå
FINLAND
Vaasa
Kotlas
Nizhniy Tagil
Perm
L. Onega
Vyborg
L. Ladoga
Turku
Helsinki
ST. PETERSBURG
Vologda
Kirov
Yekaterinburg
Chelyabinsk
UDMURTIA
Tallinn
ESTONIA
L. Chudskoye
Rybinsk Res.
Kostroma
Yaroslavl
Ivanovo
Nizhniy Novgorod
MARI EL
Kazan
Ufa
BASHKORTOSTAN
Magnitogorsk
TATARSTAN
CHUVASHIA
R U S S I A
LATVIA
Riga
MOSCOW
Simbirsk
Samara
Orenburg
MORDVINIA
Penza
LITHUANIA
Kaunas
W. Dvina
Vitebsk
Smolensk
Tula
Uralsk
Vilnius
Mahilyow
Minsk
Volga
Tambov
Saratov
Orel
BELARUS
Gomel
Kursk
Voronezh
KAZAKHSTAN
Brest
Pripet
Warsaw
Chernihiv
Ural
Atyraū
Volgograd
Lublin
Kiev
Dnieper
Kharkov
Zhytomyr
UKRAINE
Astrakhan
Lvov
Donetsk
Don
Dniester
Dnepropetrovsk
Taganrog
Rostov
KALMYKIA
Caspian Sea
Bug
Krivoy Rog
Zaporozhye
Debrecen
MOLDOVA
Kherson
Stavropol
Nikolayev
CHECHENIA
Cluj-Napoca
Kishinev
Odessa
NORTH OSSETIA
Makhachkala
CRIMEA
Krasnodar
ADYGEA
ROMANIA
Timişoara
Galaţi
DAGESTAN
Braşov
Ploieşti
Sevastopol
KARACHAY-CHERKESSIA
KABARDINO-BALKARIA
INGUSHETIA
GEORGIA
Tbilisi
Baku
Bucharest
Constanţa
Black Sea
AZERBAIJAN
Danube
ARMENIA
Yerevan
Niš
Varna
Sofia
Samsun
Araks
BULGARIA
Bosporus
Erzerum
Plovdiv
Skopje
Tabriz
İSTANBUL
T U R K E Y
Thessaloniki
Bursa
Ankara
Kayseri
IRAN
Diyarbakir
Aegean Sea
A S I A
GREECE
Izmir
Konya
Adana
IRAQ
Patra
Athens
Aleppo
Euphrates
Tigris
Antalya
SYRIA
CYPRUS
Nicosia
Baghdād
Rhodes
Crete
COPYRIGHT PHILIP'S

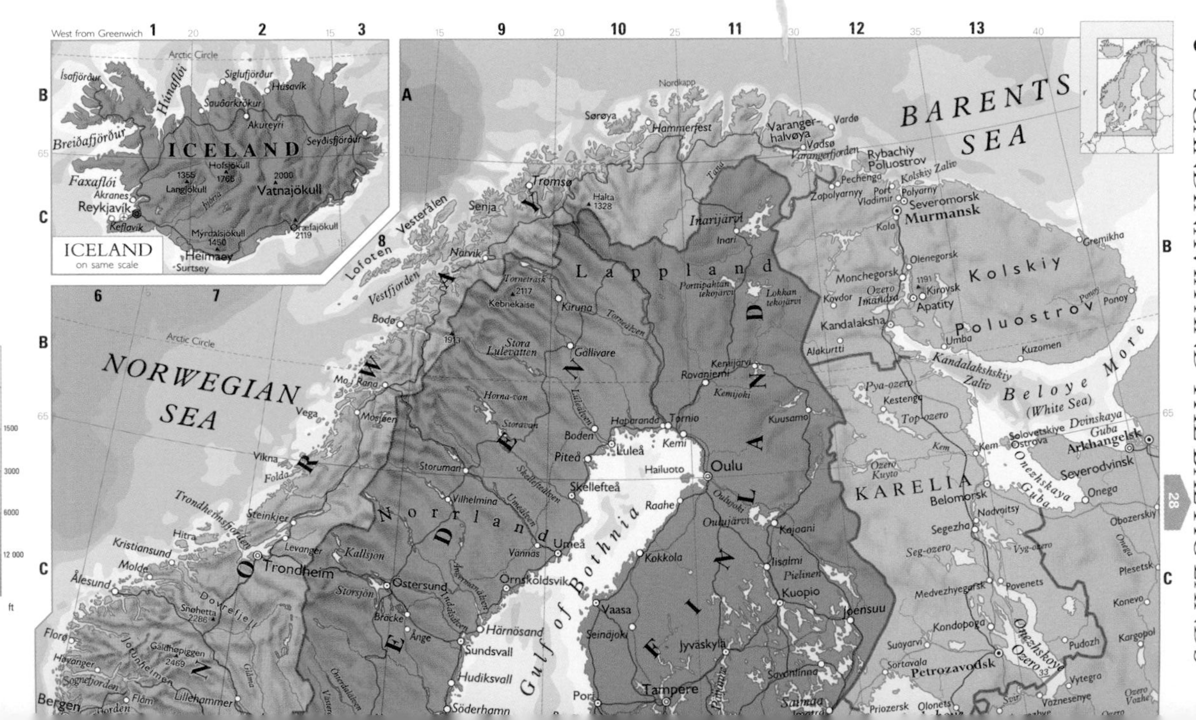
28
BARENTS SEA
NORWEGIAN SEA
Beloye More (White Sea)
Kolskiy Poluostrov
Gulf of Bothnia
Lappland
Norrland
KARELIA
Onezhskaya Guba
Onezhskoye Ozero
Kandalakshskiy Zaliv
Lofoten
Vesterålen
Vestfjorden
Trondheimsfjorden
Sognefjorden
Jotunheimen
Dovrefjell
Murmansk
Severomorsk
Kirovsk
Apatity
Monchegorsk
Kandalaksha
Arkhangelsk
Severodvinsk
Onega
Belomorsk
Petrozavodsk
Kemi
Tornio
Oulu
Kokkola
Vaasa
Tampere
Jyväskylä
Kuopio
Joensuu
Kajaani
Luleå
Piteå
Skellefteå
Umeå
Örnsköldsvik
Härnösand
Sundsvall
Hudiksvall
Söderhamn
Östersund
Kiruna
Gällivare
Boden
Haparanda
Kebnekaise 2117
Narvik
Tromsø
Hammerfest
Vardø
Vadsø
Nordkapp
Bodø
Mo i Rana
Mosjøen
Trondheim
Steinkjer
Levanger
Kristiansund
Molde
Ålesund
Bergen
Florø
Lillehammer
Galdhøpiggen 2469
Snøhetta 2286
ICELAND
ICELAND on same scale
Reykjavík
Akureyri
Húsavík
Ísafjörður
Siglufjörður
Seyðisfjörður
Vatnajökull
Hofsjökull
Langjökull
Mýrdalsjökull
Öræfajökull 2119
Faxaflói
Breiðafjörður
Húnaflói
Heimaey
Surtsey
Keflavík
Akranes
Arctic Circle
West from Greenwich
m
ft

9
Projection: Conical with two standard parallels
East from Greenwich
COPYRIGHT PHILIP'S
16
17
24
ESTONIA
LATVIA
LITHUANIA
BELARUS
POLAND
GERMANY
DENMARK
CZECH REP.
UKRAINE
RUSSIA
BALTIC SEA
Gulf of Finland
Gulf of Riga
Skagerrak
Kattegat
Svealand
Götaland
Jylland
Pripet Marshes
Helsinki
Espoo
Hanko
Kronshtadt
SANKT-PETERBURG (St. Petersburg)
Kolpino
Tikhvin
Cherepovets
Rybinsk Res.
Borovichi
Malaya Vishera
Bologoye
Vyshniy Volochek
Tver
Kimry
Staritsa
Rzhev
Zelenograd
MOSKVA (Moscow)
Odintsovo
Tallinn
Kohtla-Järve
Narva
Gdov
Luga
Novgorod
Ozero Ilmen
Ozero Chudskoye
Pärnu
Tartu
Hiiumaa (Dagö)
Saaremaa (Ösel)
Valga
Pskov
Dno
Staraya Russa
Kholm
Valdayskaya Vozvyshennost
Toropets
Velikiye Luki
Nevel
Riga
Ventspils
Jelgava
Rēzekne
Daugava
Daugavpils
Liepāja
Šiauliai
Panevėžys
Klaipėda
Nemunas
Sovetsk
Kaliningrad (Russia)
Kaunas
Vilnius
Polatsk
Vitsyebsk
Lyepyel
Orsha
Barysaw
Mahilyow
MINSK
Hrodna
Nyoman
Baranavichy
Slutsk
Babruysk
Byarezina
Zhlobin
Homyel
Pinsk
Prypyats
Mazyr
Brest
Smolensk
Vyazma
Kaluga
Belev
Oka
Roslavl
Seltso
Bryansk
Orel
Dnepr
Novhorod-Siverskyy
Chernihiv
Konotop
Sumy
Nizhyn
Pryluky
Okhtyrka
Chornobyl
Kyyivske Vdskh.
KYYIV (Kiev)
Pereyaslav-Khmelnytskyy
Bila Tserkva
Berdychiv
Zhytomyr
Korosten
Rivne
Lutsk
Kovel
Chervonohrad
Lviv
Cherkasy
Poltava
Gdynia
Gdańsk
Elbląg
Suwałki
Olsztyn
Łomża
Białystok
Koszalin
Szczecin
Świnoujście
Bydgoszcz
Toruń
Wisła
Płock
Bug
Warta
Poznań
WARSZAWA (Warsaw)
Kalisz
Łódź
Radom
Lublin
Kielce
Legnica
Wrocław
Wałbrzych
Opole
Częstochowa
Katowice
Chorzów
Kraków
Tychy
Rzeszów
Tarnów
Przemyśl
Ostrava
Cieszyn
Žilina
2655
1602 Śnieżka
Sudety
Hradec Králové
PRAHA (Prague)
Plzeň
Labe
Odra
Oder
Frankfurt
Spree
BERLIN
Potsdam
Görlitz
Dresden
Leipzig
Chemnitz
Plauen
Halle
Saale
Erfurt
Magdeburg
Braunschweig
Hannover
Osnabrück
Münster
Dortmund
Kassel
Fulda
Thüringer Wald
Frankfurt
Darmstadt
Main
Würzburg
Heidelberg
Nürnberg
Bremen
Weser
Elbe
HAMBURG
Emden
Helgoland
Lübeck
Kiel
Nord-Ostsee Kanal
Flensburg
Rostock
Stralsund
Rügen
Sassnitz
Gedser
Bornholm
KØBENHAVN (Copenhagen)
Malmö
Lund
Sjælland
Store Bælt
Fyn
Odense
Esbjerg
Holstebro
Århus
Randers
Aalborg
Limfjorden
Frederikshavn
Skagen
Göteborg (Gothenburg)
Borås
Varberg
Halmstad
Helsingborg
Trollhättan
Vänern
Vättern
Jönköping
Linköping
Norrköping
Västervik
Oskarshamn
Kalmar
Öland
Karlskrona
Gotland
Visby
Örebro
Karlstad
Västerås
Eskilstuna
Mälaren
Uppsala
Sala
STOCKHOLM
Åland (Ahvenanmaa)
Halden
Fredrikstad
Oslofjorden
Drammen
Skien
Larvik
Arendal
Kristiansand
Mandal
Lindesnes
Stavanger
Haugesund
7
8
9
10
11
12
D
E
F
15
20
25
30
50
55
0
50
100
200
300
400 km
250 miles

m
ft
2000
1000
500
200
100
50
0
6000
3000
1500
600
300
150
ATLANTIC OCEAN
NORTH SEA
Shetland Is.
(U.K.)
Yell
Unst
Fetlar
Mainland
Lerwick
Foula
Fair Isle
Orkney Is.
Westray
Sanday
Stronsay
Mainland
Kirkwall
Hoy
South Ronaldsay
Pentland Firth
C. Wrath
Thurso
Wick
Helmsdale
Lairg
Golspie
Tain
Invergordon
Dingwall
Moray Firth
Buckie
Banff
Fraserburgh
Peterhead
Nairn
Elgin
Huntly
Inverness
CAIRNGORMS
Don
Inverurie
Aberdeen
Stonehaven
Ballater
Dee
L. Ness
Aviemore
Glen More
SCOTLAND
Grampian Mts.
Ben Nevis
1342
1311
1214
1182
973
Fort William
Montrose
Arbroath
Forfar
Dundee
St. Andrews
Tay
Perth
L. LOMOND & TROSSACHS
L. Awe
L. Lomond
Stirling
Glenrothes
Kirkcaldy
Dunfermline
Dunbar
Dumbarton
Greenock
Glasgow
Edinburgh
Paisley
Motherwell
East Kilbride
Hamilton
Irvine
Kilmarnock
Arran
Uplands
Galashiels
Berwick-upon-Tweed
North West Highlands
North Minch
Ullapool
Outer Hebrides
Lewis
Stornoway
789
Harris
North Uist
Benbecula
South Uist
Barra
St. Kilda
(U.K.)
Sea of the Hebrides
Inner Hebrides
Skye
Portree
Mallaig
Rhum
Eigg
Coll
Tobermory
Tiree
Mull
Oban
L. Fyne
Colonsay
Jura
Islay
1224
316
238
NORWAY
Askøyna
Bergen
Os
Stord
Bømlo
Leirvik
Haugesund
Kopervik
Åkrahamn
Boknafjorden
Stavanger
Sandnes
Bryne
Nærbø
A
B
C
2
3
4
5
6
7
8
9
9
56
58
60

UNITED KINGDOM
IRELAND
ENGLAND
WALES
NETHERLANDS
BELGIUM
FRANCE
NORTHERN IRELAND
IRISH SEA
CELTIC SEA
English Channel
Bristol Channel
St. George's Channel
Cardigan Bay
Galway B.
Str. of Dover
The Wash
LONDON
BIRMINGHAM
MANCHESTER
Dublin
Dun Laoghaire
Belfast
Liverpool
Leeds
Sheffield
Bradford
Kingston upon Hull
Sunderland
Middlesbrough
Nottingham
Leicester
Coventry
Bristol
Cardiff
Swansea
Plymouth
Southampton
Portsmouth
Brighton
Norwich
Ipswich
Cambridge
Oxford
Cork
Limerick
Waterford
Galway
Rotterdam
's-Gravenhage (Den Haag)
Brussel (Bruxelles)
Antwerpen
Le Havre
Rouen
Caen
Amiens
Channel Is. (U.K.)
Guernsey
Jersey
I. of Man
Isles of Scilly
Land's End
Projection: Conical with two standard parallels
National Parks
East from Greenwich
West from Greenwich
COPYRIGHT PHILIP'S
12
14
2
3
4
5
6
7
E
F
G

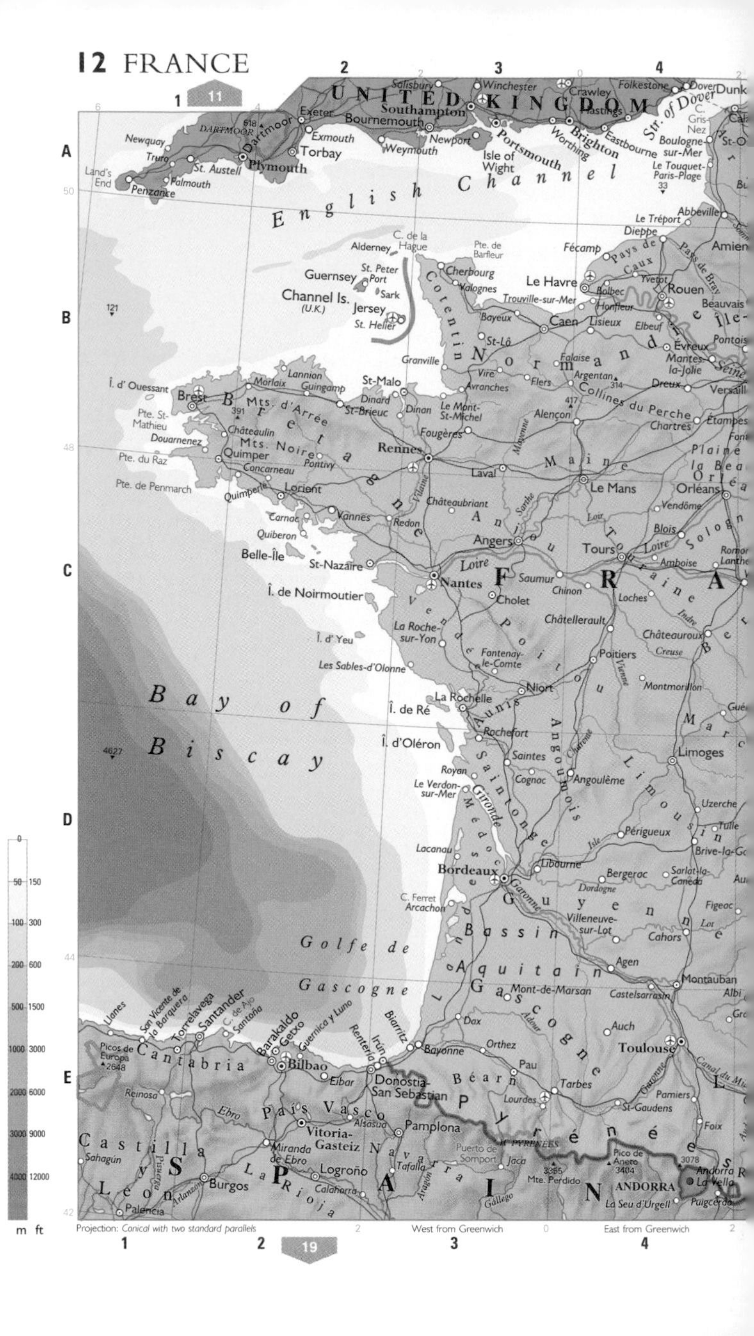
UNITED KINGDOM
Salisbury
Winchester
Crawley
Folkestone
Dover
Exeter
Bournemouth
Southampton
Hastings
Str. of Dover
DARTMOOR
Dartmoor
618
Exmouth
Newport
Portsmouth
Worthing
Brighton
Eastbourne
Boulogne-sur-Mer
Newquay
Truro
Torbay
Weymouth
Isle of Wight
Le Touquet-Paris-Plage
Land's End
Penzance
Falmouth
St. Austell
Plymouth
English Channel
Abbeville
Le Tréport
Dieppe
Amiens
C. de la Hague
Alderney
Pte. de Barfleur
Fécamp
Pays de Caux
Pays de Bray
Guernsey
St. Peter Port
Sark
Channel Is. (U.K.)
Jersey
St. Helier
Cherbourg
Valognes
Cotentin
Le Havre
Bolbec
Yvetot
Rouen
Trouville-sur-Mer
Honfleur
Beauvais
Bayeux
Caen
Lisieux
Elbeuf
Île-
St-Lô
Évreux
Mantes-la-Jolie
Seine
Pontoise
Normandie
Granville
Vire
Flers
Falaise
Argentan
314
Dreux
Versailles
121
Lannion
Morlaix
Guingamp
St-Malo
Dinard
Avranches
Collines du Perche
Î. d' Ouessant
Brest
391
Mts. d'Arrée
St-Brieuc
Dinan
Le Mont-St-Michel
417
Alençon
Chartres
Étampes
Pte. St-Mathieu
Châteaulin
Bretagne
Fougères
Mayenne
Douarnenez
Mts. Noires
Rennes
Maine
Plaine de la Beauce
Pte. du Raz
Quimper
Pontivy
Laval
Orléanais
Concarneau
Le Mans
Orléans
Pte. de Penmarch
Quimperlé
Lorient
Vilaine
Châteaubriant
Sarthe
Vendôme
Carnac
Vannes
Redon
Anjou
Loir
Sologne
Quiberon
Angers
Touraine
Blois
Belle-Île
Tours
Loire
St-Nazaire
Amboise
Nantes
Saumur
Chinon
Loches
FRANCE
Î. de Noirmoutier
Cholet
Vendée
Châtellerault
Indre
La Roche-sur-Yon
Châteauroux
Î. d' Yeu
Fontenay-le-Comte
Poitou
Poitiers
Creuse
Berry
Vienne
Les Sables-d'Olonne
Montmorillon
Bay of Biscay
La Rochelle
Niort
Î. de Ré
Aunis
Marche
Rochefort
Angoumois
Charente
Î. d'Oléron
Saintes
Limousin
Limoges
4627
Royan
Cognac
Angoulême
Le Verdon-sur-Mer
Saintonge
Gironde
Médoc
Uzerche
Tulle
Périgueux
Isle
Brive-la-Gaillarde
Lacanau
Libourne
Bordeaux
Bergerac
Sarlat-la-Canéda
Dordogne
Garonne
C. Ferret
Arcachon
Guyenne
Figeac
Villeneuve-sur-Lot
Lot
Bassin d'Aquitaine
Cahors
Landes
Golfe de Gascogne
Agen
Montauban
Gascogne
Mont-de-Marsan
Castelsarrasin
Albi
Adour
Dax
Auch
Llanes
San Vicente de la Barquera
Torrelavega
Santander
C. de Ajo
Santoña
Barakaldo
Getxo
Guernica y Luno
Rentería
Biarritz
Irún
Bayonne
Orthez
Toulouse
Picos de Europa
2648
Cantabria
Bilbao
Pau
Béarn
Canal du Midi
Eibar
Donostia-San Sebastián
Tarbes
Reinosa
Lourdes
Pamiers
Ebro
País Vasco
Alsasua
St-Gaudens
Vitoria-Gasteiz
Pamplona
Foix
Pyrénées
Castilla y León
Sahagún
Pisuerga
Miranda de Ebro
Navarra
Puerto de Somport
Jaca
PYRÉNÉES
Pico de Aneto
3404
3078
Logroño
Tafalla
3355
Mte. Perdido
Andorra
La Vella
SPAIN
Burgos
La Rioja
Calahorra
Aragón
Gállego
ANDORRA
Arlanzón
Palencia
La Seu d'Urgell
Puigcerdà
m ft
0
50 150
100 300
200 600
500 1500
1000 3000
2000 6000
3000 9000
4000 12000
Projection: Conical with two standard parallels
West from Greenwich
East from Greenwich
1 2 3 4
A B C D E
11
19

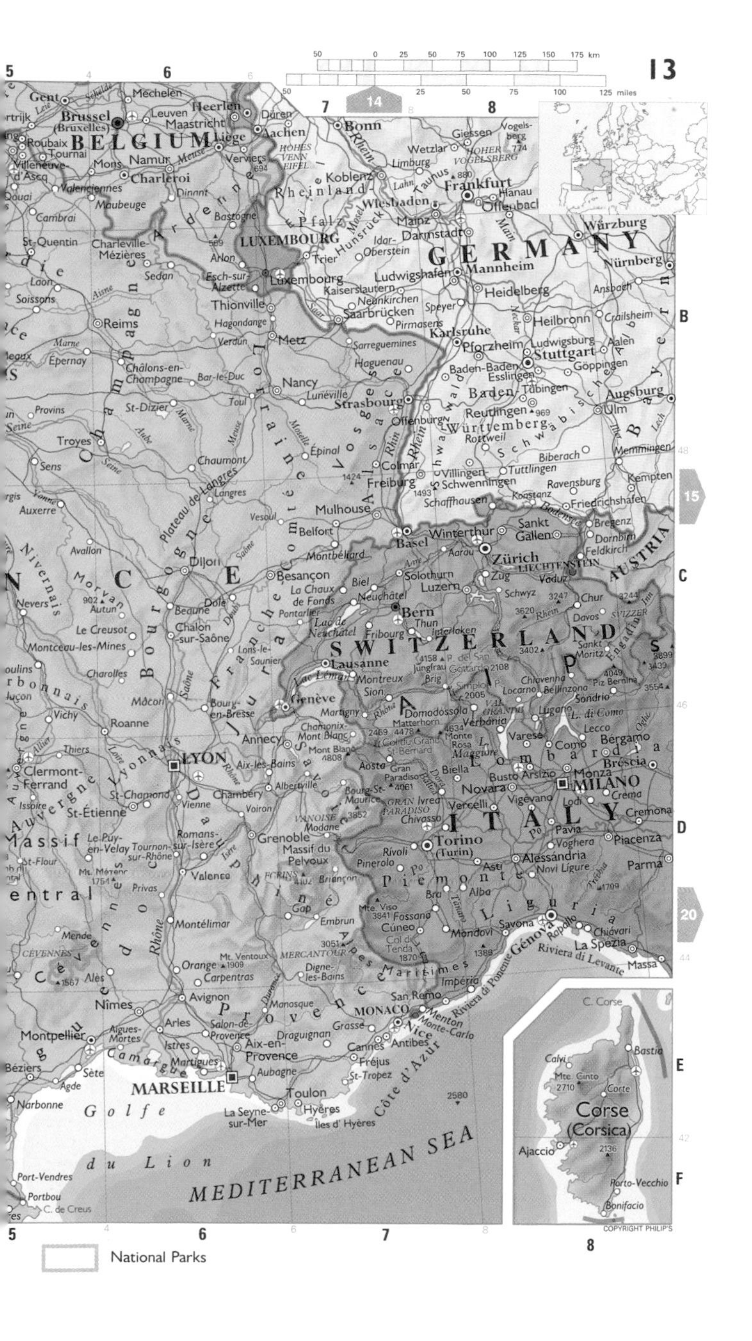

National Parks

16 CENTRAL EUROPE
GERMANY
POLAND
CZECH REP.
SLOVAK REPUBLIC
AUSTRIA
HUNGARY
SLOVENIA
CROATIA
SERBIA
BERLIN
WARSZAWA (Warsaw)
PRAHA (Prague)
WIEN (Vienna)
BUDAPEST
ZAGREB
Bratislava
Ljubljana
Zatoka Gdańska
Zalew Wiślany
Kaliningrad
Gdańsk
Gdynia
Sopot
Słupsk
Koszalin
Kołobrzeg
Szczecin
Stettiner Haff
Usedom
Wolin
Świnoujście
Neubrandenburg
Schwedt
Eberswalde-Finow
Fürstenwalde
Frankfurt
Gorzów Wielkopolski
Pojezierze Pomorskie
Pojezierze Mazurskie
Bydgoszcz
Toruń
Grudziądz
Elbląg
Olsztyn
Włocławek
Płock
Poznań
Gniezno
Wisła
Warta
Odra
Oder
Noteć
Zielona Góra
Leszno
Kalisz
Łódź
Piotrków Trybunalski
Radom
Kielce
Częstochowa
Wrocław
Legnica
Opole
Katowice
Bytom
Sosnowiec
Gliwice
Zabrze
Chorzów
Tychy
Kraków
Tarnów
Bielsko-Biała
Dresden
Görlitz
Cottbus
Chemnitz
Erzgebirge
Liberec
Ústí nad Labem
Karlovy Vary
Plzeň
České Budějovice
Hradec Králové
Pardubice
Ostrava
Olomouc
Brno
Zlín
Jihlava
Českomoravská Vrchovina
Böhmerwald
Sudety
Labe
Vltava
Žilina
Trenčín
Banská Bystrica
Košice
Prešov
Nitra
Trnava
Západné Beskydy
Nízke Tatry
Slovenské Rudohorie
Malé Karpaty
Linz
Passau
Salzburg
Sankt Pölten
Wiener Neustadt
Graz
Klagenfurt
Steiermark
Kärnten
Karawanken
Donau (Danube)
Duna (Danube)
Győr
Sopron
Szombathely
Székesfehérvár
Balaton
Bakony
Veszprém
Kecskemét
Szeged
Pécs
Miskolc
Debrecen
Szolnok
Maribor
Celje
Kranj
Trieste
Rijeka
Karlovac
Osijek
Drava
Sava
Subotica
Novi Sad
Vojvodina
Timișoara
Arad
Projection: Conical with two standard parallels
m ft

BELARUS
UKRAINE
MOLDOVA
ROMANIA
MINSK
Hrodna
Lida
Navahrudak
Baranavichy
Slonim
Vawkavysk
Białystok
Brest
Pinsk
Luninyets
Mazyr
Babruysk
Asipovichy
Dzyarzhynsk
Slutsk
Salihorsk
Svyetlahorsk
Rechytsa
Homyel
Zhlobin
Rogachow
Bykhaw
Slawharad
Kalinkavichy
Khoyniki
Pripet Marshes
Chornobyl
Ovruch
Korosten
Malyn
KYYIV (Kiev)
Irpin
Vasylkiv
Fastiv
Bila Tserkva
Zhytomyr
Berdychiv
Novohrad-Volynskyy
Rivne
Lutsk
Kovel
Volodymyr-Volynskyy
Dubno
Kremenets
Shepetivka
Lviv (Lvov)
Ternopil
Khmelnytskyy
Vinnytsya
Zhmerynka
Kamyanets-Podilskyy
Mohyliv-Podilskyy
Uman
Chernivtsi
Kolomyya
Ivano-Frankivsk
Kalush
Stryy
Drohobych
Boryslav
Sambir
Uzhhorod
Mukacheve
Khust
Podilska Vysochyna
Bălţi
Soroca
Orhei
Chişinău
Tiraspol
Tighina
Dubăsari
Cahul
Comrat
Ungheni
Izmayil
Reni
Kiliya
Vylkove
Bilhorod-Dnistrovskyy
Suceava
Botoşani
Iaşi
Vaslui
Bârlad
Roman
Piatra Neamţ
Bacău
Oneşti
Focşani
Galaţi
Brăila
Buzău
Tecuci
Braşov
Sibiu
Făgăraş
Sighişoara
Mediaş
Târgu Mureş
Cluj-Napoca
Zalău
Satu Mare
Baia Mare
Bistriţa
Alba-Iulia
Deva
Hunedoara
Petroşani
Carpaţii Meridionali
Transilvania
Moldova
Dunărea (Danube)
Dnister
Siret
Prut
Dubăsari Vdkhr.
Kyyivske Vdskh.
Ozero Sasyk
Sulina
East from Greenwich
COPYRIGHT PHILIP'S
National Parks
24
25
22

 SPAIN AND PORTUGAL

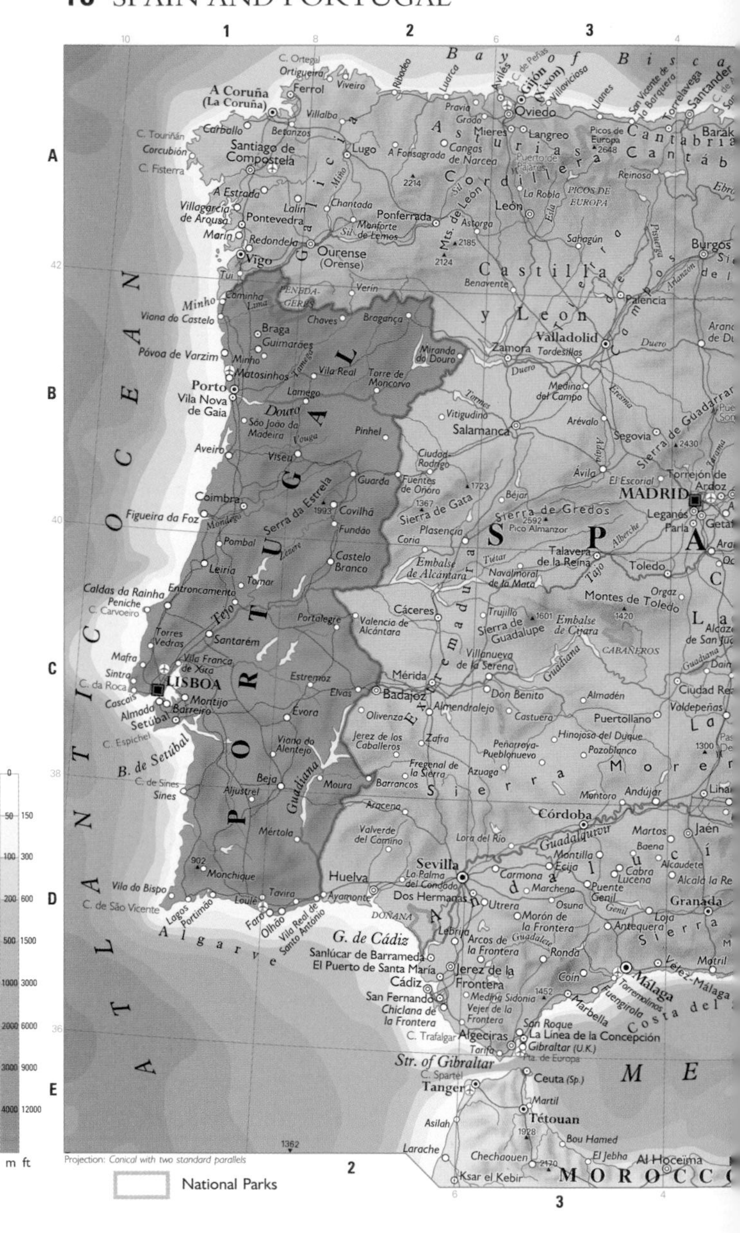

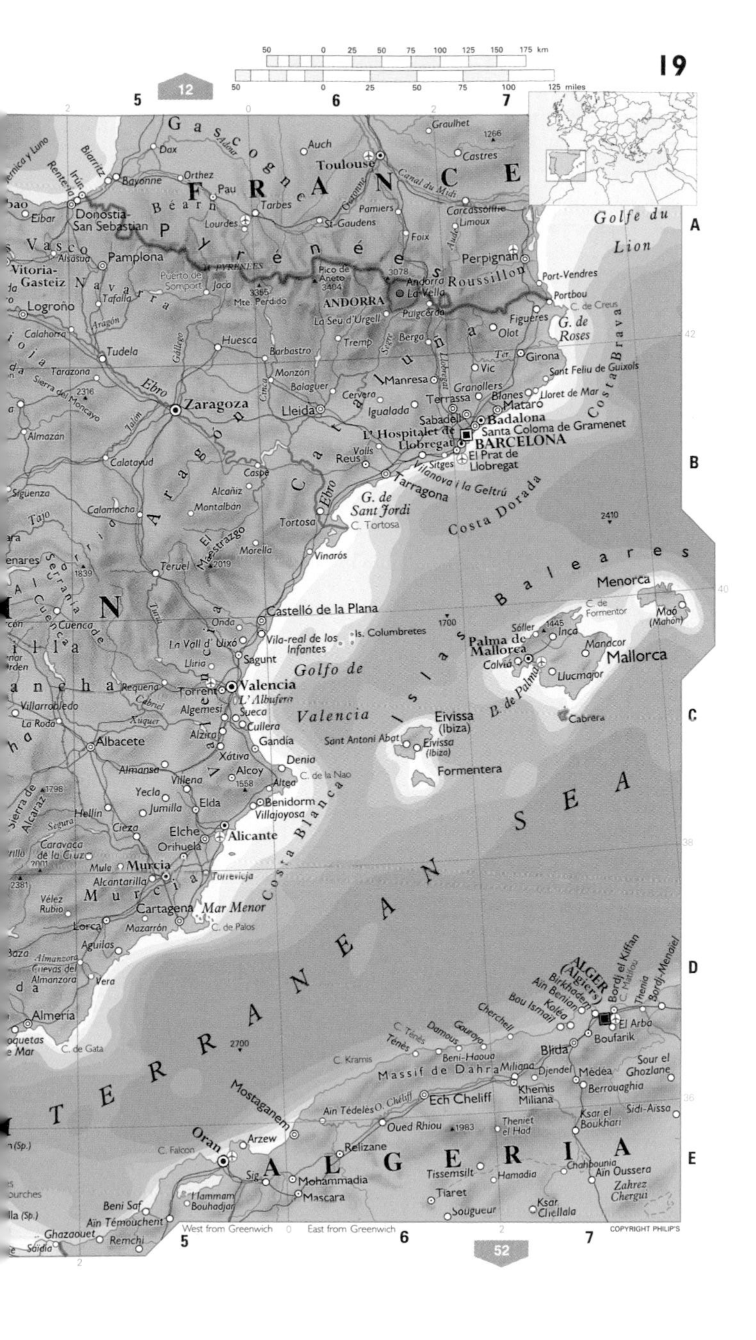

12
5
6
7
FRANCE
Gascogne
Béarn
Pyrénées
Golfe du Lion
Toulouse
Auch
Dax
Bayonne
Biarritz
Orthez
Pau
Tarbes
Lourdes
St-Gaudens
Pamiers
Foix
Carcassonne
Limoux
Castres
Graulhet
Perpignan
Roussillon
Port-Vendres
Portbou
C. de Creus
Donostia-San Sebastian
Irún
Rentería
Eibar
Alsasua
Vitoria-Gasteiz
Pamplona
Navarra
Tafalla
Logroño
Calahorra
Tudela
Tarazona
Sierra del Moncayo
Jaca
Puerto de Somport
Mte. Perdido
Pico de Aneto
ANDORRA
Andorra La Vella
La Seu d'Urgell
Puigcerdà
Tremp
Berga
Olot
Figueres
G. de Roses
Girona
Vic
Huesca
Barbastro
Monzón
Balaguer
Cervera
Manresa
Granollers
Blanes
Lloret de Mar
Sant Feliu de Guixols
Costa Brava
Terrassa
Igualada
Sabadell
Mataró
Badalona
Santa Coloma de Gramenet
L'Hospitalet de Llobregat
BARCELONA
El Prat de Llobregat
Sitges
Vilanova i la Geltrú
Valls
Reus
Tarragona
Costa Dorada
G. de Sant Jordi
C. Tortosa
Tortosa
Lleida
Ebro
Zaragoza
Aragón
Cataluña
Caspe
Alcañiz
Montalbán
Calamocha
Calatayud
Almazán
Sigüenza
Tajo
El Maestrazgo
Morella
Vinaròs
Teruel
Serranía de Cuenca
Cuenca
Castelló de la Plana
Onda
Vila-real de los Infantes
Is. Columbretes
La Vall d'Uixó
Sagunt
Llíria
Golfo de Valencia
Valencia
Torrent
L'Albufera
Requena
Algemesí
Sueca
Cullera
Alzira
Gandía
Xàtiva
Villarrobledo
La Roda
Albacete
Almansa
Alcoy
Villena
Denia
C. de la Nao
Altea
Benidorm
Villajoyosa
Yecla
Elda
Jumilla
Hellín
Cieza
Elche
Alicante
Orihuela
Caravaca de la Cruz
Mula
Murcia
Alcantarilla
Torrevieja
Costa Blanca
Cartagena
Mar Menor
C. de Palos
Mazarrón
Lorca
Vélez Rubio
Águilas
Cuevas del Almanzora
Vera
Almería
C. de Gata
Islas Baleares
Menorca
C. de Formentor
Maó (Mahón)
Sóller
Inca
Palma de Mallorca
Calvià
Manacor
Mallorca
Llucmajor
B. de Palma
Cabrera
Eivissa (Ibiza)
Sant Antoni Abat
Formentera
MEDITERRANEAN SEA
ALGER (Algiers)
Bordj el Kiffan
C. Matifou
Thenia
Bordj-Menaïel
Birkhadem
Aïn Benian
Koléa
Bou Ismaïl
Cherchell
Gouraya
Damous
C. Ténès
Ténès
Beni-Haoua
El Arba
Boufarik
Blida
Miliana
Massif de Dahra
Djendel
Médéa
Sour el Ghozlane
Khemis Miliana
Berrouaghia
C. Kramis
Mostaganem
Aïn Tédelès
O. Chéliff
Ech Cheliff
Oued Rhiou
Theniet el Had
Ksar el Boukhari
Sidi-Aïssa
Arzew
Oran
C. Falcon
Relizane
ALGERIA
Chahbounia
Aïn Oussera
Zahrez Chergui
Tissemsilt
Hamadia
Sig
Mohammadia
Mascara
Tiaret
Hammam Bouhadjar
Beni Saf
Aïn Témouchent
Ghazaouet
Remchi
Sougueur
Ksar Chellala
West from Greenwich
East from Greenwich
COPYRIGHT PHILIP'S
52

HUNGARY
ROMANIA
UKRAINE
CROATIA
BOSNIA-HERZEGOVINA
SERBIA
MONTENEGRO
KOSOVO
MACEDONIA
BULGARIA
BLACK SEA
ADRIATIC
Marmara
Transilvania
Carpații Meridionali
Vojvodina
Valahia
Dobrogea
Stara Planina
Rhodopi Planina
Pirin Planina
Suva Planina
Yıldız Dağları
İstanbul Boğazı (Bosporus)
BUCUREȘTI (Bucharest)
BEOGRAD (Belgrade)
SOFIYA
İSTANBUL
Sarajevo
Podgorica
Skopje
Priština
Tiranë
Constanța
Varna
Burgas
Galați
Brăila
Ploiești
Brașov
Sibiu
Craiova
Timișoara
Arad
Novi Sad
Subotica
Szeged
Pécs
Osijek
Tuzla
Mostar
Niš
Kragujevac
Plovdiv
Ruse
Pleven
Shumen
Dobrich
Stara Zagora
Edirne
Tekirdağ
Dubrovnik
Shkodra
Durrës
Tulcea
Focșani
Buzău
Pitești
Târgu-Jiu
Drobeta-Turnu Severin
Vidin
Vratsa
Montana
Veliko Tŭrnovo
Gabrovo
Sliven
Yambol
Kŭrdzhali
Khaskovo
Blagoevgrad
Kyustendil
Pernik
Kumanovo
Tetovo
Prilep
Peć
Prizren
Novi Pazar
Kraljevo
Čačak
Užice
Valjevo
Zrenjanin
Pančevo
Smederevo
Zenica
Vukovar
Tisa
Sava
Drava
Morava
Prut
Siret
Olt
Mureș
Dunărea (Danube)
m
ft
4000
3000
2000
1000
500
200
100
50
12000
9000
6000
3000
1500
600
300
150
0
1
2
3
4
5
6
7
A
B
C
D
17
20

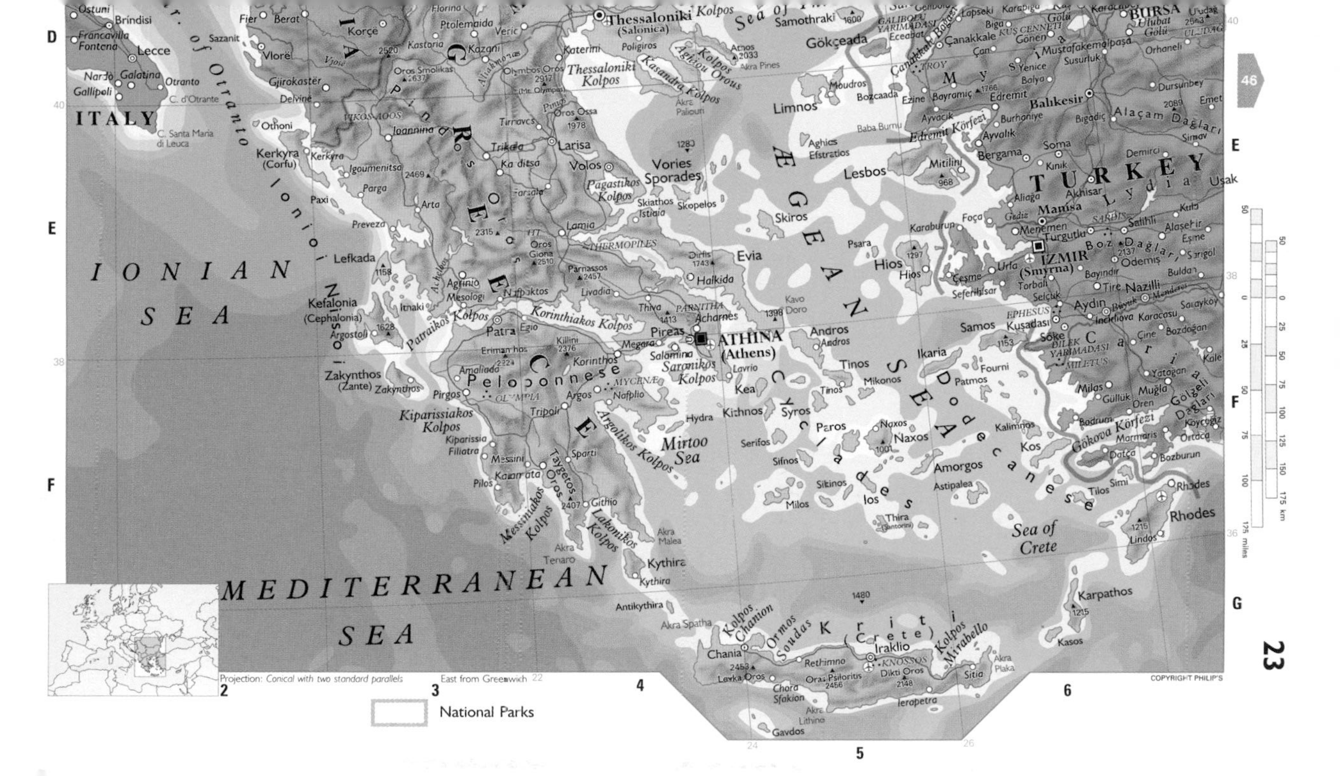
ITALY
GREECE
TURKEY
IONIAN SEA
MEDITERRANEAN SEA
AEGEAN SEA
Sea of Crete
Mirtoo Sea
Str. of Otranto
Peloponnese
Kriti (Crete)
Cyclades
Dodecanese
ATHINA (Athens)
Thessaloniki (Salonica)
IZMIR (Smyrna)
BURSA
Balıkesir
Manisa
Aydın
Nazilli
Muğla
Brindisi
Lecce
Otranto
Gallipoli
Galatina
Vlorë
Berat
Korçë
Gjirokastër
Kerkyra (Corfu)
Ioannina
Larisa
Volos
Lamia
Patra
Korinthos
Pireas
Argos
Nafplio
Tripoli
Sparti
Kalamata
Pirgos
Kefalonia (Cephalonia)
Zakynthos (Zante)
Lefkada
Evia
Halkida
Limnos
Lesbos
Mitilini
Hios
Samos
Ikaria
Naxos
Paros
Tinos
Andros
Milos
Thira (Santorini)
Amorgos
Kos
Rhodes
Karpathos
Kythira
Chania
Iraklio
Sitia
Ierapetra
Gavdos
Korinthiakos Kolpos
Saronikos Kolpos
Argolikos Kolpos
Lakonikos Kolpos
Messiniakos Kolpos
Thessaloniki Kolpos
Vories Sporades
Skiros
Gökçeada
Samothraki
Çanakkale
Edremit Körfezi
Gökova Körfezi
Projection: Conical with two standard parallels
East from Greenwich
National Parks
COPYRIGHT PHILIP'S
46
0 25 50 75 100 125 150 175 km
0 25 50 75 100 125 miles

BALTIC SEA
Gulf of Finland
Gulf of Riga
ESTONIA
LATVIA
LITHUANIA
BELARUS
POLAND
RUSSIA
TSENTRALNYY
PRIVOLZHSKIY
MORDVINIA
CHUVASHIA
TATARSTAN
UDMURTIA
Tallinn
Rīga
Vilnius
MINSK
SANKT-PETERBURG (St. Petersburg)
MOSKVA (Moscow)
KYYIV (Kiev)
KHARKIV (Kharkov)
WARSZAWA (Warsaw)
Kaliningrad (Russia)
NIZHNIY NOVGOROD
KAZAN
SAMARA
Severnyye Uvaly
Valdayskaya Vozvyshennost
Volga
Pripet Marshes

BLACK SEA
CASPIAN SEA
Sea of Azov
Caucasus Mountains
Caspian Depression
YUZHNYY
ROMANIA
MOLDOVA
BULGARIA
TURKEY
GEORGIA
ARMENIA
AZERBAIJAN
IRAN
Anadolu
Kuzey Anadolu Dağları
CRIMEA
KALMYKIA
DAGESTAN
CHECHENIA
ADYGEA
ABKHAZIA
AJARIA
KARACHEY-CHERKESSIA
KABARDINO-BALKARIA
NORTH OSSETIA
South Ossetia
Bessarabia
BUCUREŞTI (Bucharest)
Chişinău
Tiraspol
ODESA
Mykolayiv
Kherson
DONETSK
Zaporizhzhya
Mariupol
ROSTOV
Krasnodar
Stavropol
Astrakhan
Elista
Makhachkala
Groznyy
Vladikavkaz
Nalchik
TBILISI
YEREVAN
BAKI (Baku)
ANKARA
İSTANBUL
BURSA
İZMIR (Smyrna)
Sochi
Sokhumi
Batumi
Trabzon
Samsun
Sinop
Simferopol
Sevastopol
Yalta
Kerch
Feodosiya
Novorossiysk
Constanța
Varna
Burgas
Tabrīz
Van Gölü
Erzurum
Kayseri
Sivas
Malatya
Marmara Denizi
Projection: Conical with two standard parallels
East from Greenwich
COPYRIGHT PHILIP'S

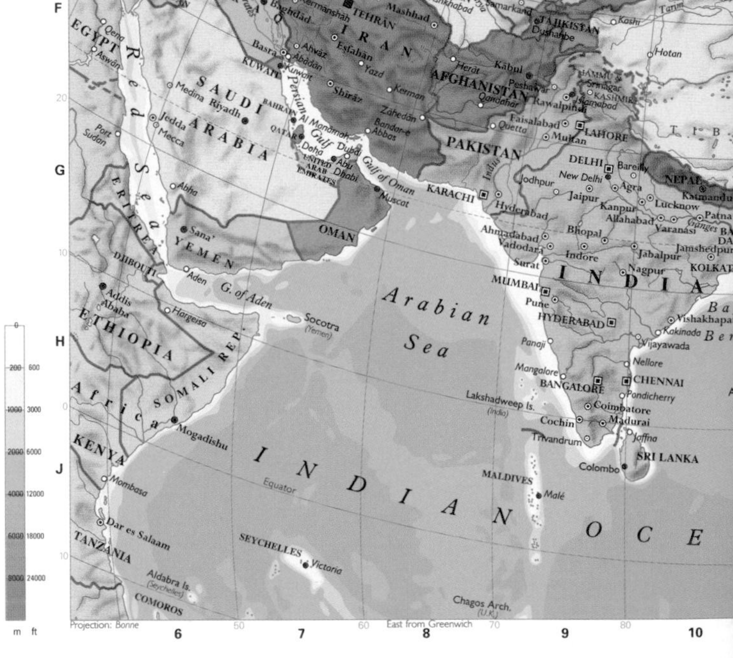
100 0 200 400 600 800 1000 1200 1400 km
100 0 200 400 600 800 1000 miles
C
B
A
D
E
F
G
H
J
6
7
8
9
10
Barents Sea
Kara Sea
Novaya Zemlya
North Sea
NORWAY
SWEDEN
FINLAND
UNITED KINGDOM
LONDON
PARIS
GERMANY
Europe
Berlin
Warsaw
ESTONIA
LATVIA
LITH.
Riga
Kaliningrad
BELARUS
ST. PETERSBURG
MOSCOW
UKRAINE
Kiev
ROMANIA
Belgrade
Danube
BULGARIA
GREECE
Athens
Odessa
Rostov
Volgograd
Black Sea
ISTANBUL
Bursa
Izmir
Ankara
Samsun
TURKEY
Erzurum
Konya
Kayseri
Adana
Gaziantep
Antalya
Krasnodar
Stavropol
KALMYKIA
GEORGIA
Tbilisi
ARM.
AZER.
Yerevan
Baku
Caspian Sea
Astrakhan
Atyraū
Ural
Aqtobe
Uralsk
Orenburg
Orsk
Murmansk
Archangelsk
Onega
KARELIA
Kotlas
Rybinsk
Vologda
Yaroslavl
Smolensk
Tula
Ryazan
Orel
Voronezh
Nizhniy Novgorod
Kirov
Glazov
Perm
Izhevsk
Kazan
Simbirsk
Samara
BASHKORTOSTAN
Ufa
Magnitogorsk
Chelyabinsk
Yekaterinburg
Kustanay
Nizhniy Tagil
Serov
Syktyvkar
Ukhta
KOMI
Naryan-Mar
Vorkuta
Amderma
Salekhard
Novyy Port
Ob
Surgut
Irtysh
Tobolsk
Tyumen
Omsk
Novosibirsk
Novokuznetsk
Pavlodar
Astana
Karaganda
Semey
Oskemen
GORNO-ALTAY
KAZAKHSTAN
Aral
Aral Sea
KARAKALPAKSTAN
UZBEKISTAN
Syrdarya
Amudarya
Urgench
TURKMENISTAN
Ashkhabad
Mashhad
L. Balkhash
Taraz
Almaty
Bishkek
KYRGYZSTAN
Tashkent
Samarkand
TAJIKISTAN
Dushanbe
Ürümqi
Tarim
Kashi
Hotan
Mediterranean Sea
Nicosia
CYPRUS
LEB.
Beirut
Tel Aviv-Jaffa
ISRAEL
Jerusalem
Amman
JORDAN
Damascus
SYRIA
Aleppo
Mosul
Kirkuk
Tigris
Euphrates
IRAQ
Baghdad
Tabriz
TEHRAN
Kermanshah
IRAN
Esfahan
Ahvaz
Abadan
Basra
KUWAIT
Kuwait
Yazd
Shiraz
Kerman
Zahedan
Bandar-e Abbas
Herat
Kabul
AFGHANISTAN
Qandahar
Peshawar
Rawalpindi
Islamabad
Srinagar
KASHMIR
JAMMU
Faisalabad
LAHORE
Quetta
Multan
PAKISTAN
Indus
KARACHI
Hyderabad
Alexandria
CAIRO
Suez
Nile
Qena
Aswan
EGYPT
Red Sea
Medina
Riyadh
SAUDI ARABIA
Jedda
Mecca
BAHRAIN
QATAR
Doha
Al Manamah
Persian Gulf
Dubai
Abu Dhabi
UNITED ARAB EMIRATES
Gulf of Oman
Muscat
OMAN
Port Sudan
Abha
ERITREA
Sana'
YEMEN
Aden
G. of Aden
DJIBOUTI
Addis Ababa
ETHIOPIA
Hargeisa
Socotra (Yemen)
SOMALI REP.
Mogadishu
Africa
KENYA
Mombasa
Dar es Salaam
TANZANIA
Aldabra Is. (Seychelles)
COMOROS
SEYCHELLES
Victoria
Arabian Sea
INDIAN OCEAN
Equator
MALDIVES
Malé
Chagos Arch. (U.K.)
Lakshadweep Is. (India)
DELHI
New Delhi
Bareilly
Jodhpur
Jaipur
Agra
Kanpur
Lucknow
Allahabad
Varanasi
Patna
Ganges
NEPAL
Katmandu
Ahmadabad
Vadodara
Bhopal
Indore
Jabalpur
Jamshedpur
KOLKATA
Surat
Nagpur
INDIA
MUMBAI
Pune
HYDERABAD
Vishakhapatnam
Kakinada
Vijayawada
Panaji
Nellore
Mangalore
BANGALORE
CHENNAI
Pondicherry
Coimbatore
Cochin
Madurai
Trivandrum
Jaffna
Colombo
SRI LANKA
Projection: Bonne
East from Greenwich
m ft
0
200 600
1000 3000
2000 6000
4000 12000
6000 18000
8000 24000

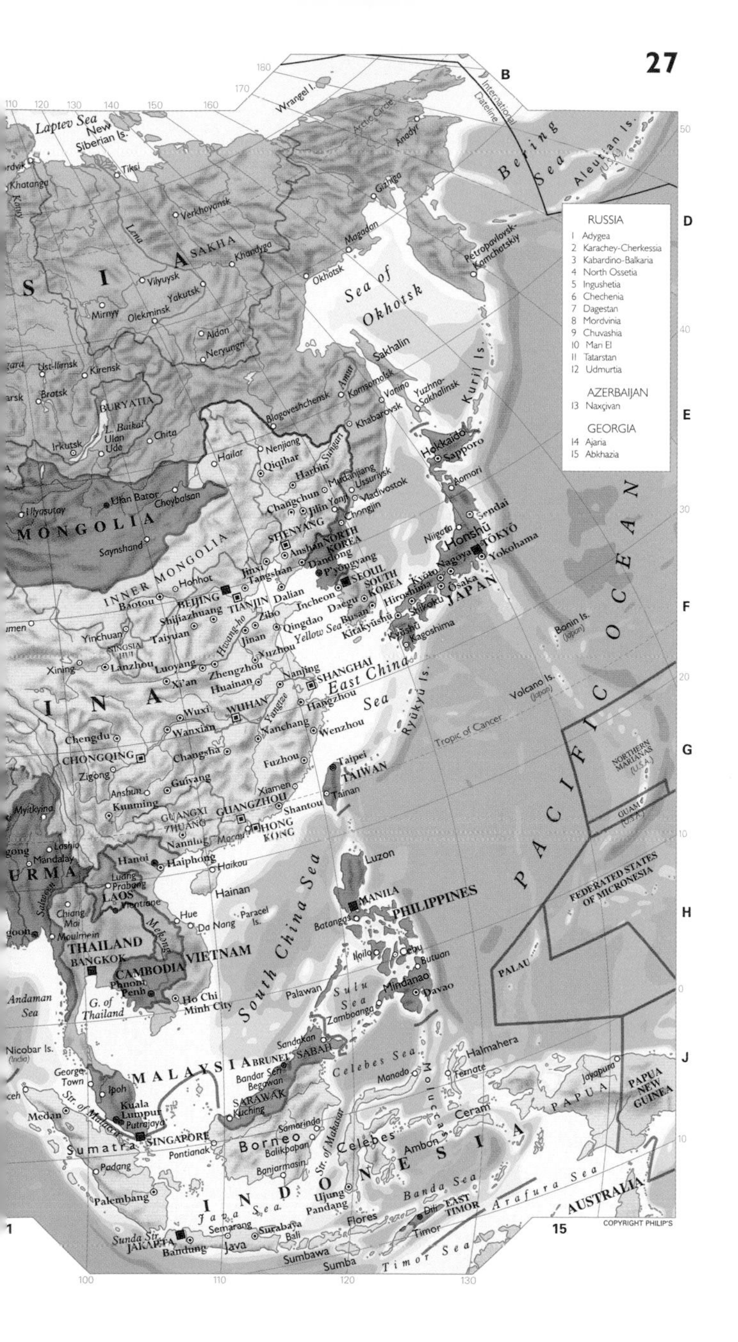
RUSSIA
1 Adygea
2 Karachey-Cherkessia
3 Kabardino-Balkaria
4 North Ossetia
5 Ingushetia
6 Chechenia
7 Dagestan
8 Mordvinia
9 Chuvashia
10 Mari El
11 Tatarstan
12 Udmurtia
AZERBAIJAN
13 Naxçivan
GEORGIA
14 Ajaria
15 Abkhazia
Laptev Sea
New Siberian Is.
Wrangel I.
International Dateline
Arctic Circle
Bering Sea
Aleutian Is. (U.S.A.)
Anadyr
Tiksi
Khatanga
Verkhoyansk
Gizhiga
Lena
SAKHA
Khandyga
Magadan
Petropavlovsk-Kamchatskiy
Okhotsk
Sea of Okhotsk
Vilyuysk
Yakutsk
Mirnyy
Olekminsk
Aldan
Neryungri
Sakhalin
Kuril Is.
Ust-Ilimsk
Kirensk
Bratsk
BURYATIA
Komsomolsk
Vanino
Yuzhno-Sakhalinsk
Amur
Blagoveshchensk
Khabarovsk
L. Baikal
Irkutsk
Ulan Ude
Chita
Hailar
Nenjiang
Qiqihar
Harbin
Sungari
Hokkaido
Sapporo
Mudanjiang
Ussuriysk
Vladivostok
Aomori
Changchun
Jilin
Yanji
Ulan Bator
Choybalsan
Ulyasutay
MONGOLIA
Saynshand
INNER MONGOLIA
Chongjin
Sendai
SHENYANG
Anshan
NORTH KOREA
Niigata
Honshū
TŌKYŌ
Yokohama
Dandong
P'yongyang
Nagoya
Kyōto
Ōsaka
Jinxi
Tangshan
SEOUL
SOUTH KOREA
Hohhot
Baotou
BEIJING
TIANJIN
Dalian
Incheon
Daegu
Hiroshima
Shikoku
JAPAN
Shijiazhuang
Taiyuan
Zibo
Jinan
Qingdao
Yellow Sea
Busan
Kitakyūshū
Kyūshū
Kagoshima
Yinchuan
NINGSIA HUI
Hwang-ho
Xuzhou
Bonin Is. (Japan)
Xining
Lanzhou
Luoyang
Zhengzhou
Xi'an
Huainan
Nanjing
SHANGHAI
East China Sea
Ryūkyū Is.
Volcano Is. (Japan)
Wuxi
WUHAN
Yangtze
Hangzhou
Wanxian
Nanchang
Wenzhou
Tropic of Cancer
Chengdu
CHONGQING
Changsha
Fuzhou
Taipei
TAIWAN
NORTHERN MARIANAS (U.S.A.)
Zigong
Anshun
Guiyang
Xiamen
Tainan
GUAM (U.S.A.)
PACIFIC OCEAN
Kunming
GUANGXI ZHUANG
GUANGZHOU
Shantou
HONG KONG
Macau
Myitkyina
Lashio
Mandalay
BURMA
Nanning
Hanoi
Haiphong
Haikou
Luzon
Luang Prabang
LAOS
Vientiane
Hainan
MANILA
PHILIPPINES
FEDERATED STATES OF MICRONESIA
Chiang Mai
Salween
Hue
Da Nang
Paracel Is.
Batangas
Moulmein
Mekong
THAILAND
BANGKOK
VIETNAM
South China Sea
Iloilo
Cebu
Butuan
PALAU
CAMBODIA
Phnom Penh
Palawan
Mindanao
Davao
Andaman Sea
G. of Thailand
Ho Chi Minh City
Sulu Sea
Zamboanga
Nicobar Is. (India)
Sandakan
SABAH
BRUNEI
Celebes Sea
Halmahera
George Town
MALAYSIA
Bandar Seri Begawan
Manado
Ternate
Jayapura
Ipoh
Kuala Lumpur
Putrajaya
SARAWAK
Kuching
Moluccas
PAPUA
PAPUA NEW GUINEA
Medan
Str. of Malacca
Samarinda
Str. of Makasar
Ceram
SINGAPORE
Sumatra
Pontianak
Borneo
Balikpapan
Celebes
Ambon
Padang
Banjarmasin
INDONESIA
Banda Sea
Arafura Sea
Palembang
Java Sea
Ujung Pandang
Dili
EAST TIMOR
AUSTRALIA
Flores
Timor
Sunda Str.
JAKARTA
Semarang
Surabaya
Bali
Bandung
Java
Sumbawa
Sumba
Timor Sea
COPYRIGHT PHILIP'S

RUSSIA
1 Adygea
2 Karachey-Cherkessia
3 Kabardino-Balkaria
4 North Ossetia
5 Ingushetia
6 Chechenia
7 Dagestan
8 Mordvinia
9 Chuvashia
10 Mari El
11 Tatarstan
12 Udmurtia
13 Khakassia
AZERBAIJAN
14 Naxçivan
GEORGIA
15 Ajaria
16 Abkhazia
UKRAINE
17 Crimea
ARCTIC OCEAN
Barents Sea
Kara Sea
Zemlya Frantsa Iosifa
Novaya Zemlya
Beloye More
Gulf of Bothnia
Gulf of Finland
Baltic Sea
North Sea
NORWAY
SWEDEN
FINLAND
ESTONIA
LATVIA
LITHUANIA
BELARUS
POLAND
UKRAINE
MOLDOVA
DENMARK
GERMANY
RUSSIA
MOSKVA
SANKT-PETERBURG
STOCKHOLM
Helsinki
Tallinn
Riga
Vilnius
MINSK
WARSZAWA
KYYIV
BERLIN
KØBENHAVN
Oslo
Murmansk
Arkhangelsk
Vorkuta
Kaliningrad

KAZAKHSTAN
UZBEKISTAN
TURKMENISTAN
KYRGYZSTAN
TAJIKISTAN
AFGHANISTAN
IRAN
IRAQ
TURKEY
GEORGIA
ARMENIA
AZERBAIJAN
CHINA
SIBIRSKIY
Caspian Sea
Aral Sea
Black Sea
Ustyurt Plateau
Garagum
Kyzyl Kum
Balqash Köl
Junggar Pendi
Pamir
ASTANA
ALMATY
BISHKEK
TOSHKENT (Tashkent)
DUSHANBE
ASHGABAT
BAKI (Baku)
TBILISI
YEREVAN
TEHRĀN
BAGHDĀD
ÜRÜMQI
OMSK
NOVOSIBIRSK
YEKATERINBURG
CHELYABINSK
VOLGOGRAD
SAMARA
UFA
ROSTOV
Orenburg
Astrakhan
Qaraghandy (Karaganda)
Pavlodar
Semey
Öskemen
Barnaul
Tomsk
Kemerovo
Novokuznetsk
Samarqand
Bukhoro
Nukus
Dashoguz
Türkmenbashi
Mary
MASHHAD
ESFAHĀN
SHĪRĀZ
TABRĪZ
AL MAWSIL (Mosul)
Kashi
Turpan
Projection: Conical Orthomorphic with two standard parallels
East from Greenwich
COPYRIGHT PHILIP'S

30 EASTERN SIBERIA
A
ARCTIC OCEAN
Zemlya Georga
Ostrov Rudolfa
Zemlya Frantsa Iosifa
Ostrov Greem-Bell
Ostrov Shmidta
Mys Arkticheskiy
Ostrov Komsomolets
Ostrov Pioner
Ostrov Oktyabrskoy Revolyutsii
965
Ostrov Bolshevik
Severnaya Zemlya
Proliv Vilkitskogo
Mys Chelyuskin
Laptev Sea
Ostrov Belkovski
3800
Novaya Zemlya
Pik Sedova 1115
Mys Sporyy Navolok
Kara Sea
Matochkin Shar
Ostrov Belyy
Poluostrov Taymyr
Gory Byrranga
1146
Oz. Taymyr
Nordvik
Ostrov Bolshoy Begichev
Ust Olenek
Olenek
Tit-Ary
Diksen
Yeniseyskiy Zaliv
Obskaya Guba
Poluostrov Yamal
Amderma
Kara
Gydanskiy Poluostrov
Pyasina
Volochanka
Kheta
Chernaya
Karaul
Ust Port
Dudinka
Norilsk
Gory Putorana
1701
Novorybnoye
Khatanga
Kotuy
Saskylakh
Anabar
Zhilinda
Khalmer Yu
Novyy Port
Labytnangi
Yar-Sale
Salekhard
Nyda
Tazovskiy
Novyy Urengoy
Nadym
Igarka
Karasino
Yessey
Moyyero
962
Arctic Circle
Turukhansk
Tarko Sale
Krasnoselkup
Taz
Pur
Yenisey
Vilyuy
Noginsk
Nizhnyaya Tunguska
Tura
Noyabrsk
Surgut
URALSKIY
Yukta
Chernyshevskiy
Mirnyy
Nizhnevartovsk
Vakh
Strezhevoy
Yerbogachen
Lensk
Taylakova
Podkamennaya Tunguska
Kuyumba
Mutoray
Sym
Yartsevo
Severo-Yeniseyskiy
Vanavara
1104
Vitim
Kargasok
Narym
SIBIRSKIY
Kezhma
Korshunovo
Mama
Tara
Kolpashevo
Ket
Belyy Yar
Yeniseysk
Angara
Boguchany
Ust-Ilimsk
Kirensk
Molchanovo
Chulym
Strelka
Makarovo
Ob
Asino
Chuna
Kondratyevo
Ust-Kut
Om
Kuybyshev
Tomsk
Anzhero-Sudzhensk
Zheleznogorsk-Ilimskiy
Magistralnyy
Tatarsk
Bogotol
Achinsk
Kansk
Ilanskiy
Bratsk
Lena
Nizhneangarsk
NOVOSIBIRSK
Kargat
Yurga
Mariinsk
Kemerovo
Leninsk-Kuznetskiy
Krasnoyarsk
Tayshet
2840
Karasuk
Cherepanovo
Berdsk
Belovo
Kamen
Prokopyevsk
Novokuznetsk
Artemovsk
Nizhneudinsk
Slavgorod
Barnaul
Novoaltaysk
Vostochnyy Sayan
Chernogorsk
Minusinsk
Tulun
Barguzin
Pavlodar
Kulunda
Aleisk
Temirtau
Abakan
Zima
Yermak
Biysk
Tashtagol
KHAKASSIA
Cheremkhovo
Ozero Baykal
455
Rubtsovsk
Abaza
Usolye Sibirskoye
Angarsk
1620
Ulan Ude
Semiyarka
Zmeinogorsk
Gorno-Altaysk
Zapadnyy Sayan
Turan
Toora-Khem
Munku-Sardyk 3491
Irkutsk
BURYATIA
Khilok
Semey
Leninogorsk
GORNO-ALTAY
Chadan
Kyzyl
Hovsgol Nuur
Slyudyanka
Petrovsk-Zabaykalskiy
TUVA
KAZAKHSTAN
Öskemen
Inya
Belukha 4506
Tannu Ola
Samagaltay
Uvs Nuur
Hatgal
Gusinoozersk
Kyakhta
Khapchera
Zyryan
Erzin
MONGOLIA
Zakamensk
Darhan
Hentiyn Nuruu
RUSSIA
28
29
34
B
C
D
E
1
2
3
4
5
6
7
8
9
10
11
12
0
200
600
2000
6000
4000
12 000
m
ft
Projection: Conical Orthomorphic with two standard parallels

East Siberian Sea
Ostrov Vrangelya
Chukchi Sea
Mys Dezhneva (East C.)
St. Lawrence I. (U.S.A.)
Anadyrskiy Zaliv
Chukotskoye Nagorye
Koryakskoye Nagorye
Bering Sea
Kolymskoye Nagorye
DALNEVOSTOCHNYY
Khrebet Cherskogo
Verkhoyanskiy Khrebet
Poluostrov Kamchatka
Sredinnyy Khrebet
Petropavlovsk-Kamchatskiy
Sea of Okhotsk
Magadan
Yakutsk
Sakhalin
Khrebet Dzhugdzhur
Stanovoy Khrebet
Kurilskiye Ostrova
Khabarovsk
Khrebet Sikhote Alin
Tatarskiy Proliv
Hokkaidō
SAPPORO
JAPAN
CHINA
Da Hinggan Ling
HARBIN
QIQIHAR
DAQING
Vladivostok
Blagoveshchensk
Komsomolsk
Yuzhno-Sakhalinsk
East from Greenwich
COPYRIGHT PHILIP'S

SEA OF JAPAN
(EAST SEA)
RUSSIA
CHINA
NORTH KOREA
Hokkaidō
Sikhote Alin
Khrebet
Wakkanai
Rebun-Tō
Rishiri-Tō
Esashi
Otoineppu
Ōmu
Mombetsu
Yūbetsu
Abashiri
Abashiri-Wan
Shari
Rausu-Dake
Nemuro
Ostrov Kunashir
Nakashibetsu
Shibecha
Akkeshi
Kushiro
Honbetsu
Kitami
Engaru
Kitami-Sammyaku
Asahigawa
Daisetsu-Zan
Ishikari-Sammyaku
Akabira
Nayoro
Shibetsu
Teshio
Embetsu
Haboro
Rumoi
Takikawa
Bibai
Iwamizawa
Ebetsu
Chitose
Obihiro
Poroshiri-Dake
Hidaka-Sammyaku
Tomakomai
Urakawa
Samani
Hiroo
Erimo-misaki
Ishikari-Wan
Atsuta
Otaru
SAPPORO
Shikotsu-Ko
Tōya-Ko
Muroran
Uchiura-Wan
Iwanai
Suttsu
Setana
Yakumo
Okushiri-Tō
Kamui-Misaki
Hakodate
Esan-Misaki
Matsumae
Shiragami-Misaki
Tsugaru Kaikyō
Shiriya-Zaki
Mutsu
Mutsu-Wan
Ohata
Aomori
Towada
Hachinohe
Towada-Ko
Kanagi
Goshogawara
Hirosaki
Henashi-Misaki
Odate
Kuji
Iwaizumi
Miyako
Kitakami-Sammyaku
Morioka
Iwate-San
Hayachine-San
Kazuno
Noshiro
Oga
Oga-Hantō
Akita
Omagari
Hanamaki
Kamaishi
Kesennuma
Mizusawa
Ichinoseki
Honjō
Chōkai-San
Sakata
Tsuruoka
Gas-San
Yamagata
Furukawa
Ishinomaki
SENDAI
Sendai-Wan
Mogami-Gawa
Terney
Plastun
Dalnegorsk
Kavalerovo
Margaritovo
Preobrazheniye
Lazo
Nakhodka
Rakitnoye
Lesozavodsk
Ariadnoye
Kirovskiy
Gornyy
Spassk Dalniy
Yakovlevka
Arsenev
Sibirtsevo
L. Khanka
Ussuriysk
Artem
Vladivostok
Zaliv Petra Velikogo
Slavyanka
Trudovoye
Pogranichnyy
Kamen-Rybolov
Novokachalinsk
Jixi
Linkou
Suifenhe
Hunchun
Khasan
Najin
Ch'ŏngjin
m
ft

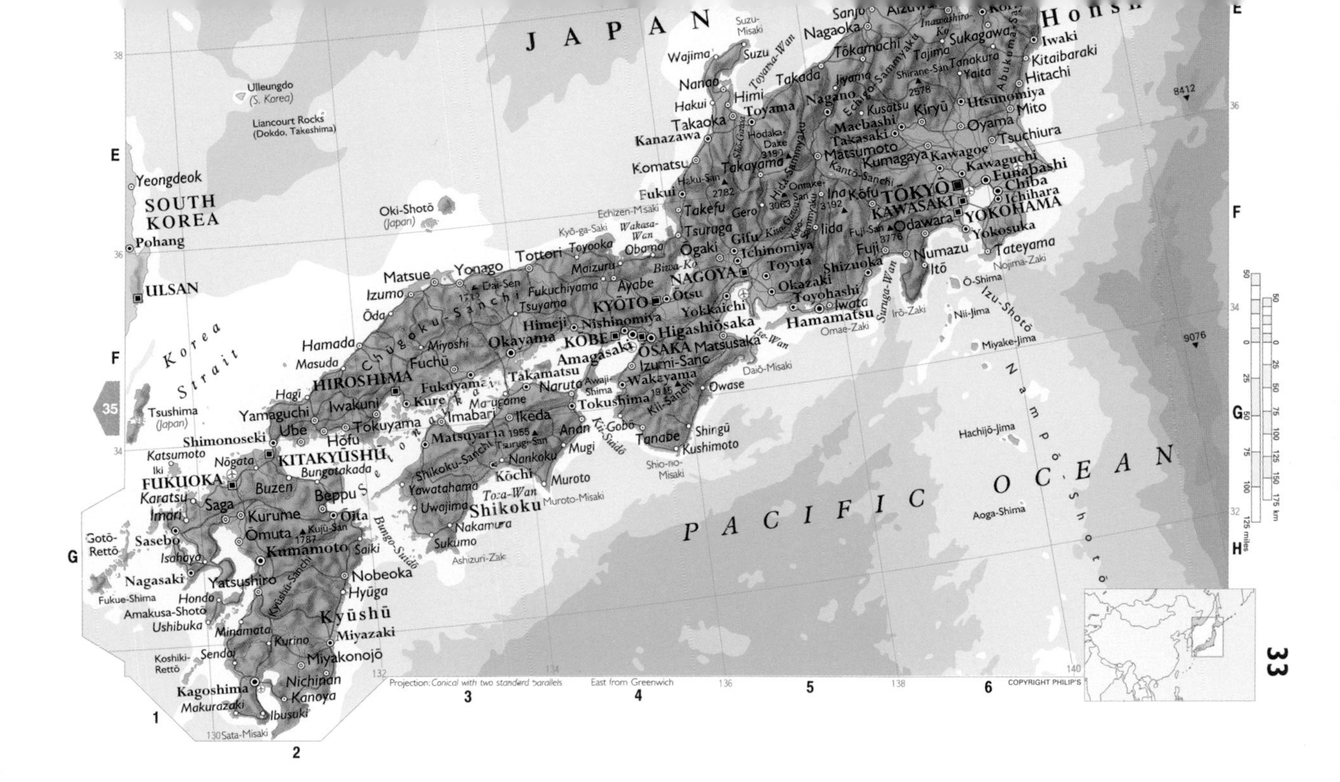

JAPAN
PACIFIC OCEAN
SOUTH KOREA
Korea Strait
Honshū
Shikoku
Kyūshū
Chūgoku-Sanchi
Nampō-Shotō
Izu-Shotō
Oki-Shotō (Japan)
Ulleungdo (S. Korea)
Liancourt Rocks (Dokdo, Takeshima)
Tsushima (Japan)
Yeongdeok
Pohang
ULSAN
TŌKYŌ
YOKOHAMA
KAWASAKI
NAGOYA
KYŌTO
ŌSAKA
KOBE
HIROSHIMA
KITAKYŪSHŪ
FUKUOKA
Chiba
Ichihara
Funabashi
Kawaguchi
Kawagoe
Yokosuka
Tateyama
Odawara
Numazu
Itō
Fuji
Fuji-San 3776
Kōfu
Shizuoka
Hamamatsu
Iwata
Toyohashi
Okazaki
Toyota
Ichinomiya
Gifu
Ōgaki
Takayama
Toyama
Himi
Takaoka
Kanazawa
Komatsu
Fukui
Takefu
Tsuruga
Nanao
Wajima
Hakui
Suzu
Nagano
Matsumoto
Maebashi
Takasaki
Kumagaya
Utsunomiya
Mito
Hitachi
Kitaibaraki
Iwaki
Oyama
Tsuchiura
Kiryū
Nagaoka
Sanjo
Tōkamachi
Takada
Ōtsu
Yokkaichi
Higashiōsaka
Matsusaka
Owase
Shingū
Kushimoto
Tanabe
Gobō
Wakayama
Izumi-Sano
Amagasaki
Nishinomiya
Himeji
Okayama
Tsuyama
Fukuchiyama
Ayabe
Maizuru
Obama
Toyooka
Tottori
Yonago
Matsue
Izumo
Ōda
Hamada
Masuda
Miyoshi
Fuchū
Fukuyama
Kure
Iwakuni
Tokuyama
Hōfu
Ube
Yamaguchi
Hagi
Shimonoseki
Takamatsu
Naruto
Tokushima
Anan
Mugi
Muroto
Kōchi
Nankoku
Ikeda
Imabari
Matsuyama
Yawatahama
Uwajima
Nakamura
Sukumo
Nobeoka
Hyūga
Miyazaki
Miyakonojō
Nichinan
Kanoya
Kagoshima
Ibusuki
Makurazaki
Sendai
Minamata
Yatsushiro
Kumamoto
Ōmuta
Kurume
Saga
Karatsu
Imari
Sasebo
Isahaya
Nagasaki
Hondo
Ushibuka
Beppu
Ōita
Buzen
Nōgata
Iki
Katsumoto
Gotō-Rettō
Fukue-Shima
Amakusa-Shotō
Koshiki-Rettō
Sata-Misaki
Ashizuri-Zaki
Muroto-Misaki
Shiono-Misaki
Daiō-Misaki
Omae-Zaki
Irō-Zaki
Nojima-Zaki
Suzu-Misaki
Echizen-Misaki
Kyō-ga-Saki
Bungo-Suidō
Kii-Suidō
Tosa-Wan
Ise-Wan
Suruga-Wan
Toyama-Wan
Wakasa-Wan
Biwa-Ko
Ō-Shima
Nii-Jima
Miyake-Jima
Hachijō-Jima
Aoga-Shima
Haku-San 2782
Ontake-San 3063
Kuju-San 1787
Shirane-San 2578
9076
8412
COPYRIGHT PHILIP'S
Projection: Conical with two standard parallels
East from Greenwich
km 0 25 50 75 100 125 150 175
miles 0 25 50 75 100 125

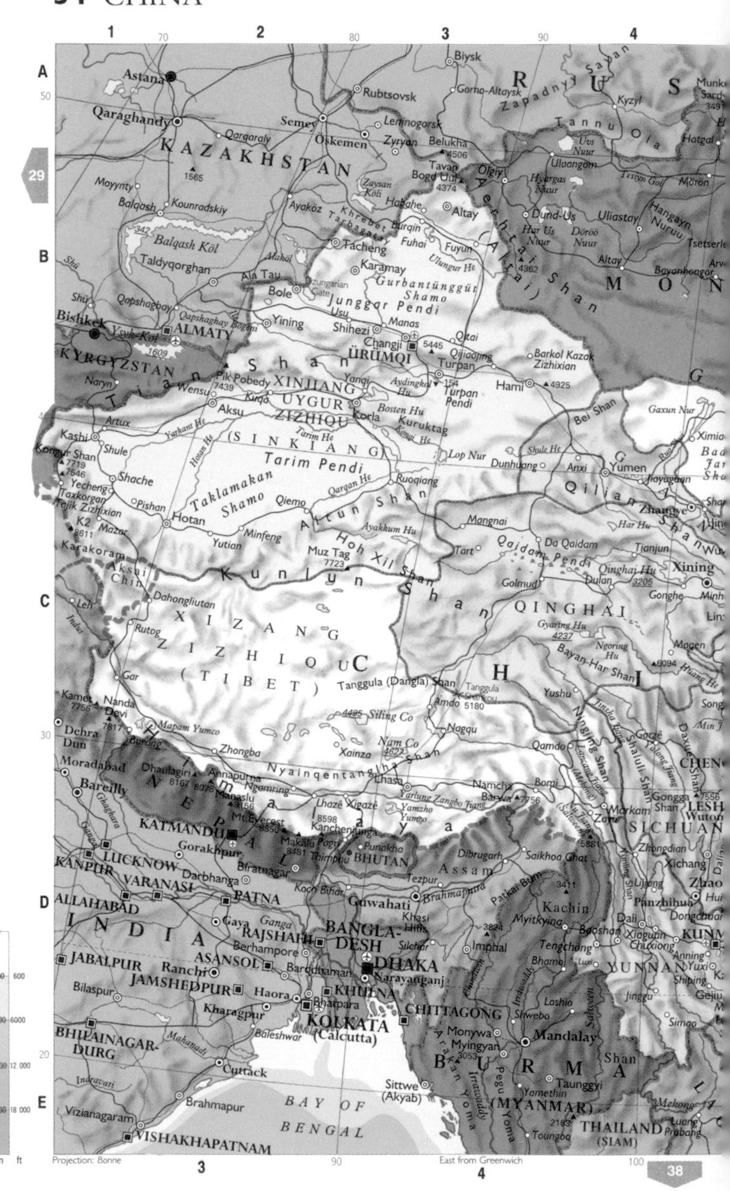
1
2
3
4
70
80
90
A
B
C
D
E
50
40
30
20
Astana
Qaraghandy
Qarqaraly
KAZAKHSTAN
1565
Moyynty
Balqash
Kounradskiy
342
Balqash Köl
Taldyqorghan
Shū
Qapshaghay
Qapshaghay Bogeni
Bishkek
Ysyk-Köl
ALMATY
1609
KYRGYZSTAN
Naryn
Artux
Kashi
Shule
Kongur Shan
7719
7546
Yecheng
Shache
Taxkorgan
Tajik Zizhixian
K2
8611
Mazar
Karakoram
Aksai Chin
Leh
Indus
Rubtsovsk
Semey
Öskemen
Leninogorsk
Zyryan
Zaysan Köli
Ayaköz
Khrebet Tarbagatay
Alaköl
Ala Tau
Tacheng
Karamay
Bole
Dzungarian Gate
Yining
Biysk
Gorno-Altaysk
Belukha
4506
Tavan Bogd Uul
4374
Habahe
Altay
Burqin
Fuhai
Fuyun
Ulungur He
Gurbantünggüt Shamo
Junggar Pendi
Usu
Shihezi
Manas
Changji
ÜRÜMQI
5445
Qitai
Qijiaojing
Turpan
Turpan Pendi
Aydingkol Hu
154
Tian Shan
Pik Pobedy
7439
Wensu
Aksu
Kuqa
Yanqi
Korla
Bosten Hu
Kuruktag
XINJIANG UYGUR ZIZHIQU
(SINKIANG)
Tarim He
Yarkant He
Hotan He
Tarim Pendi
Taklamakan Shamo
Qargan He
Qiemo
Pishan
Hotan
Minfeng
Yutian
Ruoqiang
Lop Nur
Altun Shan
Ayakkum Hu
Muz Tag
7723
Hoh Xil Shan
Kunlun Shan
Dahongliutan
Rutog
XIZANG ZIZHIQU
(TIBET)
Gar
Tanggula (Dangla) Shan
Tanggula Shankou
5180
Amdo
4495 Siling Co
Nam Co
4627
Nagqu
Xainza
Zhongba
Mapam Yumco
Nyainqentanglha Shan
Lhasa
Yarlung Zangbo Jiang
Namcha Barwa
7756
Yamzho Yumco
Lhazê
Xigazê
Ngamring
Kamet
7756
Nanda Devi
7817
Dehra Dun
Moradabad
Bareilly
Dhaulagiri
8167
Annapurna
8078
Manaslu
8156
NEPAL
Mt. Everest
8850
KATMANDU
Makalu
8481
Kanchenjunga
8598
Himalaya
Gorakhpur
LUCKNOW
KANPUR
VARANASI
Darbhanga
Biratnagar
ALLAHABAD
PATNA
Gaya
Ganga
INDIA
RAJSHAHI
Berhampore
ASANSOL
Ranchi
JAMSHEDPUR
JABALPUR
Bilaspur
Haora
Kharagpur
Bhatpara
KOLKATA
(Calcutta)
Baleshwar
Mahanadi
BHILAINAGAR-DURG
Cuttack
Brahmapur
Vizianagaram
VISHAKHAPATNAM
BAY OF BENGAL
Ghaghara
Thimphu
Punakha
BHUTAN
Koch Bihar
Guwahati
Brahmaputra
Tezpur
Assam
Dibrugarh
Saikhoa Ghat
Patkai Bum
Khasi Hills
Silchar
BANGLA-DESH
DHAKA
Narayanganj
KHULNA
CHITTAGONG
Imphal
3824
Kachin
Myitkyina
3411
5881
Chindwin
Irrawaddy
Bhamo
Lashio
Shwebo
Monywa
Myingyan
Mandalay
3053
Arakan Yoma
Pegu Yoma
Sittwe
(Akyab)
Taunggyi
Yamethin
Toungoo
BURMA
(MYANMAR)
Shan
2183
Salween
THAILAND
(SIAM)
Luang Prabang
Mekong
Zapadnyy Sayan
RUSSIA
Tannu Ola
Kyzyl
Uvs Nuur
Ulaangom
Ölgiy
Hyargas Nuur
Dund-Us
Har Us Nuur
Döröö Nuur
Uliastay
Altay
Hangayn Nuruu
4362
Aerhtai Shan (Altai)
MONGOLIA
Hatgal
Mörön
Tesiyn Gol
Bayanhongor
Barkol Kazak Zizhixian
4925
Hami
Bei Shan
Gaxun Nur
Shule He
Dunhuang
Anxi
Yumen
Jiayuguan
Qilian Shan
Zhangye
Hei He
Mangnai
Da Qaidam
Qaidam Pendi
Tianjun
Qinghai Hu
3205
Xining
Golmud
Dulan
Gonghe
QINGHAI
Gyaring Hu
4237
Ngoring Hu
Bayan Har Shan
Maqen
6094
Huang He
Yushu
CHINA
Jinsha Jiang
Ningjing Shan
Lancang Jiang (Mekong)
Shaluli Shan
Qamdo
Bomi
Markam
Zayü
Nu Jiang (Salween)
Yalong Jiang
Daxue Shan
Gongga Shan
7556
SICHUAN
Zhongdian
Xichang
Lijiang
Panzhihua
Dali
Xiaguan
Chuxiong
Baoshan
Tengchong
YUNNAN
Anning
Yuxi
Shiping
Jinggu
Simao
Projection: Bonne
East from Greenwich
100
3
4
m
ft
0
200
600
2000
6000
4000
12 000
6000
18 000

29
38

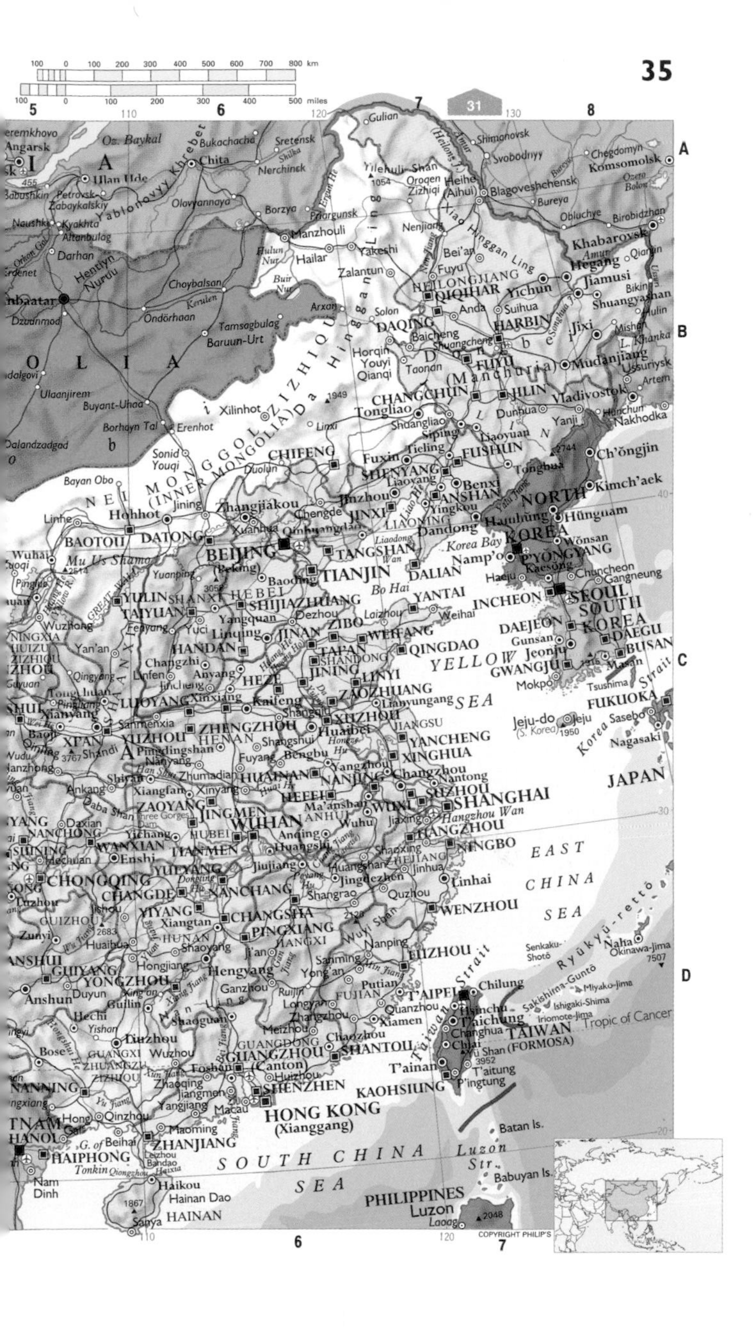
100 0 100 200 300 400 500 600 700 800 km
100 0 100 200 300 400 500 miles
5
6
7
8
31
110
120
130
A
B
C
D
Oz. Baykal
Bukachacha
Sretensk
Chita
Nerchinsk
Ulan Ude
Yablonovyy Khrebet
Olovyannaya
Borzya
Priargunsk
Manzhouli
Kyakhta
Altanbulag
Darhan
Hentiyn Nuruu
Choybalsan
Kerulen
Öndörhaan
Tamsagbulag
Baruun-Urt
Ulaanjirem
Buyant-Uhaa
Borhoyn Tal
Erenhot
Dalandzadgad
Sonid Youqi
Bayan Obo
Gulian
Yilehuli Shan
1054
Oroqen Zizhiqi
Heihe (Aihui)
Shimanovsk
Svobodnyy
Blagoveshchensk
Bureya
Chegdomyn
Komsomolsk
Obluchye
Birobidzhan
Khabarovsk
Amur
Hegang
Jiamusi
Nenjiang
Bei'an
Xiao Hinggan Ling
Hailar
Yakeshi
Hulun Nur
Buir Nur
Zalantun
Fuyu
HEILONGJIANG
QIQIHAR
Yichun
Shuangyashan
Bikin
Arxan
Solon
DAQING
Anda
Suihua
HARBIN
Jixi
Baicheng
Shuangcheng
Horqin Youyi Qianqi
Taonan
FUYU
Mudanjiang
Ussuriysk
Artem
Vladivostok
Nakhodka
CHANGCHUN
JILIN
(Manchuria)
Da Hinggan Ling
1949
NEI MONGGOL ZIZHIQU (INNER MONGOLIA)
Xilinhot
Linxi
Tongliao
Shuangliao
Siping
Liaoyuan
Dunhua
Yanji
Hunchun
Ch'ŏngjin
CHIFENG
Fuxin
Tieling
FUSHUN
SHENYANG
Liaoyang
Benxi
ANSHAN
Tonghua
Kimch'aek
NORTH KOREA
Hamhŭng
Hŭngnam
Jining
Hohhot
Zhangjiakou
Chengde
Jinzhou
JINXI
Yingkou
LIAONING
Dandong
Korea Bay
Namp'o
P'YONGYANG
Wŏnsan
Linhe
BAOTOU
DATONG
Xuanhua
Qinhuangdao
Liaodong Wan
TANGSHAN
BEIJING (Peking)
TIANJIN
DALIAN
Haeju
Kaesŏng
Chuncheon
Gangneung
SEOUL
SOUTH KOREA
Mu Us Shamo
Yuanping
Baoding
Bo Hai
YANTAI
Weihai
INCHEON
YULIN
SHANXI
HEBEI
SHIJIAZHUANG
TAIYUAN
Yangquan
Dezhou
Laizhou
ZIBO
WEIFANG
DAEJEON
DAEGU
Fenyang
Yuci
Linqing
JINAN
QINGDAO
Gunsan
Jeonju
BUSAN
HANDAN
TAI'AN
SHANDONG
YELLOW
GWANGJU
Masan
Changzhi
Anyang
JINING
LINYI
Mokpo
Tsushima
Strait
HEZE
Xinxiang
Kaifeng
ZAOZHUANG
SEA
FUKUOKA
LUOYANG
Lianyungang
Jeju-do (S. Korea)
Jeju
1950
Sasebo
Nagasaki
Sanmenxia
ZHENGZHOU
XUZHOU
Huaibei
JIANGSU
Korea Strait
XI'AN
YUZHOU
HENAN
Shangshui
YANCHENG
3767
Pingdingshan
Fuyang
Bengbu
XINGHUA
Nanyang
Yangzhou
Changzhou
Nantong
JAPAN
Ankang
Zhumadian
HUAINAN
NANJING
Xiangfan
SUZHOU
SHANGHAI
Daba Shan
ZAOYANG
HEFEI
WUXI
Hangzhou Wan
JINGMEN
Ma'anshan
ANHUI
Three Gorges Dam
WUHAN
HANGZHOU
Daxian
NANCHONG
Yichang
HUBEI
Anqing
Jiaxing
WANXIAN
Enshi
TIANMEN
Huangshi
Shaoxing
NINGBO
ZHEJIANG
EAST
Jiujiang
Jinhua
CHONGQING
YUEYANG
Jingdezhen
Linhai
CHANGDE
NANCHANG
CHINA
Luzhou
Shangrao
Quzhou
WENZHOU
YIYANG
Xiangtan
CHANGSHA
GUIZHOU
SEA
2120
Zunyi
2683
PINGXIANG
Huaihua
HUNAN
JIANGXI
Nanping
Shaoyang
Naha
Okinawa-Jima
Hongjiang
Sanming
FUZHOU
Senkaku-Shotō
7507
GUIYANG
Ryūkyū-retto
Hengyang
Yong'an
YONGZHOU
Putian
Chilung
Anshun
Duyun
Ganzhou
FUJIAN
T'AIPEI
Miyako-Jima
Guilin
Quanzhou
Hsinchu
Sakishima-Guntō
Ishigaki-Shima
Hechi
Shaoguan
Xiamen
T'aichung
Iriomote-Jima
Tropic of Cancer
Yishan
Meizhou
Zhangzhou
Changhua
TAIWAN
Liuzhou
GUANGDONG
Chaozhou
Chiai
Taiwan Strait
Bose
GUANGXI ZHUANGZU ZIZHIQU
Wuzhou
GUANGZHOU (Canton)
SHANTOU
Yü Shan (FORMOSA)
3952
Foshan
Huizhou
T'ainan
T'aitung
NANNING
Zhaoqing
SHENZHEN
KAOHSIUNG
P'ingtung
Jiangmen
Qinzhou
Yangjiang
HONG KONG (Xianggang)
Macau
Batan Is.
Maoming
HANOI
Beihai
ZHANJIANG
HAIPHONG
G. of Tonkin
Luzon Str.
SOUTH CHINA
Babuyan Is.
Nam Dinh
Haikou
Hainan Dao
SEA
PHILIPPINES
Luzon
1867
HAINAN
2048
Sanya
Laoag
COPYRIGHT PHILIP'S

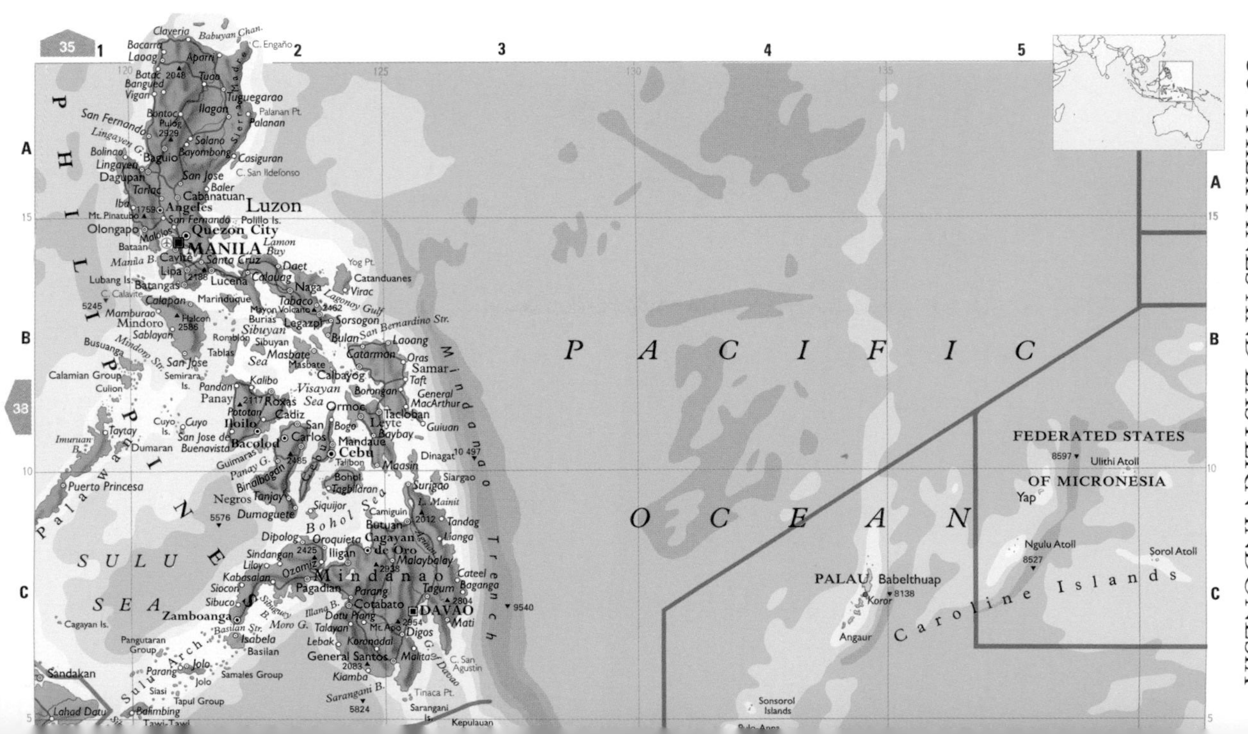

PACIFIC OCEAN
PHILIPPINES
FEDERATED STATES
OF MICRONESIA
PALAU
Caroline Islands
SULU SEA
Luzon
MANILA
Quezon City
Mindoro
Panay
Negros
Cebu
Samar
Leyte
Bohol
Mindanao
DAVAO
Zamboanga
Puerto Princesa
Iloilo
Bacolod
Tacloban
Cagayan de Oro
General Santos
Mindanao Trench
Sibuyan Sea
Visayan Sea
Bohol Sea
Yap
Ulithi Atoll
Ngulu Atoll
Sorol Atoll
Babelthuap
Koror
Angaur
Sonsorol Islands
Sandakan
Lahad Datu

100 0 100 200 300 400 500 km
100 0 50 100 150 200 250 300 350 miles
PAPUA NEW GUINEA
INDONESIA
BANDA SEA
ARAFURA SEA
FLORES SEA
SEA
MOLUCCA SEA
SERAM SEA
Lesser Sunda Is.
MALUKU
Halmahera
Sulawesi (Celebes)
Manado
Gorontalo
Teluk Tomini
Selat Makasar
UJUNG PANDANG (Makasar)
Kendari
Buton
Buru
Seram (Ceram)
Ambon
Kepulauan Sula
Kepulauan Aru
Kepulauan Tanimbar
Kepulauan Kai
IRIAN JAYA
PAPUA
Pegunungan Maoke
Jayapura
Biak
Yapen
Sorong
Waigeo
Flores
Sumba
Sawu Sea
Sumbawa
NUSA TENGGARA TIMUR
EAST TIMOR
Dili
Kupang
Alor
Wetar
Equator
East from Greenwich
Projection: Mercator
COPYRIGHT PHILIP'S

39
60

BURMA
(MYANMAR)
RANGOON
(Yangon)
G. of Martaban
THAILAND
BANGKOK
LAOS
VIETNAM
CAMBODIA
PHNOM PENH
THANH PHO HO CHI MINH
(Saigon)
Vientiane
(Viangchan)
Da Nang
Hue
Nha Trang
Cam Ranh
Qui Nhon
Buon Ma Thuot
Gulf of Thailand
Malay Pen.
PENINSULAR MALAYSIA
SOUTH CHINA SEA
ANDAMAN SEA
Straits of Malacca
Paracel Is.
Spratly Is.
PHILIPPINES
Palawan
SABAH
Kota Kinabalu
Bandar Seri Begawan
Kota Bharu
Kuala Terengganu
George Town
Butterworth
Alor Setar
Hat Yai
Songkhla
Nakhon Si Thammarat
Surat Thani
Phuket
Kho Khot Kra
(Isthmus of Kra)
Mergui
Moulmein
Nakhon Ratchasima
Khon Kaen
Udon Thani
Ubon Ratchathani
Savannakhet
Pakxe
Tonle Sap
Siemreab
Batdambang
Kampong Cham
Can Tho
Rach Gia
Ca Mau
Con Son
Sandakan
Mt. Mantalingajan
Balabac Str.
Mekong
Banda Aceh
Sabang
34
36
41

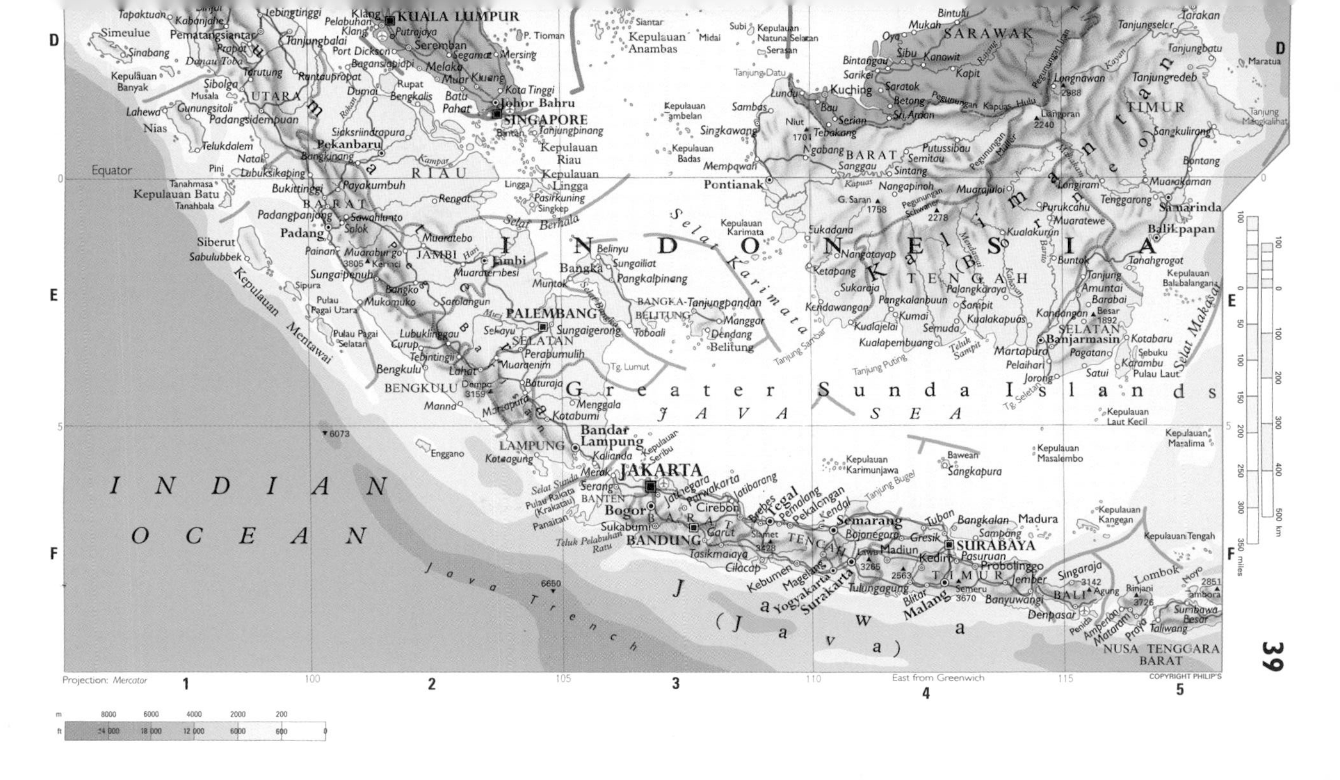
INDIAN OCEAN
INDONESIA
Sumatera
Kalimantan (Borneo)
Greater Sunda Islands
JAVA SEA
Jawa (Java)
Java Trench
Selat Karimata
Selat Makasar
Selat Sunda
Selat Bangka
Selat Berhala
SARAWAK
KUALA LUMPUR
SINGAPORE
JAKARTA
BANDUNG
SURABAYA
PALEMBANG
Pontianak
Kuching
Samarinda
Balikpapan
Banjarmasin
Semarang
Surakarta
Yogyakarta
Malang
Denpasar
Bandar Lampung
Padang
Pekanbaru
Jambi
Bengkulu
Pematangsiantar
Sibolga
Nias
Siberut
Kepulauan Mentawai
Kepulauan Riau
Kepulauan Lingga
Kepulauan Anambas
Kepulauan Natuna Selatan
Bangka
Belitung
Madura
Bali
Lombok
Sumbawa Besar
NUSA TENGGARA BARAT
RIAU
JAMBI
BENGKULU
LAMPUNG
BANTEN
UTARA
BARAT
SELATAN
TENGAH
TIMUR
BANGKA-BELITUNG
Equator
East from Greenwich
Projection: Mercator
COPYRIGHT PHILIP'S
0 100 200 300 400 500 km
0 50 100 150 200 250 300 350 miles

XIZANG
ZIZHIQU
(TIBET)
Gangdisê Shan
Nyain
Chamba
Hanle
Nganglong Kangri
7315
7026
Palampur
Kulu
Jogindar Nagar
Mandi
HIMACHAL PRADESH
Dankhar Gompa
Hoshiarpur
Bhakra Dam
Shimla
Kandaghat
Kamet 7756
Gar
Shiquan He
(Sutlej)
La'nga Co
Mapam Yumco
Ombu
Tangra Yumco
Gyaring Co
Xoin
Coqên
LUDHIANA
Chandigarh
Chakrata
Badarinath
Mussoorie
Dehra Dun
Rishikesh
Nanda Devi 7817
Patiala
Ambala
Jagadhri
UTTARANCHAL
Saharanpur
Karnal
Haridwar
Roorkee
Muzaffarnagar
Najibabad
Bijnor
Almora
Baitadi
Dandeldhura
Simikot
Mugu
Namse Shankou 4944
7059
Zhongba
Saga
Silgarhi Doti
Jumla
Kamali
Ramnagar
Haldwani
Mustang
Annapurna 8078
Muktinath
Gyala Shankou 5602
Hansi
HARYANA
Bhiwani
DELHI
New Delhi
Sonipat
MEERUT
Amroha
Moradabad
Rampur
Hapur
Ghaziabad
Sambhal
Bulandshahr
Pilibhit
Bareilly
Dhangarhi
NEPAL
Dhaulagiri 8167
Nuwakot
Pokhara
Gurkha
Xixabangma Feng 8013
Nyalam
Mt. Everest 8850
Kanchenjunga
Rewari
FARIDABAD
Aligarh
Shahjahanpur
Sarda
Lakhimpur
Nepalganj
Siwalik Range
Nawakot
KATMANDU
Bhaktapur
Ramechhap
Hathras
Alwar
Mathura
Bharatpur
Fatehgarh
UTTAR PRADESH
Hardoi
Sitapur
Bahraich
Jarwa
Nautanwa
Balrampur
Gonda
Birganj
Sun Kosi
Dhankuta
Mainpuri
Kannauj
AGRA
Firozabad
Dhaulpur
Etawah
Ganga
LUCKNOW
Faizabad
Basti
Gorakhpur
Bettiah
Raxaul
Motihari
Udaipur Garhi
Jaynagar
Shiliguri
Chambal
Bhind
Gwalior
KANPUR
Unnao
Rae Bareli
Ghaghara
Deoria
Gandak
Darbhanga
Biratnagar
Kishanganj
Sawai Madhopur
Orai
Konch
Sultanpur
Azamgarh
Siwan
Muzaffarpur
Supaul
Purnia
Sheopur
Datia
Hamirpur
Fatehpur
Bela
Jaunpur
Chhapra
BIHAR
Behariganj
Katihar
Shivpuri
Jhansi
Mau Ranipur
Banda
Yamuna
VARANASI
Ghazipur
Ara
PATNA
Bankipore
Mokama
Munger
Ganges
Baran
521
ALLAHABAD
Jahanabad
Bihar
Jamalpur
Bhagalpur
Chhatarpur
Manikpur
Mirzapur
Sasaram
Gaya
Tinpahar
Guna
Lalitpur
Tikamgarh
Panna
Satna
Mauganj
Aurangabad
Deoghar
Jhalawar
Rewa
Dudhi
Rampur Hat
INDIA
Rajgarh
Sironj
Bina-Etawah
Banda
690
Murwara
Hazaribag
Barhi
Giridih
Baharampur
Gomoh
DHANBAD
MADHYA PRADESH
Sagar
Damoh
Bharatpur
JHARKHAND
1366
ASANSOL
Raniganj
Vidisha
Vindhya Range
Bhanrer Range
Umaria
Lohardaga
Ramgarh
WEST BENGAL
Shajapur
BHOPAL
Shahdol
Chirmiri
1225
Ambikapur
Ranchi
Puruliya
Bankura
Barddhaman
Sehore
Narsimhapur
JABALPUR
Anuppur
JAMSHEDPUR
Hoshangabad
Gadarwara
Mandla
1127
Chakradharpur
Medinipur
Kannod
Birmitrapur
Chaibasa
Raurkela
Gua
Kharagpur
1353
Nainpur
Makrai
Chhindwara
Kawardha
Bilaspur
Sundargarh
Badampahar
Khandwa
Satpura Range
Betul
Balaghat
Maikala Range
Raigarh
Jharsuguda
Contai
Burhanpur
Tirodi
Katangi
CHHATTISGARH
Baleshwar
Gawilgarh Hills
Ramtek
Gondia
Khairagarh
Sarangarh
Hirakud Dam
Sambalpur
Keonjhargarh
1187
Subarnarekha
Achalpur
NAGPUR
Raipur
Bhadrakh
Amravati
Bhandara
Raj Nandgaon
BHILAINAGAR-DURG
Sonepur
Talcher
Brahmani
Mahanadi
Bramhapuri
Balangir
Dhenkanal
Kendrapara
Akola
Yavatmal
Wardha
Wainganga
Dhamtari
ORISSA
Cuttack
Paradip
Washim
Darwha
Hinganghat
Kanker
1001
Titlagarh
Russellkonda
Bhubaneshwar
Wani
Penganga
Ghugus
Chandrapur
Bhawanipatna
Puri
Hingoli
Adilabad
Asifabad
Ahiri
Bhamragarh
Chilka L.
Satmala Hills
Brahmapur
Parbhani
Nanded
Nirmal
Pranhita
Indravati
Bastar
Rayagada
1501
Chatrapur
Ichchapuram
Palam
Godavari
Jagtial
Bijapur
Jagdalpur
Jeypore
BAY OF BENGAL
Bodhan
Nizamabad
1240
Salur
Parvatipuram
Latur
Udgir
Manthani
Karimnagar
Venkatapuram
Bobbili
Tekkali
ANDHRA PRADESH
Eastern Ghats
1680
Srikakulam
Vizianagaram
Manjra
Siddipet
Warangal
Konta
Anakapalle
Bidar
Northern Circars
VISHAKHAPATNAM
Secunderabad
Kottagudem
Gulbarga
HYDERABAD
Rajahmundry
Pithapuram
Nalgonda
Suriapet
Godavari Point
Narayanpet
Eluru
Kakinada
Yadgir
Mahbubnagar
Krishna
Vijayawada
Raichur
Narasapur
Gadwal
Tenali
Machilipatnam
INDIAN OCEAN
917
Kurnool
Chirala
Bapatla
Tungabhadra
Adoni
Erramala Hills
Nallamalai Hills
Cumbum
Hospet
Nandyal
Veligonda Ra.
Ongole
1100
Bellary
Guntakal
43
Projection: Conical with two standard parallels
East from Greenwich
m ft
200 600

50 0 100 200 300 400 km
50 0 50 100 150 200 250 miles
34
38
C H I N A
Tanggula Shan
Nam Co
Nagqu
Baqên
Dêngqên
Nangqen
Gamtog
Qamdo
Baiyü
Garzê
Xinlong
SICHUAN
Yajiang
Yidun
Litang
Lhorong
Nu Jiang
Zhaxizê
Lhari
Lhinzub
Gongbo'gyamda
Lhasa
Namcha Barwa
Riga
Goqên
Ningjing
Lancang Jiang (Mekong)
Salween
Yarlung Zangbo Jiang
Brahmaputra
Jido
Dihang
Nang Xian
Mainkung
Muli Zangzu Zizhixian
Jinsha Jiang
Zhongdian
Nizamghat
Minutang
Hkakabo Razi (Thala La)
Zizhixian
Subansiri
Lhunzê
ARUNACHAL PRADESH
Murkongselek
Saikhoa Ghat
Dum Duma
Tinsukia
Hpungan Pass
Putao
Konglu
Weixi
Lijiang
Cona
Kangto
Thunkar
Punakha
Tongsa Dzong
BHUTAN
Taga Dzong
Rupa
North Lakhimpur
Dibrugarh
Sibsagar
Patkai Bum
Chaukan Pass
Bumhpa Bum
Jianchuan
Jorhat
Hukawng Valley
Maingkwan
KACHIN
Kumon Bum
Mali
Nmai
Yunlong
Tezpur
Rangia
ASSAM
Silghat
Nowgong
Mokokchung
Alipur Duar
Barpeta
Mairabari
Koch Bihar
Goalpara
Guwahati
Brahmaputra
Dhuburi
NAGALAND
Kohima
Singkaling Hkamti
Chindwin
Myitkyina
Mogaung
YUNNAN
Baoshan
Tengchong
Shillong
MEGHALAYA
Tura
Cherrapunji
Barail Range
Haflong
Ukhrul
Tamenglong
Imphal
Homalin
Longling
Changning
Rangpur
Jamalpur
Mohanganj
SYLHET
Sylhet
Silchar
MANIPUR
Churachandpur
Thaungdut
Indaw
Katha
Bhamo
Shwegu
Sirajganj
Mymensingh
Bengal
Lalaghat
Tamu
Wuntho
Tigyaing
Tropic of Cancer
Kolosib
SAGAING
Shweli
Man Na
Kunlong
Hsenwi
Pang-Long
Brahmanbaria
TRIPURA
Sairang
Aizawl
Mawlaik
Kyunhla
Tiddim
Bawdwin
Namtu
Kawnro
DHAKA
Agartala
MIZORAM
Kalewa
Lashio
Narayanganj
Comilla
Dighinala
Mogok
Muhar
Jessore
Chandpur
Madaripur
Belonia
Lungler
Paldm
Chin
Mingin
Shwebo
Madaya
Mong Yai
Gokteik
Pang-Yang
Mong Pawk
KHULNA
Barisal
BARISAL
Bhola
Maijdi
Hatia
Patuakhali
CHITTAGONG
Dohazari
CHIN Hills
Gangaw
Budalin
Alon
Monywa
Mandalay
Mong Hsu
Mong Wa
Canning
Ganges
Haringhata
Yinmabin
Sagaing
Kyaukse
Mong Kung
SHAN
Keng Tung
Kaladan
Pauk
Myingyan
Pakokku
Meiktila
Thazi
Yamethin
Taunggyi
Heho
Inle L.
Keng Tawng
Mong Nai
Mong Ton
Cox's Bazar
Paletwa
Kanpetlet
BURMA (MYANMAR)
Kyaukpadaung
Yenangyaung
Magwe
Minbu
Taungdwingyi
Mawk Mai
Mong Pan
Muang Chiang Rai
Sittwe (Akyab)
ARAKAN
MAGWE
Irrawaddy
Pyinmana
Loi-kaw
Mae Hong Son
KAYAH
Chiang Mai
THAILAND
Kyaukpyu
Thayetmyo
Bawlake
Taungoo
Salween
Muang Lamphun
Ramree I.
Letpan
Arakan Coast
Arakan Yoma
Prome
Pegu Yoma
Karen
Lampang
Taungup
Cheduba I.
Pyu
Papun
Sandoway
Myanaung
Madauk
Sittang Myit
Letpadan
Tharrawaddy
Dawna Range
Gwa
Henzada
Pegu
Thaton
Tak
Kyonggyaw
Yandoon
PEGU
Pa-an
Insein
RANGOON
Martaban
Moulmein
Bassein
Maubin
MON
Myaungmya
IRRAWADDY
Pyapon
Rangoon
G. of Martaban
Amherst
Mai Klong
Maudin Sun
Mouths of the Irrawaddy
Kalegauk
Lamaing
Ye
Sangkhla Buri
Sangkhla
Natkyizin
BAY OF BENGAL
INDIAN OCEAN
Mouths of the Ganges
Preparis North Channel
Paripari Kyun (Burma)
Preparis South Channel
Koko Kyunzu (Burma)
Moscos Is.
Maungmagan Is.
Launglon Bok
Nam Tok
Yebyu
Tavoy
COPYRIGHT PHILIP'S

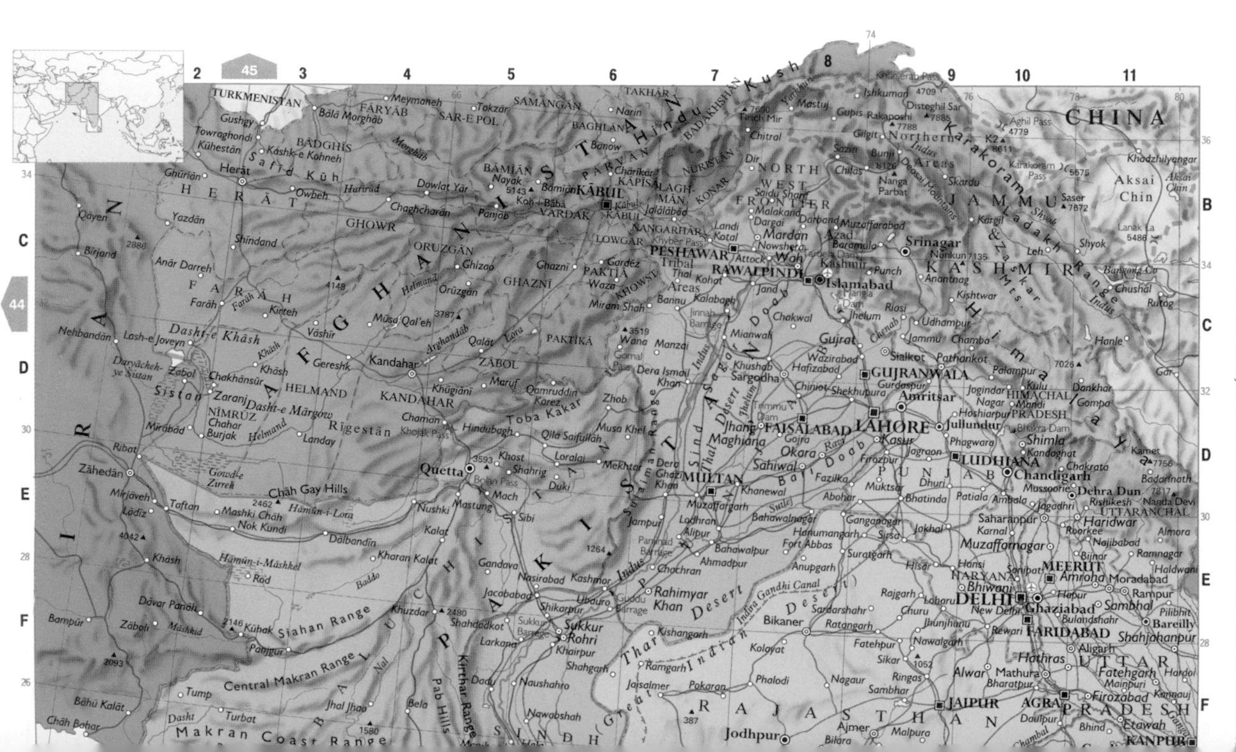
CHINA
Aksai Chin
Karakoram
JAMMU
KASHMIR
Srinagar
Islamabad
RAWALPINDI
PESHAWAR
LAHORE
GUJRANWALA
FAISALABAD
MULTAN
Amritsar
LUDHIANA
Chandigarh
Shimla
Dehra Dun
MEERUT
DELHI
New Delhi
FARIDABAD
Ghaziabad
AGRA
JAIPUR
Jodhpur
Bikaner
Thar Desert
RAJASTHAN
PUNJAB
HARYANA
UTTARANCHAL
HIMACHAL PRADESH
Sukkur
Rohri
Quetta
Kandahar
KABUL
Herat
Farah
Zahedan
Kirthar Range
Pab Hills
Central Makran Range
Makran Coast Range
Siahan Range
Chah Gay Hills
Rigestan
Hindu Kush
TURKMENISTAN
AFGHANISTAN
PAKISTAN
IRAN
Indus
45
44

43
INDIA
GUJARAT
MADHYA PRADESH
MAHARASHTRA
ANDHRA PRADESH
KARNATAKA
TAMIL NADU
KERALA
SRI LANKA
DADRA AND NAGAR HAVELI
ARABIAN SEA
INDIAN OCEAN
Rann of Kachchh
Gulf of Kachchh
Gulf of Khambhat
Gulf of Mannar
Palk Strait
Palk Bay
Adam's Bridge
Mouths of the Indus
Kathiawar
Western Ghats
Eastern Ghats
Malabar Coast
Coromandel Coast
Vindhya Range
Satpura Range
Satmala Hills
Ajanta Range
Balaghat Range
Nallamalai Hills
Erramala Hills
Velikonda Range
Cardamon Hills
Palani Hills
Gawilgarh Hills
Tropic of Cancer
MUMBAI (BOMBAY)
CHENNAI (Madras)
BANGALORE
HYDERABAD
AHMADABAD
VADODARA (Baroda)
SURAT
NAGPUR
INDORE
BHOPAL
JABALPUR
PUNE (Poona)
NASIK
COIMBATORE
MADURAI
COCHIN (Kochi)
Trivandrum (Thiruvananthapuram)
Calicut (Kozhikode)
Mysore
Mangalore
Tiruchchirappalli
Puducherry (Pondicherry)
Solapur
Colombo
Jaffna
Trincomalee
Kanyakumari (C. Comorin)
Dondra Head
Continuation Southwards on same scale
Projection: Conical with two standard parallels
East from Greenwich
COPYRIGHT PHILIP'S
40
km
miles
m
ft

Projection: Conical Orthomorphic with two standard parallels

East from Greenwich

C. M. VA B. = CHAHĀR MAHĀLL VA BAKHTĪARĪ
K. VA B. A. = KOHKĪLŪYEH VA BŪYER AḤMADI

50 0 100 200 300 400 km
50 0 50 100 150 200 250 miles
UZBEKISTAN
TAJIK
Pamir
Bukhoro
Shahrisabz
Dushanbe
Ordzhonikidzeabad
Qarshi
Guzar
Türkmenabat
Amudarya
Kŭlob
Qŭrghonteppa
Vakhsh
Khorugh
Ishkuman
Feyzābād
Qarāvol
Sherabad
Atamyrat
Tāloqān
Jorm
Eshkamesh
Rakaposhi
Gupis
7788
Mastuj
Gilgit
Termiz
KONDOZ
Kondoz
Khānābād
TAKHĀR
BADAKHSHĀN
7690
Tirich Mir
Sazin
Chitral
Chilas
Mary
Baýramaly
Ýolöten
Āqchah
BALKH
Andkhvoy
JOWZJĀN
Mazar-e Sharīf
Kholm
Aybak
Baghlān
5209
Narin
Tejen
Murgap
Sheberghān
SAMANGĀN
BAGHLĀN
Hindu Kush
PANJSHER
NURISTAN
Dir
Asmār
Muzaffarabad
Sar-e Pol
FĀRYĀB
Sarahs
Dashköpri
Meymaneh
SAR-E POL
Chārīkār
KAPISA
KONAR
NORTH
Dargai
Darband
Mardan
Nowshera
Islamabad
3494
Band-e Torkestan
Morghāb
Sayghan
BAMĪAN
PARVAN
Kābul
KĀBUL
Jalālābād
NANGARHĀR
Khyber Pass
PESHAWAR
RAWALPINDI
Serhetabat
BĀDGHĪS
Dowlat Yār
Navak
5143
Koh-i-Bābā
VARDAK
LOWGAR
Kashk-e Kohneh
Safīd Kūh
Owbeh
Harīrūd
Chaghcharān
Panjāb
Gardēz
PAKTIA
Khowst
WEST
Thal
Kohat
Jand
Chakwal
Kalabagh
Jinnah Barrage
Herāt
3588
Ghūriān
HERĀT
Tūlak
GHOWR
DAY KUNDI
Helmand
Ghazni
GHAZNI
KHOWST
Bannu
Mianwali
Khushab
Teyvareh
3519
FRONTIER
Sargodha
Chiniot
Daryācheh-i Namakzār
Yazdān
AFGHANISTAN
Mukur
Wana
Manzai
Gomal Pass
Jhelum
Shindand
ORŪZGĀN
3787
PAKTĪKĀ
Mashūray
Dera Ismail Khan
Indus
Jhang Maghiana
2886
4148
Mūsā Qal'eh
Qalāt
Lora
ZĀBOL
Zhob
Thal Desert
PUNJAB
Tabas
Farāh
Arghandāb
Ma'ruf
Musa Khel
Khanewal
FARĀH
Gereshk
Khūgīānī
Kandahar
Toba Kakar
Mekhtar
MULTAN
Dasht-e Khāsh
KANDAHAR
Chaman
Hindu Bagh
Loralai
Dera Ghazi Khan
Muzaffargarh
Lāsh-e Joveyn
Daryācheh-ye Sīstān
Chakhānsūr
HELMAND
Khojak Pass
Shahrig
Duki
Jampur
Bahawalpur
Zaranj
NĪMRŪZ
Dasht-e Mārgow
Rīgestān
3593
Quetta
Bolan Pass
Much
Sulaiman Range
Panjnad Barrage
Ahmadpur
Sīstān
Mastung
Sibi
1264
Chachran
Rahimyar Khan
Chāh Gay Hills
Nushki
Hāmūn-i-Lora
Kalat
Guddu Barrage
Gowd-e Zirreh
2462
Kashmor
Zāhedān
Dālbandin
Gandava
Ubauro
Kishangarh
Taftan
Mashki Chāh
Nok Kundi
Kharan Kalat
Jacobabad
Shikarpur
Sukkur
Rohri
Ramgarh
Lādīz
BALUCHISTAN
2480
Sukkur Barrage
Khairpur
Kūh-e Taftān
4042
Hāmūn-i-Māshkel
Baddo
Shahdadkot
Larkana
Shahgarh
387
Rod
Khāsh
Siahan Range
Khuzdar
PAKISTAN
Thar Desert
(Great Indian Desert)
INDIA
Naushahro
Kirthar Range
Dadu
SINDH
SĪSTĀN VA BALŪCHESTĀN
Dāvar Panāh
2146
Kūhak
Pab Hills
Nawabshah
Munabao
Bampūr
Īrānshahr
Zāboli
Mashkīd
Panjgur
Central Makran Range
Hala
Tando Adam
Mirpur Khas
Umarkot
Jhal Jhao
Bela
Manjhand
1580
Sarbāz
Pīp
2093
Ghulam Mohammad Barrage
Kotri
HYDERABAD
Qaşr-e Qand
Makran
Turbat
Sonmiani
Nagar Parkar
Bent
Nikshahr
Pishīn
Tump
Dasht
Makran Coast Range
Kandrach
Hab
Nadi Chauki
Tatta
Badin
Pasni
Ormara
C. Monze
KARACHI
Rann of Kachchh
Polan
Gwādar
Khavda
Chāh Bahar
Gavāter
Jiwani
Mouths of the Indus
Lakhpat
Ra's-e Tang
Bhuj
Kandla
Oman
Mandvi
Gulf of Kachchh
Jamnagar
Tropic of Cancer
ARABIAN SEA
Dwarka
Gop
Porbandar
Masqat (Muscat)
Al Qurayyāt
Tiwī
2151
Şūr
Ra's al Hadd
Al Kāmil
Al Ashkhara
42
COPYRIGHT PHILIP'S

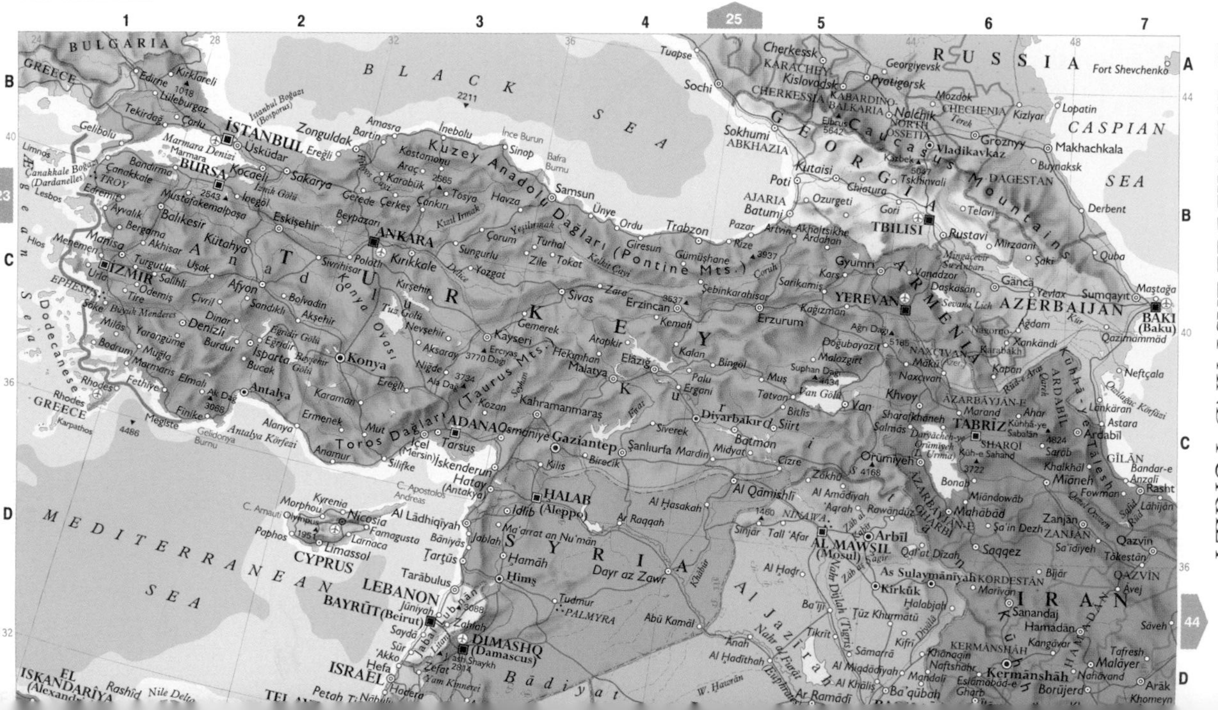
BLACK SEA
CASPIAN SEA
MEDITERRANEAN SEA
RUSSIA
GEORGIA
ARMENIA
AZERBAIJAN
TURKEY
IRAN
SYRIA
CYPRUS
LEBANON
ISRAEL
GREECE
BULGARIA
Caucasus Mountains
Kuzey Anadolu Dağları
Pontine Mts.
Toros Dağları
Taurus Mts.
Al Jazīrah
Bādiyat
TBILISI
YEREVAN
BAKI (Baku)
ANKARA
İSTANBUL
İZMİR
BURSA
ADANA
Konya
Kayseri
Samsun
Trabzon
Erzurum
Diyarbakır
Gaziantep
Antalya
Sinop
Zonguldak
Eskişehir
Sivas
Malatya
Van Gölü
TABRĪZ
Orūmīyeh
HALAB (Aleppo)
DIMASHQ (Damascus)
BAYRŪT (Beirut)
Nicosia
AL MAWSIL (Mosul)
Arbīl
Kirkūk
Hamadān
Kermānshāh
Rasht
Qazvīn
Hims
Hamāh
Tarābulus
Dayr az Zawr
Nahr Dijlah (Tigris)
Nahr al Furāt (Euphrates)
Dodecanese
Rhodes
EL ISKANDARÎYA (Alexandria)
Nile Delta

EL QÂHIRA (Cairo)
El Giza
PYRAMIDS
Benha
Zagazig
Ismâ'ilîya
Helwân
El Suweis (Suez)
Nakhl
Birket Qârûn
Sinnûris
El Faiyûm
Beni Suef
Nahr en Nîl (Nile)
Bahr Yûsef
Maghâgha
Beni Mazâr
El Minyâ
Mallawi
Dairût
Manfalût
Asyût
Abu Tig
Tahta
Sohâg
Akhmîm
Girga
Nag Hammâdi
THEBES
Qena
Qûs
El Uqsur
Idfû
Kôm Ombo
Aswân
El Shallal
Sadd el Aali (Aswan High Dam)
Buheirat en Naser (Lake Nasser)
Dunqul
El Khârga
Bârîs
El Bawiti
Wadi Halfa
EGYPT
Es Sahrâ' esh Sharqîya
Es Sînâ'
Elat
Khalîg el Suweis
Gebel Mûsa 2285
Gebel Katherina 2637
El Tûr
Sharm el Sheikh
Râs Muhammad
Hurghada
Gebel Shayib el Banât 2187
Bûr Safâga
Gebel el Sibâi 1484
Gebel Hamâta 1977
Tropic of Cancer
HALAIB TRIANGLE
Halaib
2216
Ras Hadarba
Gebeit
Muhammad Qol
SUDAN
Es Sahrâ' en Nûbîya
RED SEA
Gulf of Aqaba
Dead Sea -418
Be'er Sheva
Arish
JORDAN
PETRA
Aṭ Ṭafîlah
Bā'ir
Ma'ān
Al 'Aqabah
Ḥaql
Maqnā
2578
Rās Fartak
Ash Sharmah
2350 Jabal Dabbāgh
Al Muwayliḥ
Ḍubā
1747
Tabūk
Aṭ Ṭubayq
Wādī al Ghamah
Wādī Fajr
Qal'at al Akhḍar
Taymā
Ḥarrat al 'Uwairidh
Madā'in Ṣāliḥ
Al 'Ulā
Al Wajh
Mashābih
Shaybārā
W. al Ḥamḍ
Hanak
Ra's Abū Madd
Umm Lajj
Jazā'ir Qul'ān
Ra's Bāridī
Ras Bânâs
Khalîg Umm el Ketef
1814
Yanbu 'al Baḥr
Ra'is
Mastūrah
Rābigh
Al Qaḍīmah
Ra's al Ḥāṭibah
Dhahabān
JIDDAH (Jedda)
Ra's al Aswad
'Usfān
Zaymah
Makkah (Mecca)
'Ushayrah
2565
Aṭ Ṭā'if
As Sūq
Ḥarrat Nawāṣīf
Sahl Rakbah
'Urūq Subay'
Al Muwayh
Ḥarrat al Kishb
Al Dafīnah
Mahd adh Dhahab
Al Madīnah (Medina)
Al Ḥamrā'
Al Ḥanākīyah
Ḥarrat Khaybar
Wādī ar Rimah
Ḥulayfā'
Ṣafājah
Jabal Shammar
Ḥā'il
Fayd
Ṭābah
Al 'Uyūn
Buraydah
'Unayzah
Ar Rass
Al Qaṣīm
Az Zilfī
Al Midhnab
Al Majma'ah
Thādiq
Shaqrā'
Marāh
Al 'Uwaynid
Al Jubaylah
AR RIYĀḌ (Riyadh)
Rumāḥ
Al 'Aramah
Ad Dahnā'
Al Qā'iyah
Ad Dawādimī
'Afīf
Ar Ruwayḍah
As Sulaymānīyah
Ad Dilam
Al Ḥarīq
Al Ḥillah
Al Ḥulwah
Al Ḥamar
Al Haddār
Ghayl
Laylá
Al Badī'
Al Khunn
Wādī Sabāḥ
Ḥaraḍ
Al Jāfūrah
Al Hufūf
Al Mubarraz
Al Uqayr
Buqayq
Ayn Dār
Aẓ Ẓahrān
Ad Dammām
Al Qaṭīf
Al Fāḍilī
Al Kharsānīyah
Al Jubayl
Abū 'Alī
Manīfah
As Saffānīyah
An Nu'ayrīyah
Ra's al Mish'āb
SAUDI ARABIA
Al Ḥijāz
An Nafūd
Turabah
Ash Shu'bah
Ḥafar al Bāṭin
Nişāb
Rafḥā
Ad Duwayd
Al 'Uwayqīlah
Ṣaḥrā' al Ḥijārah
Sakākah
Al Jawf
Badanah
Al Jalāmīd
Ṭurayf
Nukhuyb
Ash Shabakah
As Salmān
An Najaf
Ash Shāmīyah
Ad Dīwānīyah
As Samāwah
Ash Shaṭrah
An Nāṣirīyah
UR
Al Kūt
Al Ḥayy
Ar Rifā'ī
Al 'Amārah
Qal'at Ṣāliḥ
Al Qurnah
Hawr al Ḥammār
AL BAṢRAH
Az Zubayr
KUWAIT
Al Jahrah
Al Kuwayt (Kuwait)
Mīnā' al Aḥmadī
Burqān
Mīnā' Su'ud
Wafrah
PERSIAN GULF
Al Fāw
Shaṭṭ al Arab
Ābādān
Khorramshahr
Bandar-e Ma'shur
Bandar-e Deylam
Behbehān
KHŪZESTĀN
Ahvāz
Jarrāhi
Āqā Jār
Sūsangerd
Naft-e Safīd
Masjed Soleymān
Haft Gel
Shūshtar
Lālī
Kārūn
4548
Khārk
Projection: Conical Orthomorphic with two standard parallels
East from Greenwich
50 0 100 200 300 400 km
50 0 50 100 150 200 250 miles

54
48
44

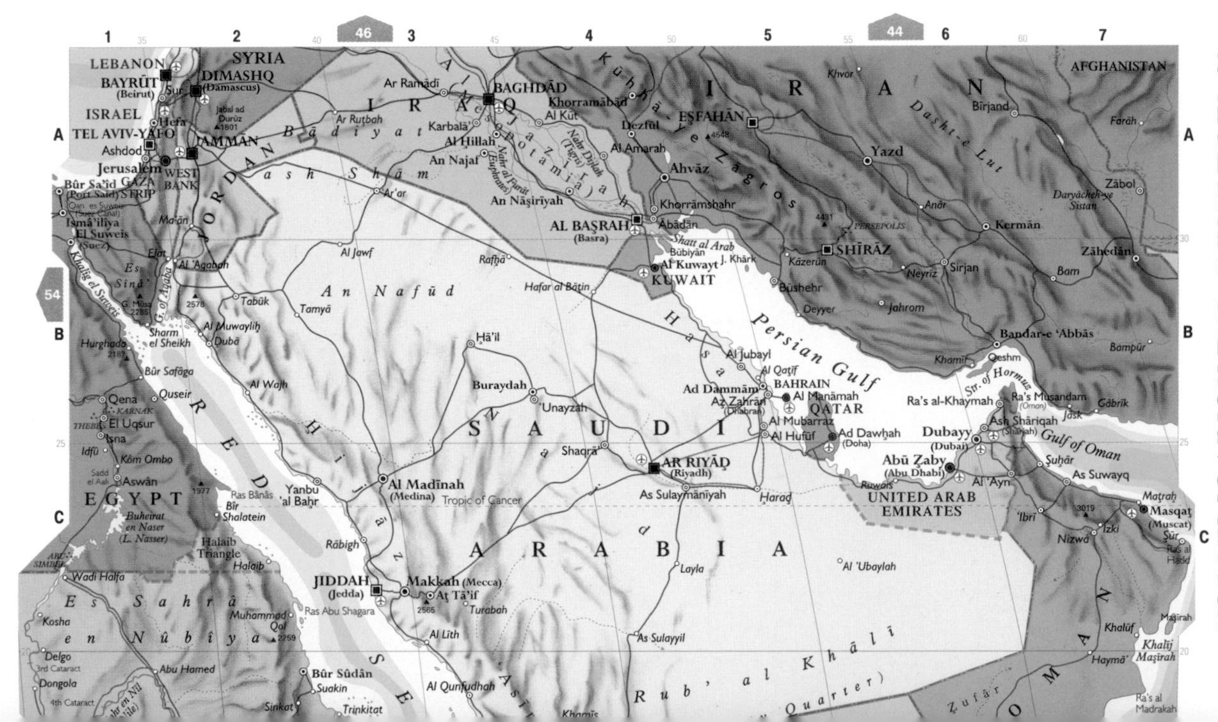
AFGHANISTAN
IRAN
Farāh
Zābol
Daryācheh-ye Sīstān
Zāhedān
Bampūr
Bīrjand
Dasht-e Lut
Kermān
Bam
Bandar-e 'Abbās
Yazd
Anār
Sīrjan
Neyrīz
Jahrom
EṢFAHĀN
Zāgros
SHĪRĀZ
PERSEPOLIS
Kāzerūn
Būshehr
Deyyer
Khvor
Qeshm
Str. of Hormuz
Ra's Musandam
(Oman)
Jāsk
Gābrīk
Gulf of Oman
Ra's al-Khaymah
Ash Shāriqah
(Sharjah)
Dubayy
(Dubai)
Abū Ẓaby
(Abu Dhabi)
Al 'Ayn
Ṣuḥār
As Suwayq
Maṭraḥ
Masqaṭ
(Muscat)
Ṣūr
Ra's al Ḥadd
Nizwá
Izki
'Ibrī
OMAN
Khalūf
Khalīj Maṣīrah
Maṣīrah
Ra's al Madrakah
Haymā'
Zufār
UNITED ARAB EMIRATES
Ruways
Persian Gulf
QATAR
Ad Dawḥah
(Doha)
BAHRAIN
Al Manāmah
Al Mubarraz
Al Hufūf
Al Qaṭīf
Ad Dammām
Aẓ Ẓahrān
(Dhahran)
Al Jubayl
Haraḍ
AR RIYĀḌ
(Riyadh)
As Sulaymānīyah
Layla
As Sulayyil
Al 'Ubaylah
Rub' al Khālī
(Empty Quarter)
KUWAIT
Al Kuwayt
Shaṭṭ al Arab
Būbiyān
J. Khārk
Ābādān
Khorramshahr
Ahvāz
Dezfūl
Khorramābād
Kūhhā-ye Zāgros
AL BAṢRAH
(Basra)
Al 'Amārah
Al Kūt
Nahr Dijlah
(Tigris)
Nahr al Furāt
(Euphrates)
An Nāṣirīyah
BAGHDĀD
Al Ḥillah
An Najaf
Karbalā'
Ar Ramādī
IRAQ
Ar Ruṭbah
Bādiyat ash Shām
Ar'ar
Rafḥā'
Ḥafar al Bāṭin
An Nafūd
Al Jawf
Tamyā
Ḥā'il
Buraydah
'Unayzah
Shaqrā'
SAUDI ARABIA
Al Madīnah
(Medina)
Tropic of Cancer
Makkah (Mecca)
Aṭ Ṭā'if
Turabah
Al Līth
Al Qunfudhah
Asir
Khamīs
JIDDAH
(Jedda)
Rābigh
Yanbu 'al Baḥr
Al Wajh
Tabūk
Al Muwayliḥ
Ḍubā
Ḥijāz
SYRIA
DIMASHQ
(Damascus)
Jabal ad Durūz
LEBANON
BAYRŪT
(Beirut)
Ṣūr
ISRAEL
Ḥefa
TEL AVIV-YAFO
Ashdod
Jerusalem
WEST BANK
GAZA STRIP
'AMMĀN
JORDAN
Ma'ān
Al 'Aqabah
G. of Aqaba
Elat
Es Sînâ'
G. Mûsa
Bûr Sa'îd
(Port Said)
Qan. es Suweis
(Suez Canal)
Ismâ'ilîya
El Suweis
(Suez)
Khalig el Suweis
Sharm el Sheikh
Hurghada
Bûr Safâga
Quseir
Qena
KARNAK
El Uqsur
THEBES
Isna
Idfû
Kôm Ombo
Aswân
Sadd el Aali
Buheirat en Naser
(L. Nasser)
EGYPT
RED SEA
Ras Bânâs
Bîr Shalatein
Halaib Triangle
Halaib
Muhammad Qol
Es Sahrâ en Nûbîya
Ras Abu Shagara
Bûr Sûdân
Suakin
Trinkitat
Sinkat
Abu Hamed
Wadi Halfa
Kosha
Delgo
3rd Cataract
Dongola
4th Cataract
ABU SIMBEL

INDIAN OCEAN
Gulf of Aden
YEMEN
Hadramawt
SANA'
Ta'izz
Ibb
Dhamar
Djebel Manar
Al Hudaydah
Hajjah
Khamir
Al Mukallā
Sayhūt
Rās Fartak
Shibām
Ahwar
Shaqrā'
Nişāb
Al 'Adan (Aden)
Madinat ash Shab
Al Mukhā
Bab el Mandeb
Kamaran
Al Luhayyah
Hanīsh
Socotra (Yemen)
Hadīboh
'Abd al Kūrī (Yemen)
ERITREA
Asmera
Mitsiwa
Dahlak Kebir
Zula
Akordat
Aseb
Danakil Desert
DJIBOUTI
Djibouti
Tadjoura
L. Assal
L. Abbé
Dikhil
ETHIOPIA
ADDIS ABEBA
Ethiopian Highlands
Ogaden
Dire Dawa
Harer
Jijiga
Nazret
Awash
Debre Zeyit
Gonder
L. Tana
Bahir Dar
Debre Markos
Debre Tabor
Dese
Mekele
Adigrat
Adwa
Aksum
Lalibela
Ras Dashen 4620
Nekemte
Bure
Jima
Gore
Metu
Dembidolo
Awasa
Yirga Alem
L. Abaya
L. Shamo
Arba Minch
Dila
Goba
Mt. Batu 4307
Ginir
Imi
Negele
Kibre Mengist
Shashemene
Asela
L. Ziway
Tendaho
Ābay (Blue Nile)
Omo
Genale
Scebeli
SOMALI REP.
Somaliland
Puntland
MUQDISHO (Mogadishu)
Hargeisa
Berbera
Burao
Zeila
Bosaso
Erigavo
Las Anod
Gardo
Garoe
Eil
Galcaio
Obbia
El Dere
Sincdogo
El Gal
Bereda
Ras Asir
Xaafuun
Ras Xaafuun
Bender Beila
Karin
Ferfer
Belet Uen
Giohar
Merca
Uanle Uen
Bur Acaba
Baidoa
Lugh Ganana
Dolo
Bardera
Giuba (Juba)
Wabi Scebeli
Giamama
Chisimaio (Kismayu)
Gelib
Dif
Equator
SUDAN
EL KHARTÛM (Khartoum)
Omdurmân
Wâd Medanî
Gezira
Kassalâ
Khashm el Girba
Gedaref
Kôstî
Ed Dueim
Umm Ruwaba
Jibalan Nubah
Ed Damazin
Roseires Res.
Singa
Nil el Azraq
Nil el Abyad
Malakâl
Sobat
Sûdd
Bahr el Jebel (Nile)
Bôr
Pibor Post
Kapoeta
Elemi Triangle
Juba
Mongalla
Torit
Tali Post
Yei
Kajo Kaji
KENYA
L. Turkana
Lokitaung
Lodwar
South Horr
Marsabit
Moyale
Wajir
El Wak
Mega
Chew Bahir
Kitale
UGANDA
Gulu
Lira
Moroto
Soroti
Mbale
Mt. Elgon 4321
L. Kyoga
L. Albert
Masindi
Pakwach
Murchison Falls
Arua
Albert Nile
Turkwel
Projection: Sanson-Flamsteed's Sinusoidal
East from Greenwich
COPYRIGHT PHILIP'S
55
57

NORTH ATLANTIC OCEAN
Azores (Port.)
Ponta Delgada
Madeira (Port.)
Funchal
Canary Is. (Sp.)
Santa Cruz de Tenerife
Las Palmas
CAPE VERDE IS.
Praia
B. of Biscay
UNITED KINGDOM
LONDON
PORTUGAL
Lisbon
SPAIN
Madrid
FRANCE
PARIS
BELG.
NETH.
GERMANY
SWITZ.
CZECH REP.
Prague
AUSTRIA
Vienna
SLOVAK REP.
HUNGARY
POLAND
Warsaw
CROATIA
BOS.-HERZ.
SERB.
MONT.
ALB.
MAC.
ROMANIA
BULGARIA
GREECE
Athens
Crete
ITALY
Rome
Corsica
Sardinia
Sicily
MALTA
Adriatic Sea
Mediterranean Sea
RUSSIA
UKRAINE
Kiev
Odessa
Volgograd
KAZAKHSTAN
Aral Sea
TURKMEN.
Black Sea
Caspian Sea
GEORGIA
ARM.
AZER.
Baku
TURKEY
Ankara
CYPRUS
SYRIA
Aleppo
Damascus
LEB.
Tel Aviv-Jaffa
Jerusalem
ISRAEL
JORDAN
IRAQ
Mosul
Baghdād
Basra
Tigris
Euphrates
IRAN
TEHRĀN
Esfahān
KUWAIT
Persian Gulf
BAHRAIN
QATAR
SAUDI ARABIA
Riyadh
Medina
Jedda
Mecca
Red Sea
YEMEN
G. of Aden
Socotra (Yemen)
Ras Asir
DJIBOUTI
Djibouti
ERITREA
Asmera
Massawa
L. Tana
Blue Nile
White Nile
SUDAN
Khartoum
Omdurmân
Wad Medani
Port Sudan
Atbara
'Atbara
El Obeid
El Fâsher
Wadi Halfa
EGYPT
CAIRO
Alexandria
Port Said
Suez
El Faiyûm
Asyût
Aswân
Nile
LIBYA
Tripoli
Mişrātah
Benghazi
Sabhā
Marzūq
Al Jawf
Ghadāmes
TUNISIA
Tunis
Sfax
Chott Djerid
ALGERIA
Algiers
Oran
Annaba
Constantine
In Salah
MOROCCO
Rabat
Casablanca
Marrakesh
Fès
Tétouan
Sahara
Tropic of Cancer
WESTERN SAHARA
El Aaiún
Dakhla
MAURITANIA
Nouakchott
Fdérik
Ras Nouâdhibou
SENEGAL
Dakar
St-Louis
C. Vert
Senegal
GAMBIA
Banjul
GUINEA-BISSAU
Bissau
GUINEA
MALI
Bamako
Tombouctou
Niger
BURKINA FASO
Ouagadougou
NIGER
Niamey
Agadès
CHAD
Ndjamena
Abéché
L. Chad
Kano
Maiduguri

SOUTH ATLANTIC OCEAN
INDIAN OCEAN
Gulf of Guinea
Bight of Benin
Mozambique Channel
ANGOLA
CONGO
CONGO (DEM. REP. OF THE)
GABON
EQUATORIAL GUINEA
SÃO TOMÉ & PRÍNCIPE
KENYA
UGANDA
RWANDA
BURUNDI
TANZANIA
ZAMBIA
MALAWI
MOZAMBIQUE
ZIMBABWE
NAMIBIA
BOTSWANA
SOUTH AFRICA
LESOTHO
SWAZ.
MADAGASCAR
COMOROS
SEYCHELLES
MAURITIUS
Ascension I. (U.K.)
St. Helena (U.K.)
Tristan da Cunha (U.K.)
Annobón
Aldabra Is.
Mayotte (Fr.)
Réunion (Fr.)
KINSHASA
Luanda
Lobito
Huambo
Namibe
Brazzaville
Pointe Noire
CABINDA (Angola)
Matadi
Libreville
Douala
Yaoundé
Malabo
Port Harcourt
Bangui
Kisangani
Mbandaka
Kananga
Mbuji-Mayi
Lubumbashi
Likasi
Kampala
Kisumu
Nairobi
Mombasa
Mogadishu
Kismayu
Kigali
Bujumbura
Dodoma
Zanzibar
Dar es Salaam
Lusaka
Ndola
Lilongwe
Blantyre
Harare
Bulawayo
Livingstone
Moçambique
Beira
Maputo
Mbabane
Windhoek
Gaborone
Pretoria (Tshwane)
Johannesburg
Kimberley
Maseru
Durban (eThekwini)
East London
Port Elizabeth
Cape Town
C. of Good Hope
C. Agulhas
C. Fria
C. Lopez
C. Delgado
Moroni
Mamoudzou
Antsiranana
Mahajanga
Toamasina
Antananarivo
Fianarantsoa
St Denis
Port Louis
Victoria
Abidjan
Sekondi-Takoradi
Accra
L. Turkana
L. Albert
L. Edward
L. Victoria
L. Kivu
L. Tanganyika
L. Mweru
L. Malawi
Congo
Oubangui
Lualaba
Kasai
Cuango
Cubango
Cunene
Zambezi
Limpopo
Vaal
Orange
Juba
Tana
Equator
Tropic of Capricorn
Projection: Azimuthal Equidistant
West from Greenwich
East from Greenwich
Dakar Capital Cities
COPYRIGHT PHILIP'S
m ft
0
200 600
1000 3000
2000 6000
4000 12000
200 0 200 400 600 800 1000 1200 1400 1600 1800 km
200 0 200 400 600 800 1000 1200 miles
1 2 3 4 5 7 8 9
G H J K

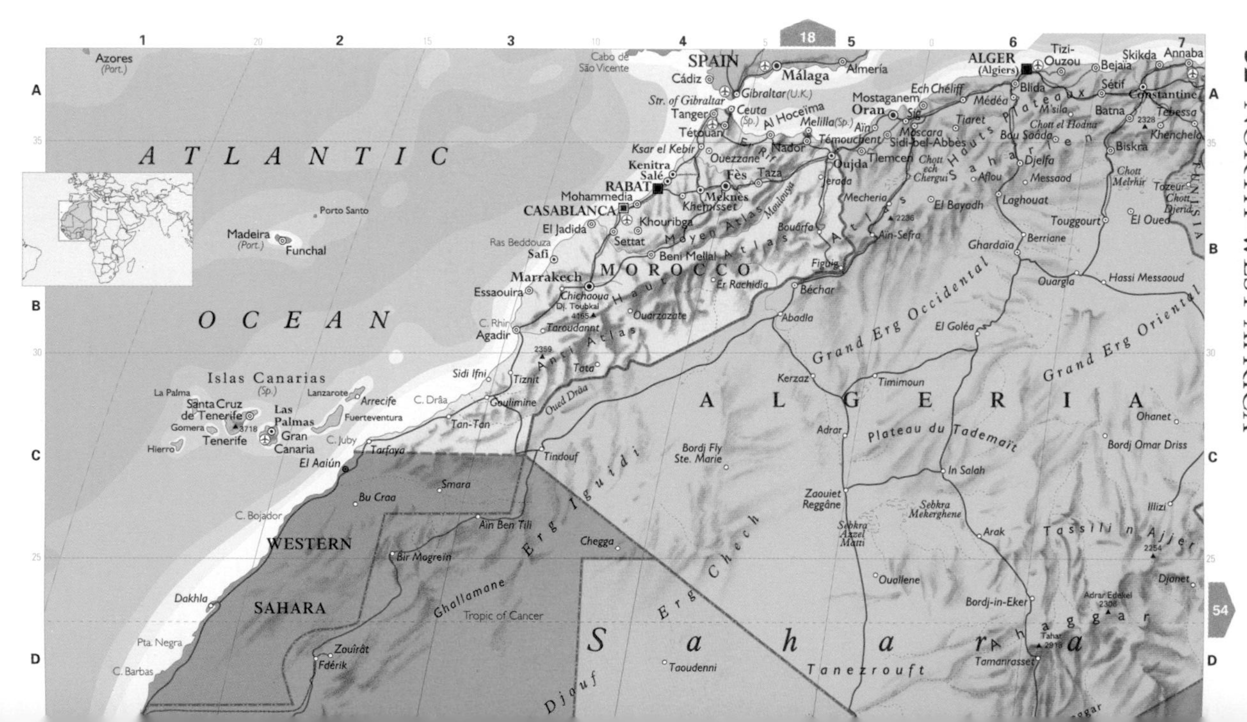

A T L A N T I C
O C E A N
Azores (Port.)
Madeira (Port.)
Funchal
Porto Santo
Islas Canarias (Sp.)
La Palma
Santa Cruz de Tenerife
Tenerife
Gomera
Hierro
Las Palmas
Gran Canaria
Lanzarote
Arrecife
Fuerteventura
C. Juby
El Aaiún
C. Bojador
Dakhla
Pta. Negra
C. Barbas
WESTERN SAHARA
Bu Craa
Smara
Aïn Ben Tili
Bir Mogreïn
Zouîrât
Fdérik
Ghallamane
Tropic of Cancer
Tarfaya
Tan-Tan
Sidi Ifni
Goulimine
Tiznit
Agadir
C. Rhir
C. Drâa
Oued Drâa
Essaouira
Marrakech
Safi
Ras Beddouza
El Jadida
CASABLANCA
Mohammedia
RABAT
Salé
Kenitra
Settat
Khouribga
Ksar el Kebir
Tanger
Tétouan
Str. of Gibraltar
Gibraltar (U.K.)
Ceuta (Sp.)
Málaga
Cádiz
SPAIN
Almería
Cabo de São Vicente
MOROCCO
Meknès
Khemisset
Fès
Taza
Ouezzane
Al Hoceïma
Melilla (Sp.)
Nador
Oujda
Jerada
Beni Mellal
Bouârfa
Figuig
Er Rachidia
Ouarzazate
Chichaoua
Dj. Toubkal 4165
Taroudannt
Tata
Anti Atlas
Haut Atlas
Moyen Atlas
Moulouya
Tindouf
Chegga
Bordj Fly Ste. Marie
Taoudenni
Djouf
A L G E R I A
S a h a r a
Oran
Mostaganem
Mascara
Sidi-bel-Abbès
Tlemcen
Témouchent
Sig
Ech Chéliff
Médéa
ALGER (Algiers)
Blida
Tizi-Ouzou
Bejaïa
Skikda
Annaba
Sétif
Constantine
M'sila
Chott el Hodna
Batna
Biskra
Tebessa
Khenchela
Tiaret
Bou Saâda
Djelfa
Aflou
Chott ech Chergui
El Bayadh
Laghouat
Messaad
Ghardaïa
Berriane
Touggourt
Ouargla
Hassi Messaoud
El Oued
Chott Melrhir
Tozeur
Chott Djerid
Mecheria
Aïn-Sefra
Béchar
Abadla
Kerzaz
Adrar
Timimoun
El Goléa
In Salah
Zaouiet Reggâne
Arak
Bordj-in-Eker
Tamanrasset
Tahat 2918
Adrar Edekel 2308
Illizi
Djanet
Ohanet
Bordj Omar Driss
Hauts Plateaux
Saharan Atlas
Grand Erg Occidental
Grand Erg Oriental
Plateau du Tademaït
Tanezrouft
Erg Chech
Erg Iguidi
Tassili n Ajjer
Ahaggar
Ouallene
Sebkra Mekerghene
Sebkra Azzel Matti
TUNISIA
18
54

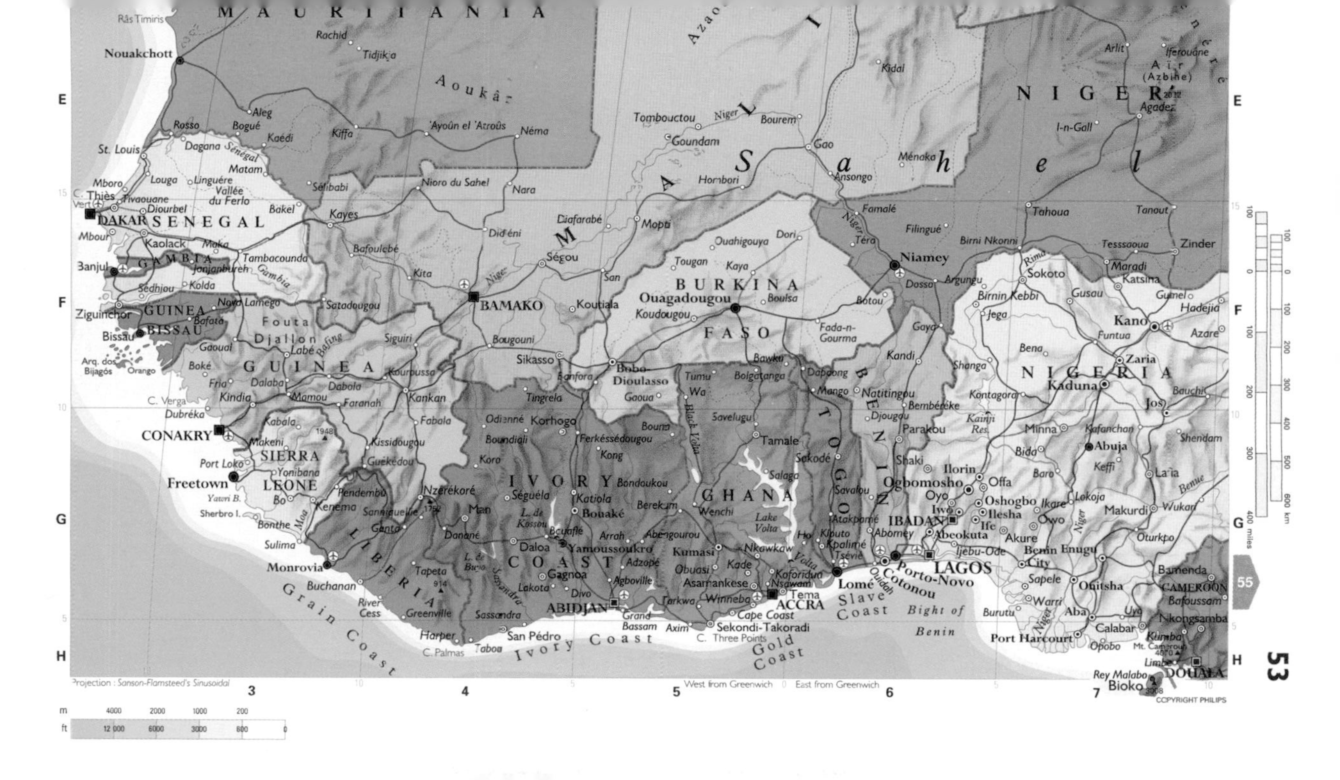

100 0 100 200 300 400 500 600 km
100 0 100 200 300 400 miles
55
E
F
G
H
MAURITANIA
Aoukâr
Nouakchott
Râs Timiris
Rachid
Tidjikja
Aleg
Bogué
Kaédi
Kiffa
Sélibabi
'Ayoûn el 'Atroûs
Néma
Nara
Nioro du Sahel
Rosso
Dagana
Sénégal
Matam
Bakel
Kayes
St. Louis
Louga
Linguère
Vallée du Ferlo
SENEGAL
Thiès
Mboro
DAKAR
C. Vert
Mbour
Diourbel
Tivaouane
Kaolack
Tambacounda
GAMBIA
Banjul
Janjanbureh
Gambia
Ziguinchor
Sédhiou
Kolda
GUINEA-BISSAU
Bissau
Bafatá
Nova Lamego
Arq. dos Bijagós
Orango
GUINEA
Fouta Djallon
Labé
Bafing
Boké
Gaoual
Kindia
Fria
Dalaba
Mamou
Dabola
Faranah
Siguiri
Kouroussa
Kankan
Fabala
Kissidougou
Guékédou
CONAKRY
Dubréka
C. Verga
SIERRA LEONE
Freetown
Port Loko
Makeni
Kabala
Yonibana
Bo
Kenema
Pendembu
Bonthe
Sherbro I.
Yawri B.
Sulima
Moa
LIBERIA
Monrovia
Buchanan
River Cess
Greenville
Harper
C. Palmas
Ganta
Sanniquellie
Tapeta
Nzérékoré
Grain Coast
MALI
Sahel
Tombouctou
Goundam
Niger
Bourem
Gao
Ansongo
Kidal
Ménaka
Hombori
Mopti
Diafarabé
San
Ségou
Didiéni
BAMAKO
Kita
Bafoulabé
Satadougou
Bougouni
Koutiala
Sikasso
Azaouad
BURKINA FASO
Ouagadougou
Ouahigouya
Kaya
Dori
Boulsa
Tougan
Koudougou
Bobo-Dioulasso
Banfora
Gaoua
Fada-n-Gourma
Bawku
Bolgatanga
Tumu
Wa
NIGER
Niamey
Filingué
Dosso
Gaya
Birni Nkonni
Tahoua
I-n-Gall
Agadez
Arlit
Iferouâne
Aïr (Azbine)
Maradi
Tessaoua
Tanout
Zinder
Téra
Famalé
Botou
Kandi
BENIN
Natitingou
Djougou
Parakou
Bembèrèkè
Savalou
Abomey
Porto-Novo
Cotonou
Ouidah
TOGO
Lomé
Sokodé
Dapaong
Mango
Atakpamé
Kpalimé
Tsévié
Slave Coast
Bight of Benin
GHANA
Tamale
Salaga
Savelugu
Black Volta
Lake Volta
Wenchi
Berekum
Kumasi
Obuasi
Kade
Koforidua
Nsawam
Nkawkaw
Ho
Kpandu
ACCRA
Tema
Winneba
Cape Coast
Sekondi-Takoradi
Tarkwa
Axim
C. Three Points
Gold Coast
Asamankese
IVORY COAST
Korhogo
Ferkéssédougou
Kong
Boundiali
Odienné
Tingrela
Bondoukou
Bouna
Katiola
Bouaké
Séguéla
Man
Danané
Daloa
Gagnoa
Yamoussoukro
Abengourou
Agboville
Adzopé
Arrah
Divo
Lakota
ABIDJAN
Grand Bassam
San Pédro
Sassandra
Tabou
Ivory Coast
NIGERIA
Sokoto
Gusau
Birnin Kebbi
Jega
Katsina
Kano
Zaria
Funtua
Kaduna
Jos
Bauchi
Azare
Hadejia
Gumel
Kontagora
Kainji Res.
Bida
Minna
Abuja
Keffi
Lafia
Makurdi
Ilorin
Offa
Ogbomosho
Oshogbo
Oyo
Ilesha
Ife
IBADAN
Abeokuta
Ijebu-Ode
LAGOS
Akure
Owo
Benin City
Sapele
Warri
Onitsha
Enugu
Aba
Port Harcourt
Calabar
Oturkpo
Lokoja
Benue
CAMEROON
Bamenda
Bafoussam
Kumba
DOUALA
Limbe
Bioko
Rey Malabo
Mt. Cameroun
Nkongsamba
Projection : Sanson-Flamsteed's Sinusoidal
West from Greenwich 0 East from Greenwich
COPYRIGHT PHILIPS
m 4000 2000 1000 200
ft 12 000 6000 3000 600 0

MEDITERRANEAN SEA
RED SEA
TURKEY
SYRIA
IRAQ
JORDAN
SAUDI ARABIA
LEBANON
ISRAEL
CYPRUS
GREECE
ITALY
MALTA
TUNISIA
ALGERIA
LIBYA
EGYPT
ADANA
HALAB (Aleppo)
DIMASHQ (Damascus)
BAYRŪT (Beirut)
TEL AVIV-YAFO
Jerusalem
AMMĀN
EL QÂHIRA (Cairo)
EL ISKANDARÎYA (Alexandria)
TARĀBULUS (Tripoli)
TUNIS
Banghāzī
Valletta
Antalya
Nicosia
Misrātah
Surt
Ajdābiya
Tubruq
Sabhā
Aswân
El Gîza
Bûr Sa'îd
Sicilia
Kriti
Rhodes
Cyrenaica
Tripolitania
Fezzan
Sahrâ' Lîbîya
Tropic of Cancer
Khalīj Surt
Golfe de Gabès
Es Sahra Esh Sharqîya
El Wâhât el-Khârga
El Wâhât el-Dakhla
Munkhafed el Qattâra
Siwa
Halaib Triangle
Wadi Halfa

NIGER
CHAD
SUDAN
ERITREA
ETHIOPIA
NIGERIA
CAMEROON
CENTRAL AFRICAN REPUBLIC
CONGO (DEM. REP. OF THE)
KENYA
Sahel
Fachi
Bilma
Grand Erg de Bilma
Borkou
Ounianga Sérir
Depression du Mourdi
Faya-Largeau
Dépression du Bodélé
Erg du Djourab
Fada
Ennedi
1310
Zagaoua
Oum Chalouba
Dongola
Bir 'Atrun
Kareima
4th Cataract
5th Cataract
6th Cataract
Ed Debba
Nahr en Nil (Nile)
Berber
Atbara
Adarama
Wad Hamid
Shendi
Nahr 'Atbara
El Khartûm Bahrî
EL KHARTÛM (Khartoum)
Omdurmân
Kassalâ
Khashm el Girba
Suakin
Sinkat
Trinkitat
Haiya
Karora
2780
Nakfa
Akordat
W. Howar (Shau)
Malha
1954
El Wuz
Sodiri
Kutum
Wâd Medanî
Gedaref
Gezira
Ed Dueim
Boultoum
Nguigmi
Zigey
Mao
Lac Tchad
Bahr el Ghazal
Biltine
Moussoro
Bosso
Kumaganum
Gashua
Nguru
Geidam
Titiwa
Maiduguri
Potiskum
346
Massakory
Abéché
Ati
Oum Hadjer
Al Junaynah
Dârfûr
J. Marrah 3088
Zalingei
Nyâlâ
El Fâsher
Umm Keddada
Kordofân
El Obeid
En Nahud
El Odaiya
Abu Zabad
Er Rahad
Umm Ruwaba
Jibalan Nubah
1325
Kâdugli
Kôstî
Singa
Nil el Azraq (Blue Nile)
Nil el Abyad (White Nile)
Ed Damazin
Roseires Res.
Gonder
1830
L. Tana
Bahir Dar
Bure
Abay (Blue Nile)
Debre Markos
Ndjamena
Kousseri
Bama
Goniri
Chibuk
Maroua
Duku
Bajoga
Gombe
Biu
Kumo
Mubi
Guider
Bokoro
Mongo
Goz Beïda
Massenya
Bitkine
Abou-Deïa
Chari
Bousso
Am Timan
Bongor
Numan
Yola
Garoua
Pala
Kélo
Logone
Laï
Sarh
Koumra
Moundou
Doba
Goré
Harazé
Birao
Mt. Toussoro 1226
Massif des Bongos
Ndélé
Songo
Bahr el Arab
Sa'id Bundas
Bahr el Ghazâl
Jur
Râgâ
Gogriâl
Wâw
Tonj
Sûdd
Malakâl
Sobat
Bahr el Jebel (Nile)
Rumbêk
Toinya
Amadi
Tali Post
Bôr
Pibor Post
Nekemte
3202
Dembidolo
Metu
Gore
Jima
3598
Omo
L. Abaya
Arba Minch
L. Shamo
Chew Bahir
Jalingo
Rés. de Lagdo
2042
1960
Baïbokoum
Gashaka
2419
Banyo
Ngaoundéré
Rés. de Mbakaou
Meiganga
Massif de l'Adamaoua
Tibati
Bétaré Oya
Foumban
Yoko
Bouar
Baboua
Bossangoa
Bozoum
Paoua
Batangafo
Kaga Bandoro
Yalinga
Bria
Ippy
Bakouma
Kotto
Chinko
Ouarra
Obo
Sibut
Bambari
Carnot
Bossembélé
Sanaga
Bertoua
Nanga-Eboko
Batouri
YAOUNDÉ
Abong-Mbang
Berbérati
Bangui
Bimbo
Mbaïki
Zongo
Libenge
Bosobolo
Oubangi
Mobaye
Mobayi
Bangassou
Bomu
Uele
Bondo
Ango
Dungu
Faradje
Yambio
El Istiwa'iya
Yei
Jûbâ
Mongalla
Kajo Kaji
3187
Torit
Kapoeta
Elemi Triangle
Lokitaung
L. Turkana
375
Projection : Sanson-Flamsteed's Sinusoidal
East from Greenwich
COPYRIGHT PHILIPS
E
F
G
H
1
2
3
4
5
6
15
10
5
20
25
30
53
56
49
57
m 4000 2000 1000 200
ft 12 000 6000 3000 600 0
100 0 100 200 300 400 500 600 km
100 0 100 200 300 400 miles

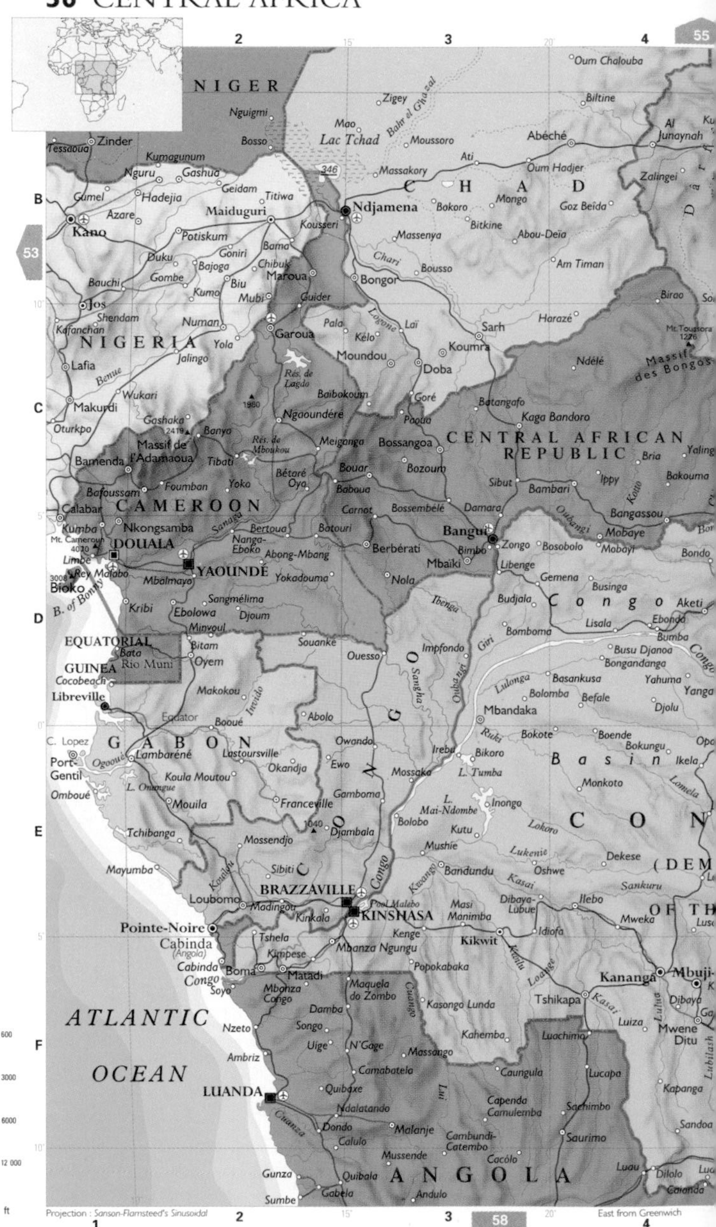
NIGER
NIGERIA
CHAD
CAMEROON
CENTRAL AFRICAN REPUBLIC
EQUATORIAL GUINEA
GABON
CONGO
ANGOLA
ATLANTIC OCEAN
Congo Basin
Lac Tchad
Oum Chalouba
Biltine
Zigey
Bahr el Ghazal
Mao
Moussoro
Abéché
Al Junaynah
Nguigmi
Bosso
Zinder
Tessaoua
Kumagunum
Nguru
Gashua
Geidam
Massakory
Ati
Oum Hadjer
Zalingei
Gumel
Hadejia
Titiwa
Maiduguri
Ndjamena
Bokoro
Mongo
Goz Beïda
Kano
Azare
Potiskum
Kousseri
Bitkine
Massenya
Abou-Deïa
Duku
Goniri
Bama
Bajoga
Chibuk
Chari
Bousso
Am Timan
Bauchi
Gombe
Biu
Maroua
Bongor
Kumo
Mubi
Guider
Birao
Jos
Shendam
Numan
Kafanchan
Pala
Laï
Sarh
Harazé
Mt. Toussoro 1276
Garoua
Kélo
Logone
Yola
Koumra
Moundou
Ndélé
Massif des Bongos
Lafia
Jalingo
Doba
Benue
Rés. de Lagdo
Wukari
Baïbokoum
Goré
Batangafo
Kaga Bandoro
Makurdi
1960
Oturkpo
Ngaoundéré
Gashaka
2419
Paoua
Banyo
Rés. de Mboukou
Meiganga
Bossangoa
Massif de l'Adamaoua
Bamenda
Tibati
Bozoum
Bria
Yalinga
Bétaré Oya
Bouar
Ippy
Bakouma
Sibut
Bambari
Bafoussam
Foumban
Yoko
Baboua
Kotto
Calabar
Carnot
Bossembélé
Damara
Bangassou
Kumba
Nkongsamba
Sanaga
Bertoua
Batouri
Oubangi
Mobaye
Mt. Cameroun 4070
DOUALA
Nanga-Eboko
Bangui
Zongo
Bosobolo
Mobayi
Limbe
Abong-Mbang
Berbérati
Bimbo
Bondo
3008
Rey Malabo
YAOUNDÉ
Mbaïki
Libenge
Gemena
Bioko
Mbalmayo
Yokadouma
Nola
Businga
B. of Bonny
Kribi
Sangmélima
Ibenga
Budjala
Aketi
Ebolowa
Djoum
Lisala
Ebonda
Minvoul
Bomboma
Bumba
Bata
Bitam
Souanké
Impfondo
Giri
Busu Djanoa
Rio Muni
Oyem
Ouesso
Bongandanga
Cocobeach
Sangha
Lulonga
Basankusu
Yahuma
Libreville
Makokou
Ivindo
Bolomba
Befale
Yanga
Ubangi
Djolu
Equator
Booué
Abolo
Mbandaka
C. Lopez
Owando
Ruki
Bokote
Boende
Lambaréné
Lastoursville
Irebu
Bikoro
Bokungu
Ikela
Port-Gentil
Ogooué
Okandja
Ewo
Mossaka
L. Tumba
Koula Moutou
Monkoto
Omboué
L. Onangue
Lomela
Mouila
Franceville
Gamboma
L. Mai-Ndombe
Inongo
1040
Djambala
Bolobo
Kutu
Lokoro
Tchibanga
Mossendjo
Mushie
Lukenie
Dekese
Mayumba
Kouilou
Sibiti
Bandundu
Oshwe
Congo
Kwango
Kasai
Sankuru
BRAZZAVILLE
Pool Malebo
Masi Manimba
Dibaya-Lubue
Ilebo
Loubomo
Madingou
Kinkala
KINSHASA
Mweka
Pointe-Noire
Kenge
Kikwit
Idiofa
Cabinda (Angola)
Tshela
Mbanza Ngungu
Kwilu
Kimpese
Popokabaka
Cabinda
Boma
Matadi
Loange
Kananga
Mbuji-
Soyo
Mbanza Congo
Maquela do Zombo
Cuango
Tshikapa
Dibaya
Damba
Kasongo Lunda
Lulua
Nzeto
Songo
Luiza
Mwene Ditu
Uige
N'Gage
Kahemba
Luachimo
Lubilash
Ambriz
Massango
Camabatela
Caungula
Lucapa
Quibaxe
Lui
Kapanga
LUANDA
Ndalatando
Capenda Camulemba
Sachimbo
Dondo
Malanje
Sandoa
Cuanza
Calulo
Cambundi-Catembo
Saurimo
Mussende
Cacólo
Gunza
Quibala
Luau
Dilolo
Caianda
Sumbe
Gabela
Andulo
15°
20°
10°
5°
0°
10°
1
2
3
4
B
C
D
E
F
53
55
58
m
ft
200
600
1000
3000
2000
6000
4000
12 000
Projection : Sanson-Flamsteed's Sinusoidal
East from Greenwich

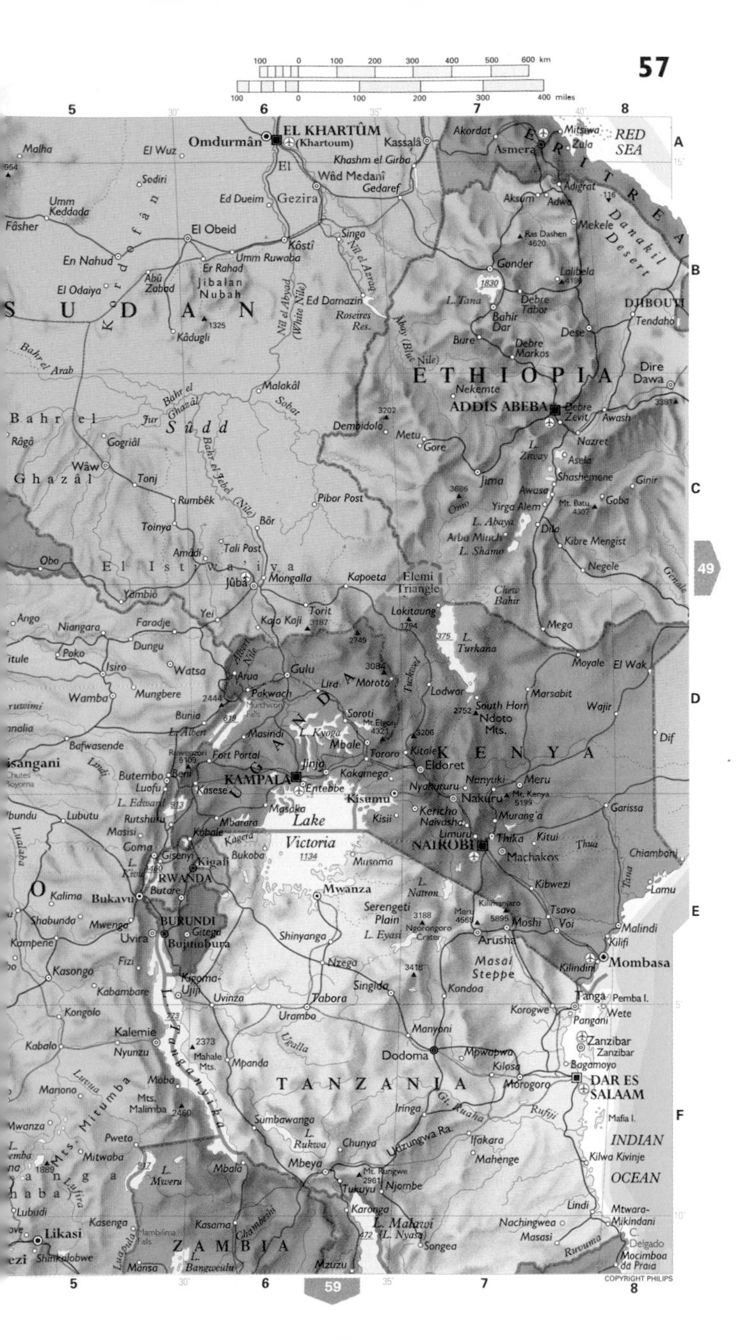

100 0 100 200 300 400 500 600 km
100 0 100 200 300 400 miles
5
6
7
8
A
B
C
D
E
F
RED SEA
ERITREA
EL KHARTÛM
(Khartoum)
Omdurmân
Kassalâ
Akordat
Asmera
Mitsiwa
Zula
Malha
El Wuz
Sodiri
Khashm el Girba
El Gezira
Wâd Medanî
Gedaref
Ed Dueim
Umm Keddada
Fâsher
El Obeid
Kordofân
Adigrat
Aksum
Adwa
Mekele
Danakil Desert
Ras Dashen 4620
Singa
Kôstî
Umm Ruwaba
En Nahud
Er Rahad
Abû Zabad
Jibalan Nubah
El Odaiya
Nil el Azraq
Gonder
Lalibela
1830
L. Tana
Debre Tabor
Bahir Dar
DJIBOUTI
Tendaho
SUDAN
Ed Damazin
Roseires Res.
Nil el Abyad (White Nile)
1325
Kâdugli
Abay (Blue Nile)
Bure
Debre Markos
Dese
Bahr el Arab
ETHIOPIA
Dire Dawa
Malakâl
Nekemte
ADDIS ABEBA
Debre Zevit
Awash
Bahr el Ghazâl
Sobat
Jur
Sûdd
3202
Dembidolo
Metu
Gore
Bahr el Ghazâl
Râgâ
Gogriâl
Bahr el Jebel (Nile)
L. Zíway
Nazret
Asela
Wâw
Tonj
Jima
Shashemene
Ginir
Awasa
Rumbêk
Pibor Post
3686
Omo
Yirga Alem
Mt. Batu 4307
Goba
Toinya
Bôr
L. Abaya
Dila
Arba Minch
L. Shamo
Kibre Mengist
Amâdi
Tali Post
Obo
El Istiwa'iya
Negele
Genale
Jûba
Mongalla
Kapoeta
Elemi Triangle
Yambiô
Chew Bahir
Torit
Lokitaung
Ango
Niangara
Faradje
Yei
Kajo Kaji
3187
Mega
Poko
Dungu
2749
375
L. Turkana
Albert Nile
Isiro
Watsa
Gulu
Moyale
El Wak
Arua
3084
Moroto
Lira
UGANDA
Turkwel
Wamba
Mungbere
Pakwach
Lodwar
Marsabit
2444
Murchison Falls
South Horr
Wajir
Bunia
619
Soroti
2752
Ndoto Mts.
L. Albert
Masindi
L. Kyoga
Mt. Elgon 4321
3206
Dif
Bafwasende
Mbale
KENYA
Ruwenzori 5109
Fort Portal
Kitale
Kisangani
Lindi
Beni
Tororo
Eldoret
Butembo
Jinja
Nyahururu
Nanyuki
Meru
Luofu
KAMPALA
Kakamega
Kasese
Entebbe
Kisumu
Nakuru
Mt. Kenya 5199
L. Edward
913
Lubutu
Rutshuru
Masaka
Kisii
Kericho
Naivasha
Murang'a
Garissa
Lualaba
Masisi
Mbarara
Lake Victoria
Limuru
Kabale
Kagera
NAIROBI
Thika
Kitui
Thua
Goma
Gisenyi
Kigali
Bukoba
1134
Musoma
Machakos
Chiamboni
L. Kivu
1460
RWANDA
Tana
Butare
Mwanza
L. Natron
Kibwezi
Lamu
Kalima
Bukavu
Serengeti Plain
Kilimanjaro 5895
Tsavo
Shabunda
Mwenga
BURUNDI
3188
Meru 4565
Moshi
Voi
Malindi
Uvira
Gitega
Bujumbura
Shinyanga
L. Eyasi
Ngorongoro Crater
Arusha
Kilifi
Kampene
Fizi
Nzega
Masai Steppe
Kilindini
Mombasa
Kasongo
3418
Kigoma-Ujiji
Singida
Kondoa
Kabambare
Uvinza
Tabora
Tanga
Pemba I.
Korogwe
Wete
Kongolo
Urambo
Pangani
773
L. Tanganyika
Kalemie
2373
Manyoni
Ugalla
Zanzibar
Kabalo
Nyunzu
Mahale Mts.
Mpanda
Dodoma
Mpwapwa
Kilosa
Bagamoyo
Moba
TANZANIA
Morogoro
DAR ES SALAAM
Manono
Luvua
Mts. Malimba
2460
Iringa
Gt. Ruaha
Rufiji
Mafia I.
Mwanza
Mts. Mitumba
Sumbawanga
L. Rukwa
Chunya
Udzungwa Ra.
Ifakara
INDIAN OCEAN
Pweto
Mitwaba
917
L. Mweru
Mahenge
Kilwa Kivinje
1889
Mbala
Mbeya
Mt. Rungwe 2961
Tukuyu
Njombe
Lufira
Lubudi
Karonga
Lindi
Mtwara-Mikindani
Kasenga
Kasama
Chambeshi
L. Malawi (L. Nyasa)
Nachingwea
Likasi
Mambilima Falls
472
Masasi
C. Delgado
Luapula
ZAMBIA
Songea
Ruvuma
Mocimboa da Praia
Shinkolobwe
Mansa
L. Bangweulu
Mzuzu
30°
35°
40°
15°
5°
10°

49
59

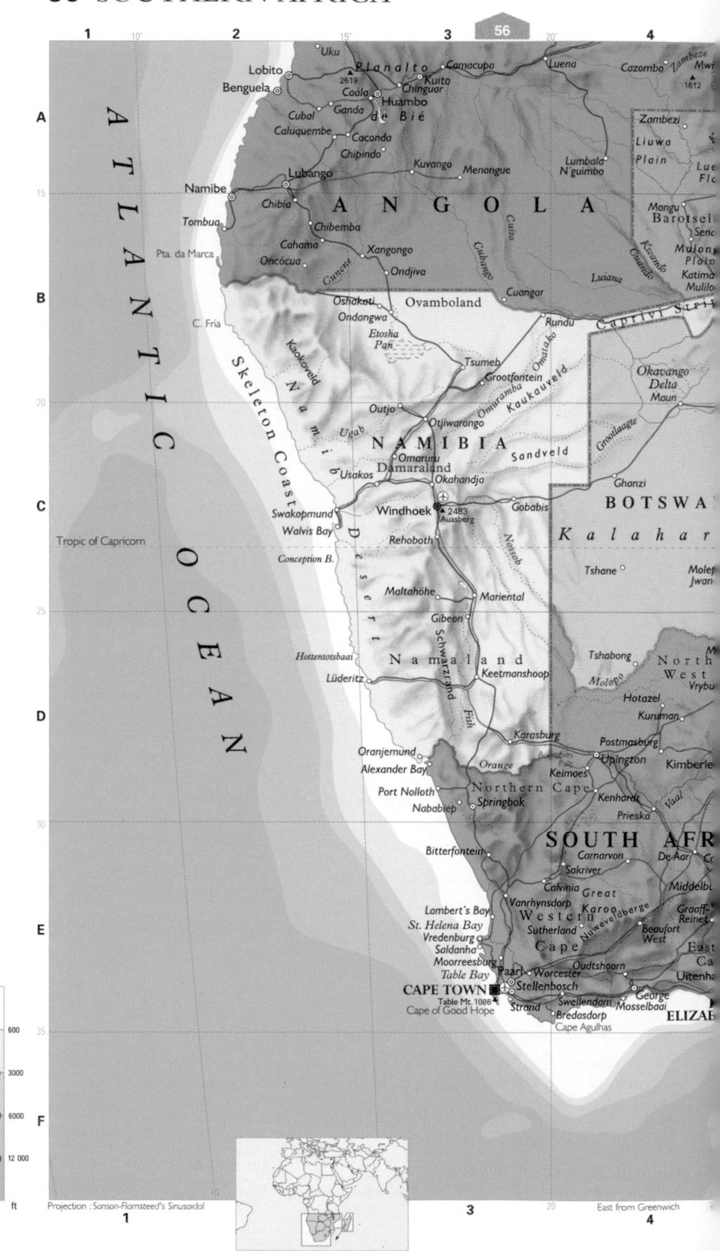
ATLANTIC OCEAN
ANGOLA
NAMIBIA
BOTSWANA
SOUTH AFRICA
Lobito
Benguela
Huambo
Kuito
Lubango
Namibe
Tombua
Menongue
Ondjiva
Ovamboland
Etosha Pan
Tsumeb
Grootfontein
Outjo
Otjiwarongo
Omaruru
Damaraland
Okahandja
Usakos
Swakopmund
Walvis Bay
Windhoek
Rehoboth
Gobabis
Kalahari
Mariental
Gibeon
Namaland
Keetmanshoop
Lüderitz
Karasburg
Oranjemund
Alexander Bay
Port Nolloth
Springbok
Northern Cape
Upington
Kimberley
Bitterfontein
Calvinia
Vanrhynsdorp
Western Cape
Lambert's Bay
Saldanha
Paarl
Worcester
CAPE TOWN
Stellenbosch
Swellendam
Oudtshoorn
George
Mosselbaai
Cape of Good Hope
Cape Agulhas
Skeleton Coast
Namib Desert
Tropic of Capricorn
Projection : Sanson-Flamsteed's Sinusoidal
East from Greenwich

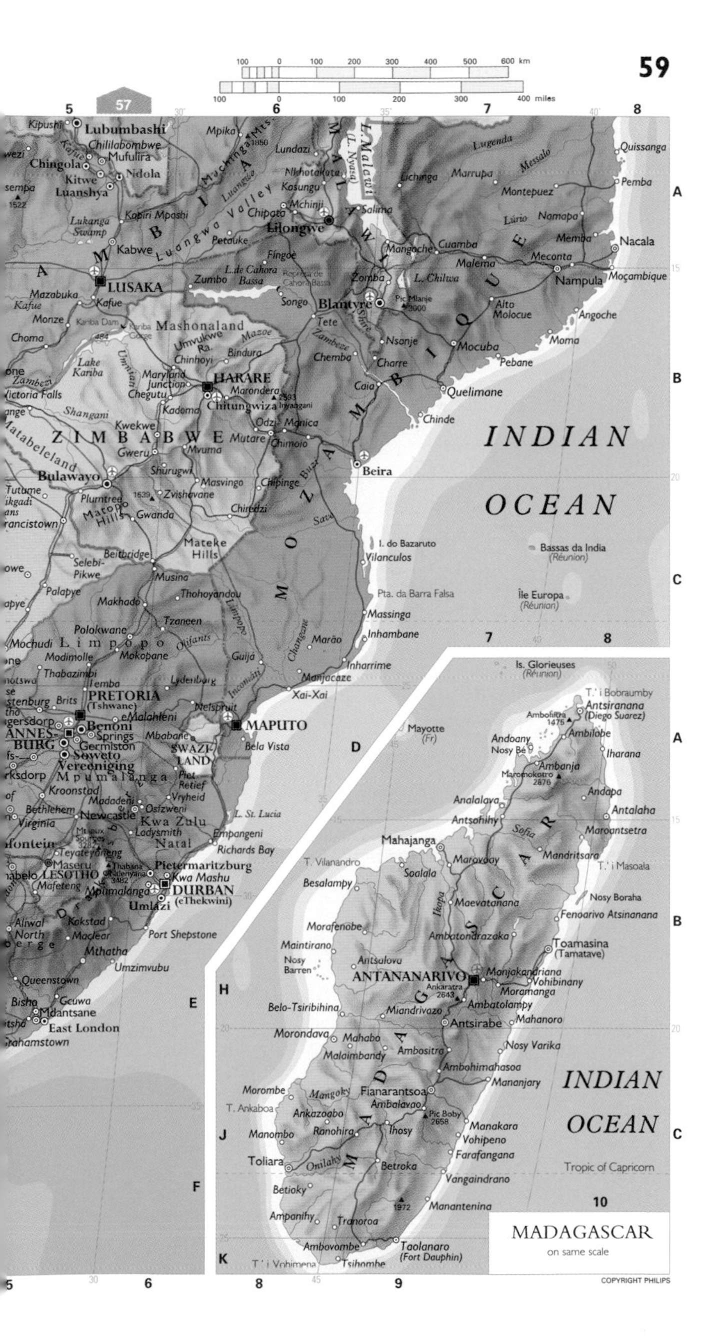

INDIAN OCEAN
MOZAMBIQUE
ZIMBABWE
ZAMBIA
MALAWI
MADAGASCAR
LUSAKA
HARARE
MAPUTO
PRETORIA (Tshwane)
ANTANANARIVO
Lilongwe
Lubumbashi
Blantyre
Beira
Bulawayo
DURBAN (eThekwini)
Pietermaritzburg
LESOTHO
SWAZILAND
Nampula
Quelimane
Mahajanga
Toamasina (Tamatave)
Antsiranana (Diego Suarez)
Toliara
Fianarantsoa
Taolanaro (Fort Dauphin)
Mayotte (Fr)
Bassas da India (Réunion)
Île Europa (Réunion)
Is. Glorieuses (Réunion)
Tropic of Capricorn
MADAGASCAR
on same scale

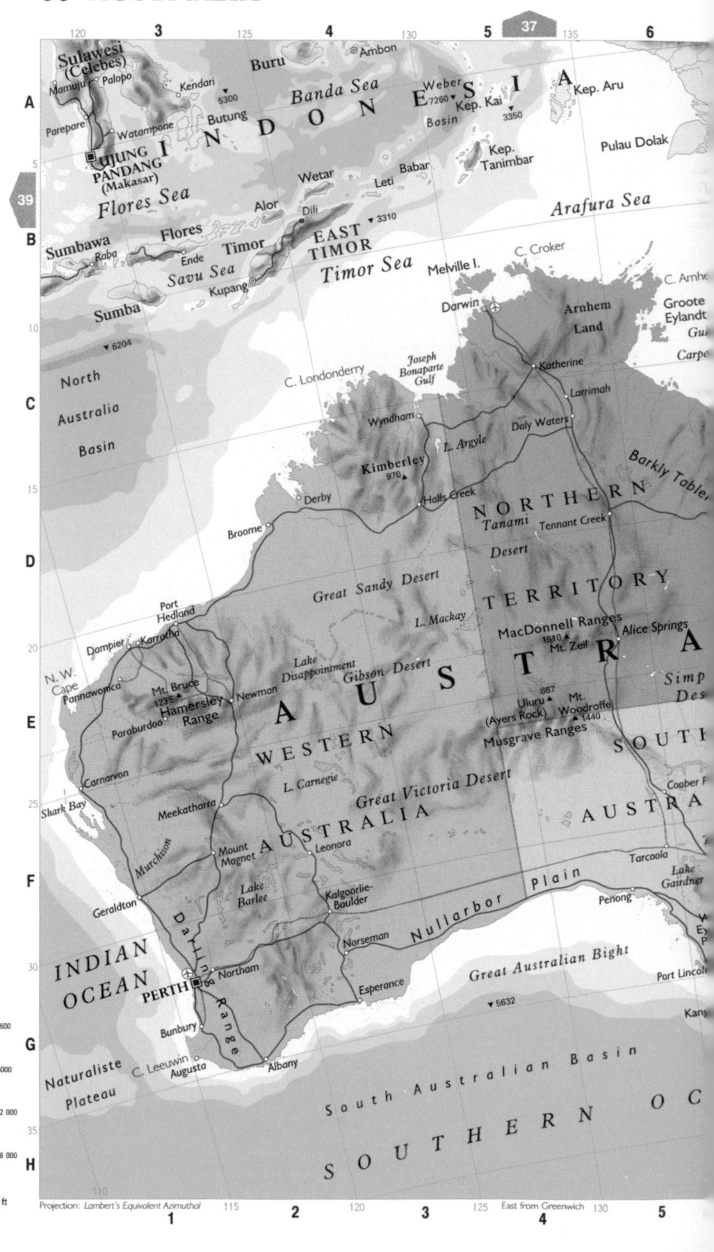
Sulawesi (Celebes)
Mamuju
Palopo
Kendari
Buru
Ambon
Banda Sea
Weber Basin
Kep. Kai
Kep. Aru
Parepare
Watampone
Butung
I N D O N E S I A
UJUNG PANDANG (Makasar)
Kep. Tanimbar
Pulau Dolak
Wetar
Babar
Leti
Flores Sea
Alor
Dili
Arafura Sea
Sumbawa
Raba
Flores
Ende
Timor
EAST TIMOR
Savu Sea
Kupang
Timor Sea
Melville I.
C. Croker
Sumba
Darwin
Arnhem Land
Groote Eylandt
North Australia Basin
C. Londonderry
Joseph Bonaparte Gulf
Katherine
Larrimah
Wyndham
Daly Waters
L. Argyle
Kimberley
Barkly Tableland
Derby
Halls Creek
NORTHERN TERRITORY
Tanami Desert
Tennant Creek
Broome
Great Sandy Desert
Port Hedland
L. Mackay
MacDonnell Ranges
Mt. Zeil
Alice Springs
Dampier
Karratha
N.W. Cape
Pannawonica
Mt. Bruce
Hamersley Range
Newman
Lake Disappointment
Gibson Desert
A U S T R A
Uluru (Ayers Rock)
Mt. Woodroffe
Simpson Desert
Paraburdoo
WESTERN AUSTRALIA
Musgrave Ranges
SOUTH AUSTRALIA
Carnarvon
L. Carnegie
Great Victoria Desert
Coober Pedy
Shark Bay
Meekatharra
Mount Magnet
Leonora
Tarcoola
Murchison
Lake Barlee
Kalgoorlie-Boulder
Nullarbor Plain
Penong
Lake Gairdner
Geraldton
Darling Range
Norseman
INDIAN OCEAN
Northam
PERTH
Great Australian Bight
Port Lincoln
Esperance
Bunbury
Augusta
C. Leeuwin
Albany
Naturaliste Plateau
South Australian Basin
SOUTHERN OCEAN
Projection: Lambert's Equivalent Azimuthal
East from Greenwich
m ft

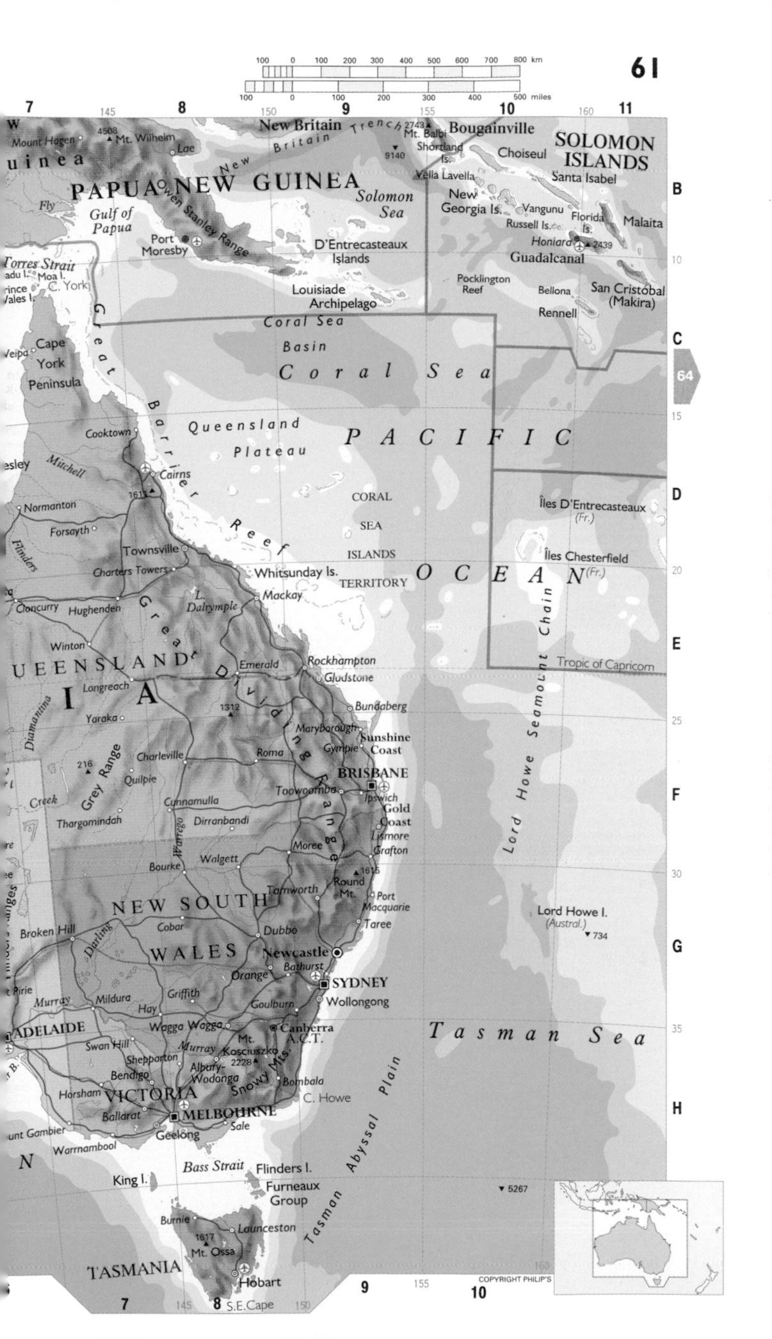

PAPUA NEW GUINEA
Mount Hagen
Mt. Wilhelm
Lae
New Britain
New Britain Trench
Owen Stanley Range
Gulf of Papua
Port Moresby
Solomon Sea
D'Entrecasteaux Islands
Louisiade Archipelago
Bougainville
Mt. Balbi
Shortland Is.
Choiseul
SOLOMON ISLANDS
Santa Isabel
Vella Lavella
New Georgia Is.
Vangunu
Russell Is.
Florida Is.
Malaita
Honiara
Guadalcanal
Pocklington Reef
Bellona
Rennell
San Cristóbal (Makira)
Torres Strait
Moa I.
C. York
Cape York Peninsula
Coral Sea Basin
Coral Sea
Great Barrier Reef
Queensland Plateau
PACIFIC OCEAN
CORAL SEA ISLANDS TERRITORY
Îles D'Entrecasteaux (Fr.)
Îles Chesterfield (Fr.)
Cooktown
Mitchell
Cairns
Normanton
Forsayth
Flinders
Townsville
Charters Towers
Whitsunday Is.
Mackay
L. Dalrymple
Cloncurry
Hughenden
Winton
QUEENSLAND
Great Dividing Range
Emerald
Rockhampton
Gladstone
Longreach
Bundaberg
Yaraka
Maryborough
Gympie
Sunshine Coast
Roma
BRISBANE
Ipswich
Toowoomba
Gold Coast
Charleville
Quilpie
Grey Range
Diamantina
Cunnamulla
Dirranbandi
Thargomindah
Lismore
Grafton
Moree
Walgett
Bourke
Round Mt.
Tamworth
Port Macquarie
Taree
NEW SOUTH WALES
Broken Hill
Darling
Cobar
Dubbo
Newcastle
Bathurst
Orange
SYDNEY
Wollongong
Griffith
Mildura
Hay
Murray
Goulburn
Canberra A.C.T.
ADELAIDE
Wagga Wagga
Swan Hill
Mt. Kosciuszko
Shepparton
Albury-Wodonga
Snowy Mts.
Bendigo
Bombala
Horsham
VICTORIA
C. Howe
Ballarat
MELBOURNE
Sale
Geelong
Warrnambool
Bass Strait
Flinders I.
King I.
Furneaux Group
Burnie
Launceston
Mt. Ossa
TASMANIA
Hobart
S.E.Cape
Lord Howe Seamount Chain
Tropic of Capricorn
Lord Howe Rise
Lord Howe I. (Austral.)
Tasman Sea
Tasman Abyssal Plain
Tasman Basin
COPYRIGHT PHILIP'S

SOUTH AUSTRALIA
Abminga
WITJIRA
Pedirka
Hamilton
Indulkana
Chandler
Marla
Alberga
Mintabie
Oodnadatta
Cadney Park
Peake Cr.
Lora Cr.
Warrina
L. Conway
Neales
L. Cadibarrawirracanna
William Creek
Coober Pedy
Stuart Range
Lake Eyre (North)
LAKE EYRE
Lake Eyre (South)
Marree
L. Thomas
Peera Peera Poolanna L.
Macumba
Warburton
Goyder Lagoon
Sturt Stony Desert
L. Howitt
Cooper Cr.
L. Kittakittaooloo
L. Hope
L. Florence
L. Gregory
L. Blanche
Strzelecki Creek
Strzelecki Desert
L. Callabonna
L. Cooninnie
L. Yamma Yamma
Innamincka
Noccundra
STURT
Tibooburra
Milparinka
Salt L.
Farina
Lyndhurst
Andamooka
Olympic Dam
Roxby Downs
Leigh Creek
Lake Torrens
LAKE TORRENS
Arkaroola
Benbonyathie Hill 1064
GAMMON RANGES
Lake Frome
Beltana
Parachilna
FLINDERS RANGES
Flinders Ranges
Wilpena Cr.
St. Mary Pk. 1188
Hawker
Malbooma
Tarcoola
L. Labyrinth
Kingoonya
L. Younghusband
L. Hanson
Woomera
Pimba
L. Harris
L. Hart
Island Lagoon
Pernatty Lagoon
Lake Gairdner
LAKE GAIRDNER
L. Everard
L. Acraman
L. Macfarlane
Koonibba
Ceduna
Denial B.
Thevenard
Smoky Bay
Pt. Brown
Nuyts Arch.
Streaky B.
C. Bauer
Pt. Westall
Streaky Bay
C. Blanche
C. Radstock
Wirrulla
Poochera
Nukey Bluff 472
Minnipa
Wudinna
Port Kenny
Kyancutta
Anxious Bay
C. Finniss
Elliston
Flinders I.
Investigator Group
Mount Hope
Drummond Pt.
Coffin Bay Pen.
Coffin Bay
COFFIN BAY
Port Lincoln
C. Carnot
Sleaford B.
LINCOLN
Kopi
Lock
Rudall
Cleve
Cowell
Kimba
Eyre Peninsula
Arno Bay
Ungarra
Cummins
Wangary
Tumby Bay
Spencer Gulf
C. Donington
Thistle I.
L. Gilles
Buckleboo
Iron Knob
Iron Baron
MT. REMARKABLE
Whyalla
Port Augusta
Quorn
Carrieton
Cradock
Wilmington
Orroroo
Mt. Remarkable
Port Germein
Port Pirie
Crystal Brook
Port Broughton
Peterborough
Terowie
Jamestown
Gladstone
Hallett
Mt. Bryan 934
Spalding
Snowtown
Burra
Kadina
Wallaroo
Moonta
Clare
Balaklava
Port Wakefield
Robertstown
Morgan
Riverton
Kapunda
Waikerie
Maitland
Hamley Bridge
Ardrossan
Yorke Pen.
Corny Pt.
Tanunda
Nuriootpa
Angaston
Elizabeth
Salisbury
Gawler
ADELAIDE
Brighton
Mt. Barker
Mannum
Murray Bridge
Swan Reach
MURRAY RIVER
Loxton
Barmera
Berri
Renmark
Murray
Yorketown
Edithburgh
West Pt.
INNES
Gambier Is.
C. Spencer
Investigator Str.
Gulf St. Vincent
Willunga
Victor Harbor
Strathalbyn
L. Milang
Alexandrina
Goolwa
Fleurieu Pen.
Kingscote
Kangaroo I.
C. Borda
FLINDERS CHASE
C. du Couedic
D'Estrees Bay
C. Gantheaume
Encounter Bay
Tailem Bend
L. Albert
Meningie
Karoonda
Coonalpyn
Tintinara
Lameroo
Pinnaroo
Keith
Bordertown
COORONG
Younghusband Peninsula
The Coorong
LITTLE DESERT
Lacepede Bay
Kingston S.E.
C. Jaffa
Naracoorte
Lucindale
Robe
Beachport
Rivoli B.
Millicent
L. Bonney
L. George
Mt. Burr
Penola
Casterton
Mount Gambier
C. Northumberland
Port MacDonnell
Discovery Bay
C. Bridgewater
C. Nelson
Portland
Portland Bay
Port Fairy
Warrnambool
Port Campbell
PORT CAMPBELL
Apollo Bay
Bass
SOUTHERN OCEAN
King Island
C. Wickham
Olary
Mannahill
Yunta
Cockburn
Stephens Creek
Broken Hill
Barrier Range
472
MUTAWINTJI
Menindee L.
Menindee
Cawndilla L.
Tandou L.
KINCHEGA
Darling
Popio L.
Popiltah L.
Travellers L.
Pooncarie
MUNGO
L. Victoria
Wentworth
Mildura
Merbein
Red Cliffs
Meringur
Werrimull
MURRAY-SUNSET
Hattah
Alawoona
Peebinga
Underbool
Ouyen
Cowangie
Patchewollock
WYPERFELD
Yaapeet
L. Albacutya
L. Hindmarsh
L. Tyrrell
Hopetoun
Birchip
Jeparit
Kaniva
Nhill
Warracknabeal
Dimboola
Donald
Horsham
Natimuk
Murtoa
St. Arnaud
Edenhope
Glenelg
Balmoral
GRAMPIANS
The Grampians
Halls Gap
Ararat
Stawell
Cavendish
Maroona
Coleraine
Hamilton
MT. ECCLES
Penshurst
LOWER GLENELG
Heywood
Mortlake
Terang
Camperdown
Colac
BRISBANE
Ballarat
MELBOURNE
on same scale
Bass Strait
Curtis Group
Kent Group
Deal I.
Currie
King Island
Grassy
Stokes Pt.
Flinders Island
Palana
Prime Seal I.
Furneaux Group
Whitemark
Cape Barren I.
C. Keraudren
Three Hummock I.
Hunter I.
Robbins I.
Smithton
Stanley
Marrawah
Wynyard
Burnie
Penguin
Ulverstone
Devonport
Beaconsfield
George Town
Clarke I.
Banks Strait
MT. WILLIAM
C. Naturaliste
Eddystone Pt.
Bridport
Scottsdale
Arthur
CRADLE MT.-LAKE ST. CLAIR
Latrobe
Railton
Sandy C.
Savage River
Waratah
Deloraine
Launceston
Westbury
St. Helens
BEN LOMOND
1522
Longford
St. Marys
Rosebery
Mt. Ossa 1617
Zeehan
Strahan
Queenstown
TASMANIA
Macquarie Harbour
Hibbs Bay
FRANKLIN-GORDON WILD RIVERS
Tarraleah
Bothwell
Campbell Town
Ross
Conara
DOUGLAS APSLEY
Bicheno
FREYCINET
Freycinet Pen.
Swansea
Oatlands
Kempton
Triabunna
Schouten I.
Maria I.
MARIA I.
New Norfolk
Bridgewater
Glenorchy
Sorell
Hobart
Forestier Pen.
Tasman Pen.
Port Arthur
SOUTHWEST
Port Davey
Bathurst Harbour
TASMANIAN WILDERNESS WORLD HERITAGE AREA
Huonville
Cygnet
Dover
South Bruny I.
Storm Bay
South West C.
South East C.
m ft
0
200 600
2000 6000
4000 12 000
Projection: Bonne
East from Greenwich
1 2 3 4
A B C D
135 140 145
30 35 40
60

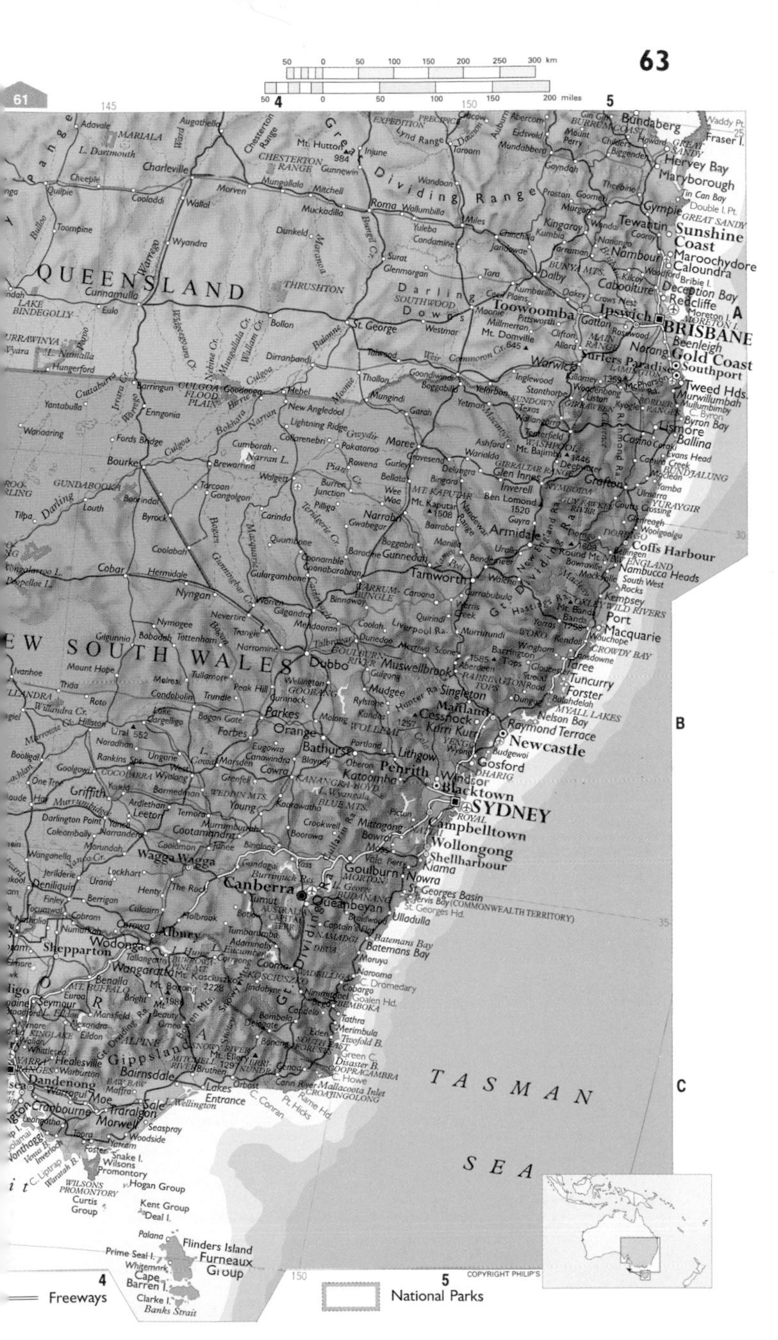
50
0
50
100
150
200
250
300 km
50
0
50
100
150
200 miles
61
145
150
4
5
A
B
C
QUEENSLAND
NEW SOUTH WALES
TASMAN
SEA
Great Dividing Range
Darling Downs
Bundaberg
Hervey Bay
Maryborough
Gympie
Sunshine Coast
Nambour
Maroochydore
Caloundra
Caboolture
Toowoomba
Ipswich
BRISBANE
Redcliffe
Beenleigh
Gold Coast
Southport
Surfers Paradise
Tweed Hds.
Murwillumbah
Lismore
Ballina
Byron Bay
Grafton
Coffs Harbour
Nambucca Heads
Kempsey
Port Macquarie
Taree
Tuncurry
Forster
Newcastle
Maitland
Cessnock
Gosford
Windsor
Blacktown
SYDNEY
Campbelltown
Wollongong
Shellharbour
Kiama
Nowra
St. Georges Basin
Jervis Bay (COMMONWEALTH TERRITORY)
Ulladulla
Batemans Bay
Moruya
Narooma
Tathra
Merimbula
Eden
Twofold B.
Green C.
Disaster B.
C. Howe
Mallacoota Inlet
Pt. Hicks
C. Conran
Lakes Entrance
Orbost
Bairnsdale
Sale
Traralgon
Moe
Morwell
Warragul
Dandenong
Cranbourne
Wilsons Promontory
Hogan Group
Kent Group
Curtis Group
Flinders Island
Furneaux Group
Cape Barren I.
Clarke I.
Banks Strait
Canberra
Queanbeyan
Goulburn
Cooma
Mt. Kosciuszko 2228
Albury
Wodonga
Wangaratta
Benalla
Shepparton
Seymour
Gippsland
Wagga Wagga
Griffith
Leeton
Narrandera
Young
Cowra
Orange
Bathurst
Lithgow
Penrith
Katoomba
Parkes
Forbes
Dubbo
Mudgee
Muswellbrook
Singleton
Tamworth
Armidale
Gunnedah
Narrabri
Moree
Inverell
Glen Innes
Tenterfield
Warwick
Dalby
Kingaroy
Goondiwindi
St. George
Roma
Charleville
Cunnamulla
Bourke
Cobar
Nyngan
Walgett
Coonamble
Coonabarabran
Deniliquin
Cootamundra
Tumut
Freeways
National Parks
COPYRIGHT PHILIP'S

NEW ZEALAND, CENTRAL AND SOUTH-WEST PACIFIC

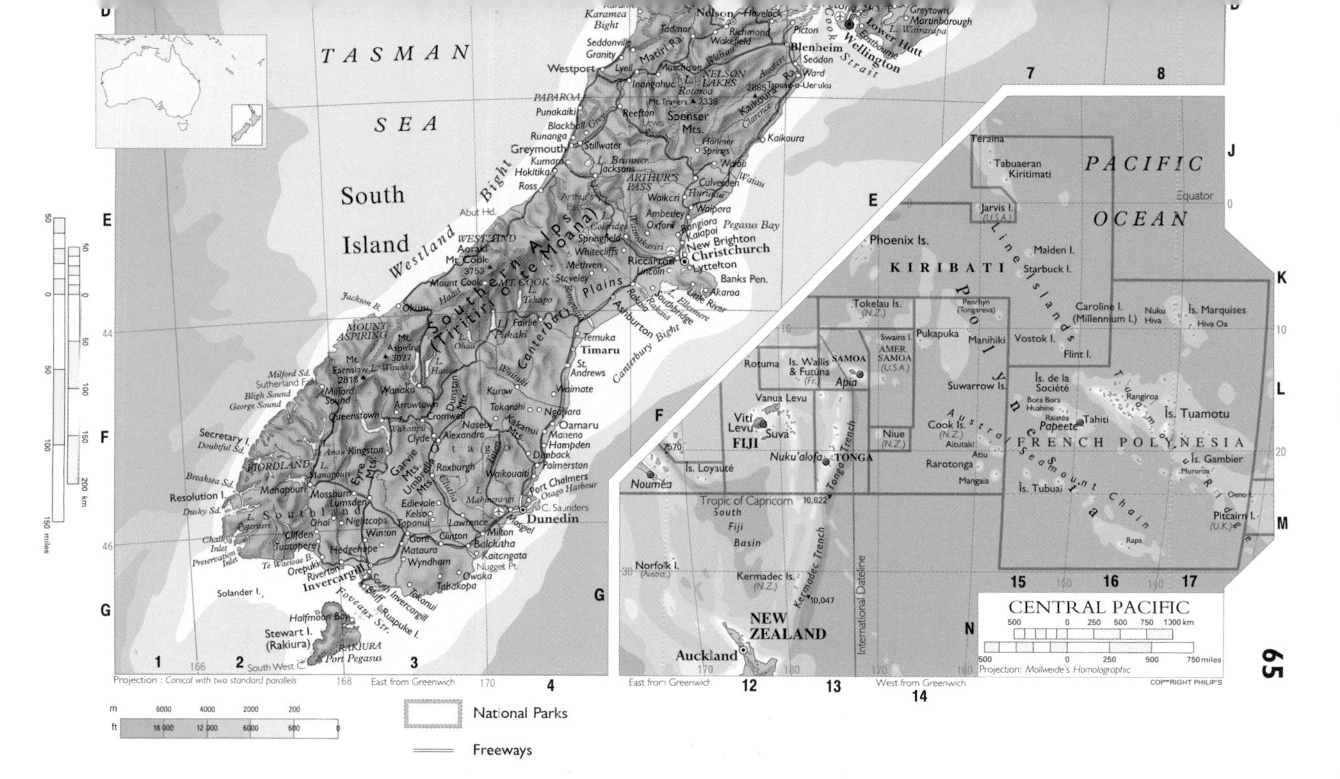

TASMAN
SEA
South
Island
Westland Bight
Southern Alps (Tiritiri o te Moana)
Canterbury Plains
Canterbury Bight
Pegasus Bay
Cook Strait
Wellington
Lower Hutt
Christchurch
Dunedin
Invercargill
Timaru
Nelson
Blenheim
Greymouth
Westport
Queenstown
Oamaru
Stewart I. (Rakiura)
Foveaux Str.
FIORDLAND
Southland
Otago
Projection : Conical with two standard parallels
East from Greenwich
National Parks
Freeways
PACIFIC
OCEAN
KIRIBATI
Line Islands
Polynesia
FRENCH POLYNESIA
Austral Seamount Chain
Tuamotu Ridge
FIJI
TONGA
SAMOA
NEW ZEALAND
Auckland
Tonga Trench
Kermadec Trench
International Dateline
Tropic of Capricorn
Equator
CENTRAL PACIFIC
Projection: Mollweide's Homolographic
West from Greenwich
COPYRIGHT PHILIP'S

ARCTIC OCEAN
Beaufort Sea
Baffin Bay
Davis Strait
Denmark Strait
Hudson Strait
Hudson Bay
Bering Sea
Bering Strait
Gulf of Alaska
GREENLAND
(Denmark)
ICELAND
Reykjavík
Nuuk
Ellesmere I.
Queen Elizabeth Is.
Victoria I.
Baffin Island
NUNAVUT
NORTHWEST TERRITORIES
YUKON TERRITORY
ALASKA
(U.S.A.)
CANADA
BRITISH COLUMBIA
ALBERTA
SASKATCHEWAN
MANITOBA
ONTARIO
QUEBEC
NEWFOUNDLAND & LABRADOR
NOVA SCOTIA
PRINCE EDWARD I.
NEW BRUNSWICK
St.-Pierre et Miquelon
St. John's
Charlottetown
Halifax
Fredericton
Québec
St. Lawrence
Eastmain
L. Winnipeg
Nelson
Churchill
L. Athabasca
Great Slave L.
Great Bear L.
Yellowknife
Mackenzie
Arctic Circle
Back
Dubawnt
Athabasca
Peace
Edmonton
Calgary
Regina
Saskatchewan
Fraser
Vancouver
Victoria
Skeena
Liard
Whitehorse
Juneau
Porcupine
Fairbanks
Anchorage
Mt. McKinley
6194
Yukon
Kodiak I.
St. Lawrence I.
International Date Line
RUSSIA
Asia
A
B
C
D
E
50
60
70
80

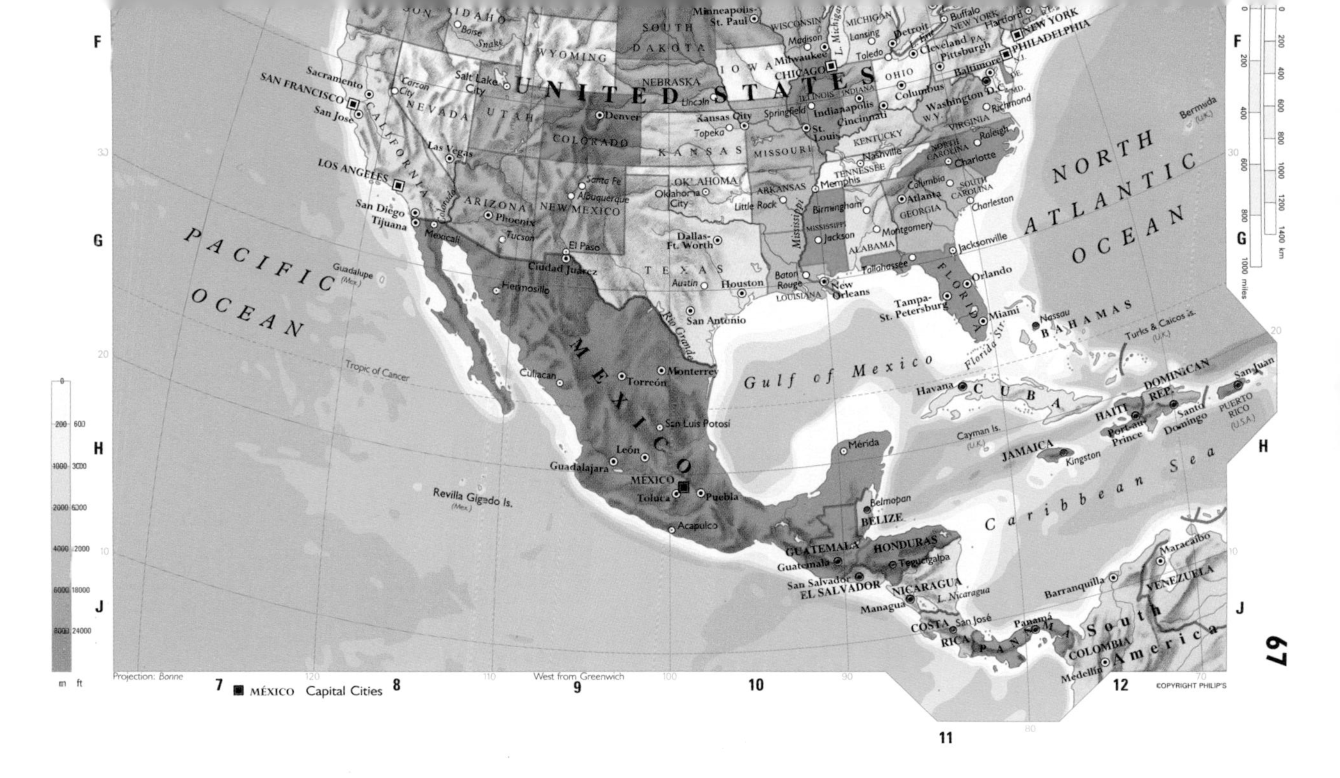
UNITED STATES
MEXICO
PACIFIC OCEAN
NORTH ATLANTIC OCEAN
Gulf of Mexico
Caribbean Sea
South America
CUBA
BAHAMAS
JAMAICA
HAITI
DOMINICAN REP.
PUERTO RICO (U.S.A.)
BELIZE
GUATEMALA
HONDURAS
EL SALVADOR
NICARAGUA
COSTA RICA
PANAMA
COLOMBIA
VENEZUELA
WASHINGTON D.C.
NEW YORK
PHILADELPHIA
CHICAGO
LOS ANGELES
SAN FRANCISCO
MÉXICO
Guatemala
San Salvador
Tegucigalpa
Managua
San José
Panamá
Havana
Nassau
Kingston
Port-au-Prince
Santo Domingo
San Juan
Belmopan
Medellín
Barranquilla
Maracaibo
Mérida
Monterrey
Torreón
Culiacan
Hermosillo
Ciudad Juárez
Mexicali
Tijuana
Guadalajara
León
San Luis Potosí
Toluca
Puebla
Acapulco
Revilla Gigedo Is. (Mex.)
Guadalupe (Mex.)
Tropic of Cancer
Bermuda (U.K.)
Turks & Caicos Is. (U.K.)
Cayman Is. (U.K.)
Florida Str.
Rio Grande
Mississippi
Colorado
Snake
L. Michigan
L. Nicaragua
Sacramento
San Jose
Carson City
Salt Lake City
Las Vegas
San Diego
Phoenix
Tucson
El Paso
Santa Fe
Albuquerque
Denver
Boise
Minneapolis-St. Paul
Milwaukee
Madison
Lansing
Detroit
Toledo
Cleveland
Buffalo
Hartford
Pittsburgh
Baltimore
Richmond
Columbus
Cincinnati
Indianapolis
Springfield
St. Louis
Kansas City
Topeka
Lincoln
Oklahoma City
Dallas-Ft. Worth
Austin
San Antonio
Houston
Baton Rouge
New Orleans
Jackson
Little Rock
Memphis
Nashville
Birmingham
Montgomery
Atlanta
Tallahassee
Jacksonville
Orlando
Tampa-St. Petersburg
Miami
Columbia
Charleston
Charlotte
Raleigh
IDAHO
WYOMING
SOUTH DAKOTA
NEBRASKA
IOWA
WISCONSIN
MICHIGAN
OHIO
INDIANA
ILLINOIS
KENTUCKY
TENNESSEE
MISSOURI
KANSAS
COLORADO
UTAH
NEVADA
CALIFORNIA
ARIZONA
NEW MEXICO
OKLAHOMA
TEXAS
ARKANSAS
LOUISIANA
MISSISSIPPI
ALABAMA
GEORGIA
FLORIDA
SOUTH CAROLINA
NORTH CAROLINA
VIRGINIA
W.V.
PA.
NEW YORK
N.J.
DE.
MD.
0 200 400 600 800 1000 1200 1400 km
0 200 400 600 800 1000 miles
m ft
0
200 600
1000 3000
2000 6000
4000 12000
6000 18000
8000 24000
F G H J
7 8 9 10 11 12
30 20 10
120 110 100 90 80 70
West from Greenwich
Projection: Bonne
■ MÉXICO Capital Cities
COPYRIGHT PHILIP'S

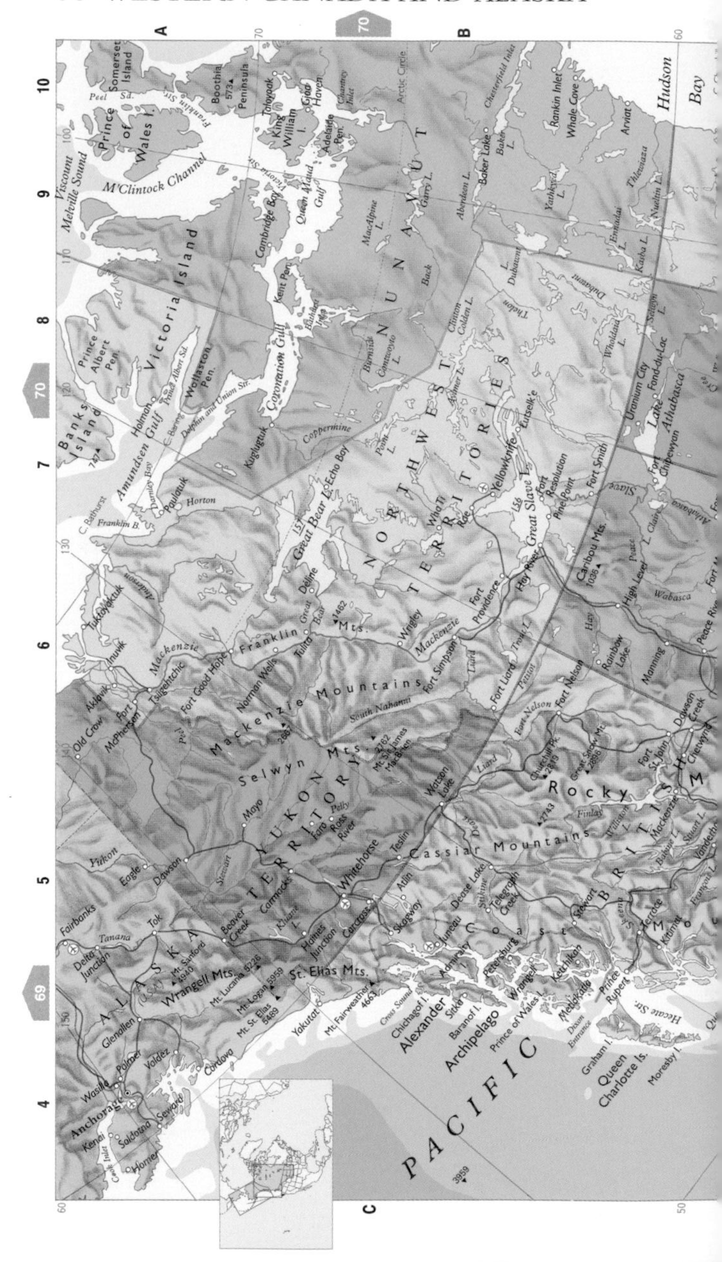

A
B
C
70
69
4
5
6
7
8
9
10
Somerset Island
Boothia Peninsula
Prince of Wales I.
Viscount Melville Sound
M'Clintock Channel
Victoria Island
Prince Albert Pen.
Wollaston Pen.
Banks Island
Amundsen Gulf
Holman
Coronation Gulf
Cambridge Bay
King William I.
Gjoa Haven
Taloyoak
Queen Maud Gulf
Adelaide Pen.
Kent Pen.
Kugluktuk
Coppermine
Dolphin and Union Str.
Arctic Circle
N U N A V U T
Baker Lake
Rankin Inlet
Whale Cove
Arviat
Chesterfield Inlet
Hudson Bay
Aberdeen L.
Garry L.
MacAlpine L.
Back
Dubawnt L.
Dubawnt
Thelon
Clinton Colden L.
Aylmer L.
Contwoyto L.
Yathkyed L.
Ennadai L.
Kasba L.
Nueltin L.
N O R T H W E S T T E R R I T O R I E S
Great Bear L.
Echo Bay
Great Slave L.
Yellowknife
Lutselk'e
Fort Resolution
Pine Point
Fort Smith
Hay River
Fort Providence
Wha Ti
Rae
Fort Simpson
Wrigley
Deline
Tulita
Norman Wells
Fort Good Hope
Franklin Mts.
Mackenzie
Mackenzie Mountains
Tsiigehtchic
Inuvik
Tuktoyaktuk
Aklavik
Fort McPherson
Old Crow
Paulatuk
Horton
Franklin B.
C. Bathurst
Darnley Bay
Anderson
Fort Liard
Fort Nelson
South Nahanni
Lake Athabasca
Fort Chipewyan
Uranium City
Fond-du-Lac
Wholdaia L.
Caribou Mts.
High Level
Peace
Wabasca
Rainbow Lake
Manning
Peace River
Dawson Creek
Fort St. John
Chetwynd
Rocky
Y U K O N T E R R I T O R Y
Selwyn Mts.
Mt. St. James MacBrien
Mayo
Faro
Ross River
Pelly
Watson Lake
Whitehorse
Carmacks
Teslin
Atlin
Dawson
Eagle
Yukon
Stewart
Beaver Creek
Kluane L.
Haines Junction
Carcross
Skagway
Cassiar Mountains
Dease Lake
Telegraph Creek
Stikine
Coast
Juneau
Admiralty I.
Petersburg
Wrangell
Ketchikan
Metlakatla
Sitka
Baranof I.
Chichagof I.
Alexander Archipelago
Prince of Wales I.
Dixon Entrance
Prince Rupert
Hecate Str.
Graham I.
Queen Charlotte Is.
Moresby I.
Terrace
Kitimat
Stewart
Mackenzie
Williston L.
Finlay
B R I T I S H
A L A S K A
Fairbanks
Tanana
Tok
Delta Junction
Mt. Sanford 4940
Wrangell Mts.
Mt. Lucania 5226
Mt. Logan 5959
St. Elias Mts.
Mt. St. Elias 5489
Mt. Fairweather 4663
Yakutat
Cross Sound
Glennallen
Valdez
Palmer
Wasilla
Anchorage
Cordova
Seward
Soldotna
Kenai
Homer
Cook Inlet
P A C I F I C
3959

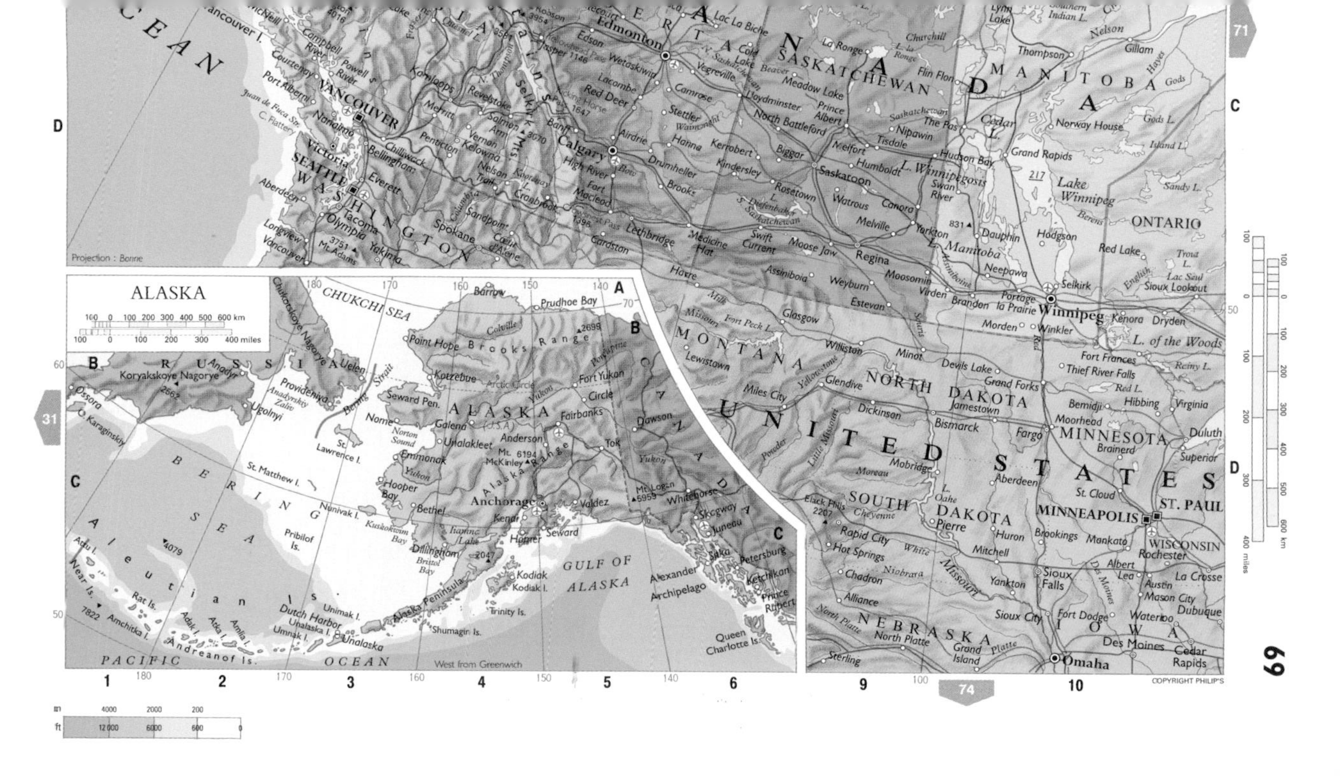
ALASKA
CHUKCHI SEA
BERING SEA
GULF OF ALASKA
PACIFIC OCEAN
Aleutian Is.
Brooks Range
Alaska Range
Anchorage
Fairbanks
Juneau
Barrow
Prudhoe Bay
Nome
Kodiak
Valdez
Seward
Mt. McKinley 6194
UNITED STATES
MONTANA
NORTH DAKOTA
SOUTH DAKOTA
MINNESOTA
NEBRASKA
IOWA
WISCONSIN
WASHINGTON
MANITOBA
SASKATCHEWAN
ONTARIO
Edmonton
Calgary
Regina
Saskatoon
Winnipeg
VANCOUVER
Victoria
SEATTLE
Spokane
MINNEAPOLIS
ST. PAUL
Omaha
Des Moines
Lake Winnipeg
L. of the Woods
Projection : Bonne
West from Greenwich
COPYRIGHT PHILIP'S

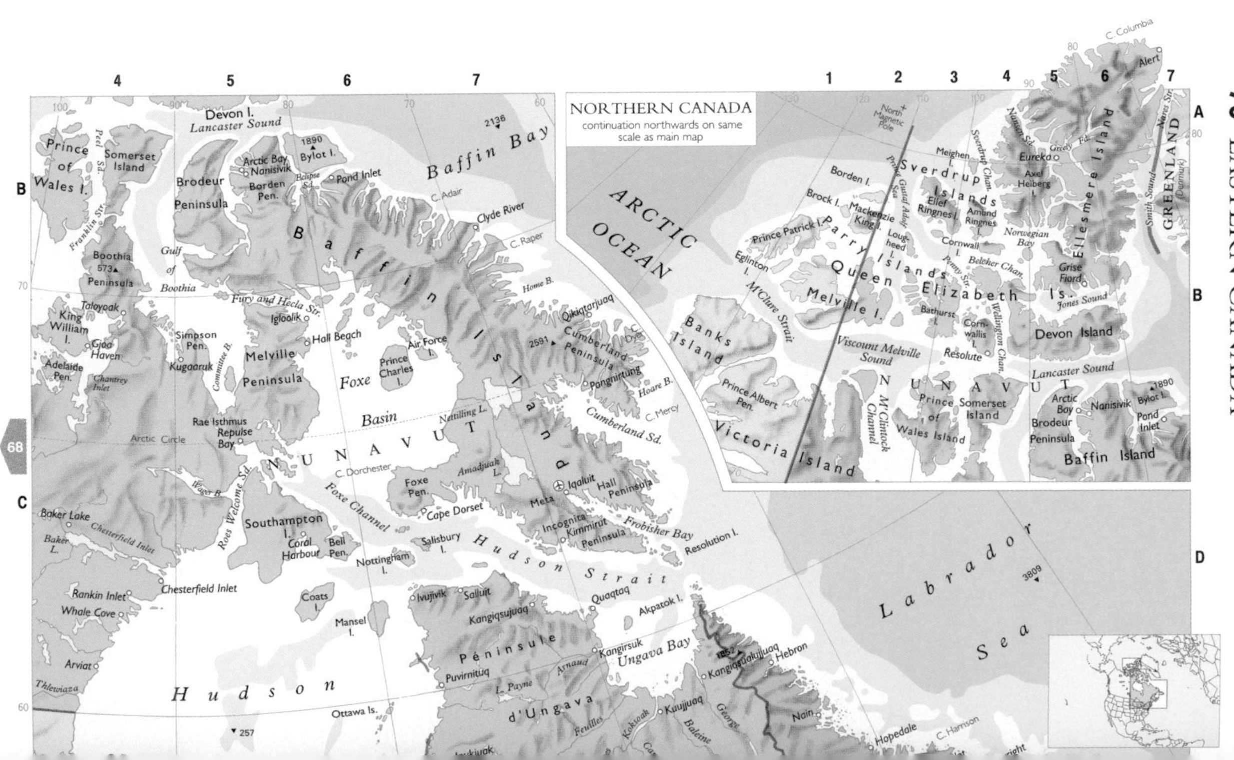
NORTHERN CANADA
continuation northwards on same scale as main map
ARCTIC OCEAN
GREENLAND
(Denmark)
Alert
C. Columbia
Nares Str.
Smith Sound
Ellesmere Island
Eureka
Axel Heiberg I.
Nansen Sd.
Sverdrup Chan.
Sverdrup Islands
Meighen I.
Ellef Ringnes I.
Amund Ringnes I.
Norwegian Bay
Cornwall I.
Belcher Chan.
Grise Fiord
Jones Sound
Devon Island
Lancaster Sound
Queen Elizabeth Is.
Parry Islands
Wellington Chan.
Cornwallis I.
Resolute
Penny Str.
Bathurst I.
Lougheed I.
Prince Gustaf Adolf Sea
North Magnetic Pole
Borden I.
Mackenzie King I.
Brock I.
Prince Patrick I.
Melville I.
Viscount Melville Sound
M'Clintock Channel
M'Clure Strait
Eglinton I.
Banks Island
Prince Albert Pen.
Victoria Island
Prince of Wales Island
Somerset Island
NUNAVUT
Arctic Bay
Nanisivik
Pond Inlet
Bylot I.
1890
Brodeur Peninsula
Baffin Island
Labrador Sea
3809
Baffin Bay
2136
Clyde River
C. Adair
C. Raper
Home B.
Qikiqtarjuaq
Cumberland Peninsula
2591
Pangnirtung
Hoare B.
C. Mercy
Cumberland Sd.
Baffin Island
Hall Peninsula
Iqaluit
Frobisher Bay
Resolution I.
Meta Incognita Peninsula
Kimmirut
Hudson Strait
Akpatok I.
Quaqtaq
Ungava Bay
Kangirsuk
Kangiqsualujjuaq
Hebron
Nain
Hopedale
C. Harrison
George
Baleine
Kuujjuaq
Koksoak
Arnaud
Feuilles
Péninsule d'Ungava
Kangiqsujuaq
Salluit
Ivujivik
L. Payne
Puvirnituq
Amadjuak L.
Nettilling L.
Cape Dorset
Foxe Pen.
Salisbury I.
Nottingham I.
Foxe Basin
Prince Charles I.
Air Force I.
Hall Beach
Igloolik
Fury and Hecla Str.
Melville Peninsula
Foxe Channel
C. Dorchester
Southampton I.
Coral Harbour
Bell Pen.
Coats I.
Mansel I.
Ottawa Is.
Hudson Bay
257
Roes Welcome Sd.
Repulse Bay
Rae Isthmus
Committee B.
Wager B.
Simpson Pen.
Kugaaruk
Arctic Circle
Chesterfield Inlet
Devon I.
Lancaster Sound
Eclipse Sd.
Borden Pen.
Gulf of Boothia
Boothia Peninsula
573
Peel Sd.
Franklin Str.
Prince of Wales I.
Taloyoak
Gjoa Haven
King William I.
Chantrey Inlet
Adelaide Pen.
Baker Lake
Baker L.
Rankin Inlet
Whale Cove
Arviat
Thlewiaza
A
B
C
D
1
2
3
4
5
6
7
68

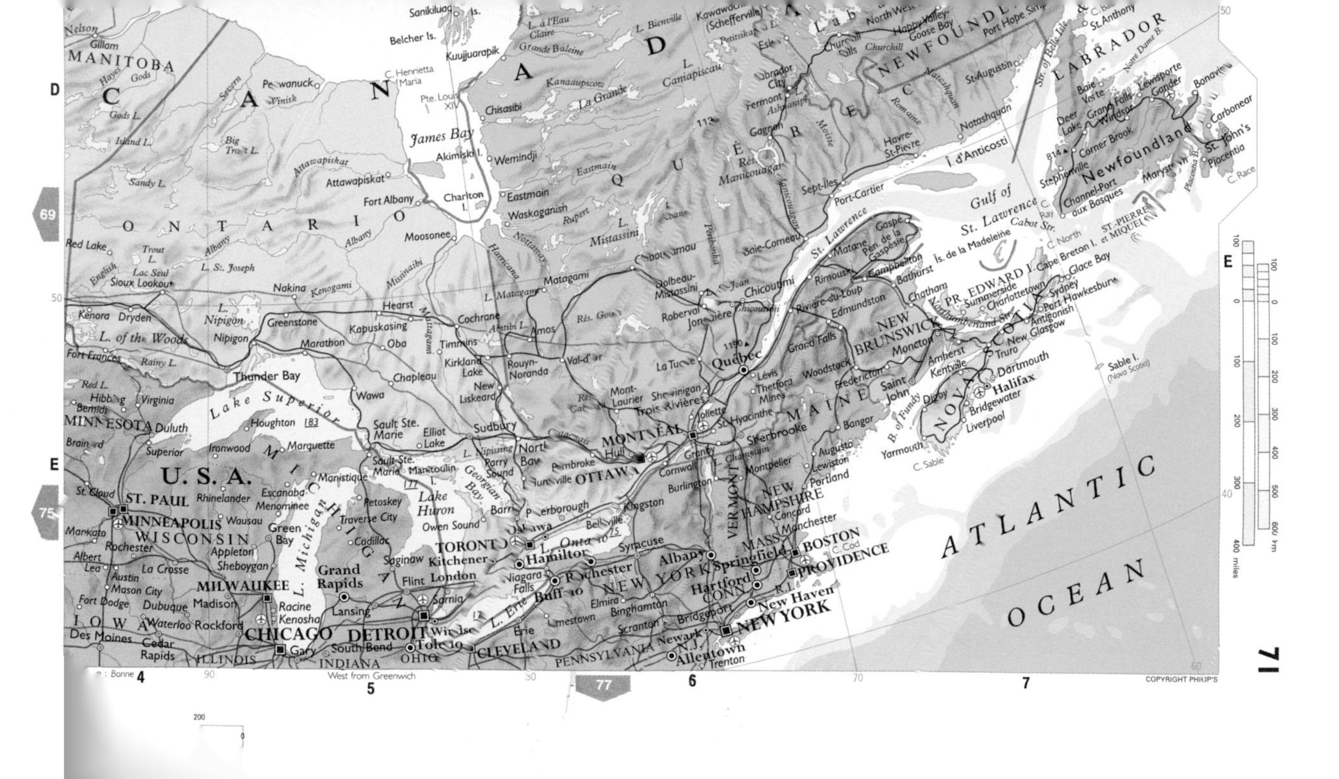
CANADA
MANITOBA
ONTARIO
QUEBEC
LABRADOR
NEWFOUNDLAND
Newfoundland
NEW BRUNSWICK
NOVA SCOTIA
PR. EDWARD I.
U.S.A.
MINNESOTA
WISCONSIN
MICHIGAN
IOWA
ILLINOIS
INDIANA
OHIO
PENNSYLVANIA
NEW YORK
VERMONT
NEW HAMPSHIRE
MAINE
MASS.
CONN.
R.I.
N.J.
ATLANTIC OCEAN
Gulf of St. Lawrence
James Bay
Lake Superior
Lake Huron
L. Michigan
L. Ontario
L. Erie
Georgian Bay
L. of the Woods
B. of Fundy
Cabot Str.
Str. of Belle Isle
Î. d'Anticosti
Îs. de la Madeleine
Pén. de la Gaspésie
Sable I. (Nova Scotia)
ST. PIERRE et MIQUELON
C. Race
C. North
C. Ray
C. Sable
C. Cod
C. Henrietta Maria
Belcher Is.
Akimiski I.
Charlton I.
Manitoulin I.
Res. Manicouagan
L. Mistassini
L. Nipigon
L. Nipissing
L. Champlain
L. Caniapiscau
L. Bienville
Kuujjuarapik
Chisasibi
Wemindji
Eastmain
Waskaganish
Moosonee
Fort Albany
Attawapiskat
Peawanuck
Nakina
Hearst
Kapuskasing
Cochrane
Timmins
Kirkland Lake
Rouyn-Noranda
Val-d'Or
Amos
Matagami
Chibougamau
Chicoutimi
Jonquière
Roberval
Dolbeau-Mistassini
Baie-Comeau
Sept-Îles
Port-Cartier
Havre-St-Pierre
Natashquan
St-Augustin
Fermont
Gagnon
Labrador City
Churchill Falls
Goose Bay
Happy Valley-Goose Bay
North West River
Port Hope Simpson
Schefferville
St. Anthony
Corner Brook
Deer Lake
Grand Falls-Windsor
Gander
Lewisporte
Carbonear
St. John's
Placentia
Channel-Port aux Basques
Stephenville
Matane
Rimouski
Rivière-du-Loup
Edmundston
Grand Falls
Campbellton
Bathurst
Chatham
Moncton
Fredericton
Saint John
Woodstock
Summerside
Charlottetown
Sydney
Glace Bay
Port Hawkesbury
Antigonish
New Glasgow
Truro
Amherst
Kentville
Dartmouth
Halifax
Bridgewater
Liverpool
Yarmouth
Digby
Québec
Lévis
Thetford Mines
Sherbrooke
St-Hyacinthe
Trois Rivières
Shawinigan
Joliette
Montréal
Mont-Laurier
Hull
Ottawa
Pembroke
North Bay
Sudbury
Elliot Lake
Sault Ste. Marie
Wawa
Chapleau
Marathon
Thunder Bay
Nipigon
Greenstone
Kenora
Dryden
Fort Frances
Red Lake
Sioux Lookout
Gillam
Nelson
Toronto
Hamilton
Kitchener
London
Windsor
Sarnia
Owen Sound
Barrie
Peterborough
Oshawa
Belleville
Kingston
Cornwall
Granby
Burlington
Montpelier
Concord
Manchester
Portland
Lewiston
Augusta
Bangor
Boston
Providence
Springfield
Hartford
New Haven
New York
Newark
Bridgeport
Trenton
Allentown
Scranton
Binghamton
Elmira
Albany
Syracuse
Rochester
Buffalo
Niagara Falls
Erie
Cleveland
Toledo
Detroit
Flint
Saginaw
Lansing
Grand Rapids
Cadillac
Traverse City
Petoskey
Manistique
Escanaba
Menominee
Marquette
Houghton
Ironwood
Green Bay
Appleton
Sheboygan
Milwaukee
Racine
Kenosha
Chicago
Gary
South Bend
Madison
Rockford
Wausau
Rhinelander
Duluth
Superior
Virginia
Hibbing
Bemidji
Brainerd
St. Cloud
St. Paul
Minneapolis
Mankato
Rochester
Albert Lea
Austin
Mason City
Fort Dodge
Des Moines
Cedar Rapids
Waterloo
Dubuque
La Crosse
West from Greenwich
COPYRIGHT PHILIP'S
0 100 200 300 400 500 600 km
0 100 200 300 400 miles

72
NORTH-WEST USA
1
2
3
4
5
6
B
C
D
E
F
VANCOUVER
Nanaimo
Vancouver Island
Duncan
Surrey
New Westminster
Coquitlam
Chilliwack
Victoria
Juan de Fuca Strait
PACIFIC RIM NAT. PARK
Port Renfrew
C. Flattery
Neah Bay
Blaine
Ferndale
Lynden
Bellingham
Mt. Baker 3285
Ross L.
NORTH CASCADES NAT. PARK
Oliver
Osoyoos
Grand Forks
Rossland
Trail
BRITISH CO
Esquimalt
Oak Hr.
Anacortes
Sedro-Woolley
Mount Vernon
Concrete
Burlington
Port Angeles
Port Townsend
Sequim
La Push
Forks
Olympic Mts.
Mt. Olympus 2428
OLYMPIC NAT. PARK
Everett
Arlington
Darrington
Snohomish
Glacier Peak 3213
Winthrop
Okanogan
Omak
Oroville
Tonasket
Republic
Franklin D. Roosevelt L.
Northport
Metaline Falls
Kettle Falls
Colville
Chewelah
Newport
Priest River
Sandpoint
Edmonds
SEATTLE
Bellevue
Bremerton
Poulsbo
Skykomish
Leavenworth
Chelan
L. Chelan
Pateros
Brewster
Grand Coulee
Grand Coulee Dam
LAKE ROOSEVELT NAT. REC. AREA
Deer Park
Spokane
Post Falls
Coeur d'Alene
Opportunity
Cheney
Sprague
Nelton
Moclips
Hoodsport
Shelton
Tacoma
Renton
Kent
WASHINGTON
Waterville
Wenatchee
Coulee City
Davenport
Hoquiam
Aberdeen
Grays Harbor
Westport
Elma
Montesano
Olympia
Lacey
Tumwater
Puyallup
Enumclaw
Ephrata
Columbia
Columbia Basin
Willapa B.
Raymond
Ocean Park
Long Beach
C. Disappointment
Centralia
Chehalis
Mt. Rainier 4392
MOUNT RAINIER NAT. PARK
Ellensburg
Quincy
Odessa
Moses Lake
Ritzville
Rosalia
Plummer
Tekoa
Astoria
Warrenton
Toledo
Morton
Naches
HANFORD REACH NAT. REC. AREA
Othello
Lind
Oakesdale
Cathlamet
Longview
Kelso
Mt. St. Helens 2550
Selah
Yakima
Wapato
Union Gap
Connell
Garfield
Colfax
Pullman
Moscow
Seaside
Wheeler
Rainier
Kalama
MOUNT ST. HELENS NAT. VOLCANIC MON.
Mt. Adams 3751
Toppenish
Sunnyside
Grandview
Prosser
Richland
Kennewick
Pasco
Snake
Waitsburg
Pomeroy
Clarkston
Dayton
Lewiston
St. Helens
PORTLAND
Hillsboro
Vancouver
Battle Ground
Klickitat
Camas
Goldendale
C. Meares
Tillamook
Beaverton
Gresham
Cascade Locks
Hood River
Umatilla
Wallula
Walla Walla
Newberg
Milwaukie
Oregon City
The Dalles
Mt. Hood 3427
Wasco
Arlington
Hermiston
Milton-Freewater
Lincoln City
McMinnville
Canby
Deschutes
Pendleton
Weston
HELLS CANYON NAT. REC. AREA
Salem
Keizer
Woodburn
Grass Valley
Condon
Heppner
Pilot Rock
Elgin
Wallowa
Dallas
Monmouth
Stayton
Maupin
Newport
Toledo
Corvallis
Albany
Lebanon
Brownsville
Mt. Jefferson 3200
JOHN DAY FOSSIL BEDS NAT. MON.
Fossil
John Day
Spray
La Grande
Enterprise
Wallowa Mts.
Waldport
Philomath
Blue Mountains
North Powder
Haines
Baker City
Mapleton
Florence
Junction City
Sweet Home
Madras
Long Creek
OREGON DUNES NAT. REC. AREA
Reedsport
Eugene
Springfield
Three Sisters 3156
Sisters
Prineville
Mitchell
Dayville
Redmond
Cottage Grove
Oakridge
OREGON
Bend
John Day
Prairie City
North Bend
Coos Bay
Drain
NEWBERRY NAT. VOLCANIC MON.
Brothers
Brogan
Huntington
Coquille
Sutherlin
La Pine
Weiser
Ontario
Payette
Myrtle Point
Green
Roseburg
Silvies
Vale
Nyssa
New Plymouth
C. Blanco
Camas Valley
Myrtle Creek
Chemult
Riley
Burns
Malheur
Juntura
Parma
Caldwell
Eagle
Port Orford
Canyonville
Harney Basin
Crane
Homedale
Garden City
Boise
Gold Beach
Rogue
Crater L.
Silver Lake
CRATER LAKE NAT. PARK
Harney L.
Malheur L.
L. Owyhee
Nampa
Meridian
Grants Pass
Gold Hill
White City
Mt. McLoughlin 2894
Fort Klamath
Summer L.
Brookings
Central Point
Medford
Paisley
Murphy
Jordan Valley
Mountain Home
SMITH RIVER NAT. REC. AREA
Talent
Ashland
Upper Klamath L.
L. Abert
Valley Falls
Steens Mountain
Burns Junction 2962
Crescent City
Happy Camp
Klamath Falls
Altamont
Merrill
Bly
Bruneau
Hornbrook
Dorris
Lakeview
Alvord Desert
REDWOOD NAT. PARK
Yreka
Clear Lake Res.
Goose Lake
LAVA BEDS NAT. MON.
Klamath Mts.
Mt. Shasta 4317
Weed
Mount Shasta
Upper Alkali L.
McDermitt
CALIFORNIA
Dunsmuir
McCloud
Canby
Alturas
Santa Rosa Range
Owyhee
McKinleyville
Arcata
Eureka
Fortuna
Thompson Pk. 2724
WHISKEYTOWN-SHASTA-TRINITY NAT. REC. AREA
Weaverville
Pit
Bieber
Middle Alkali L.
Lower Alkali L.
Warner Mts.
Paradise Valley
Mountain City
Scotia
Cape Mendocino
Weott
Redding
Anderson
Shasta L.
Burney
LASSEN VOLCANIC NAT. PARK & WILDERNESS
Lassen Peak 3187
Eagle L.
Winnemucca
Little Humboldt
Independence Mts.
Garberville
Red Bluff
Chester
Susanville
Almanor L.
Westwood
Greenville
Gerlach
Rye Patch Res.
Imlay
Golconda
Humboldt
Elko
Laytonville
Corning
Orland
Chico
Paradise
Quincy
Honey L.
Winnemucca L.
Lovelock
Battle Mountain
Dunphy
Carlin
Spring Creek
Ruby Mts.
Ft. Bragg
Willits
Mendocino
Willows
Sierra Nevada
Portola
Pyramid L.
Trinity Range
Great Basin
Franklin L.
Ruby L.
Ukiah
Upper Lake
Lakeport
Hopland
Colusa
Sacramento
Feather
Oroville
Palermo
Gridley
Downieville
Wadsworth
Reno
Fernley
Carson Sink
Stillwater Ra.
Reese
Diamond Mts.
Clear L.
Arbuckle
Clearlake
Yuba City
Marysville
Truckee
Nevada City
Grass Valley
Sparks
Incline
Virginia City
Tahoe City
L. Tahoe
Fallon
Shoshone Mountains
Toiyabe Ra.
Austin
Woodland
Olivehurst
Auburn
Carson City
Minden
Gardnerville
Yerington
NEVADA
Eureka
McGill
Calistoga
St. Helena
Davis
Roseville
Camino
Placerville
South Lake Tahoe
Schurz
Walker L.
Ely
Napa
Vacaville
Arden
SACRAMENTO
Elk Grove
Ione
Jackson
Mt. Grant 3426
Hawthorne
Luning
Mt. Jefferson 3599
Round Mountain
Hot Creek Ra.
Currant
Egan Range
Fairfield
Concord
Lodi
San Andreas
Richmond
124
120
118
116
46
44
42
with two standard parallels
78
Freeways
State Capitals
National Parks

ALBERTA
SASKATCHEWAN
CANADA
MONTANA
IDAHO
WYOMING
UTAH
COLORADO
ROCKY MTS.
Lethbridge
Medicine Hat
Missoula
Helena
Great Falls
Butte
Bozeman
Billings
Havre
Kalispell
Lewistown
Sheridan
Casper
Laramie
Rock Springs
Green River
Idaho Falls
Pocatello
Logan
Ogden
Salt Lake City
Provo
Orem
Great Salt Lake
Yellowstone National Park
Glacier National Park
Bighorn Mountains
Uinta Mountains
Wind River Range
Absaroka Range
Fort Peck Lake
Snake River Plain
West from Greenwich
COPYRIGHT PHILIP'S

69
74
79

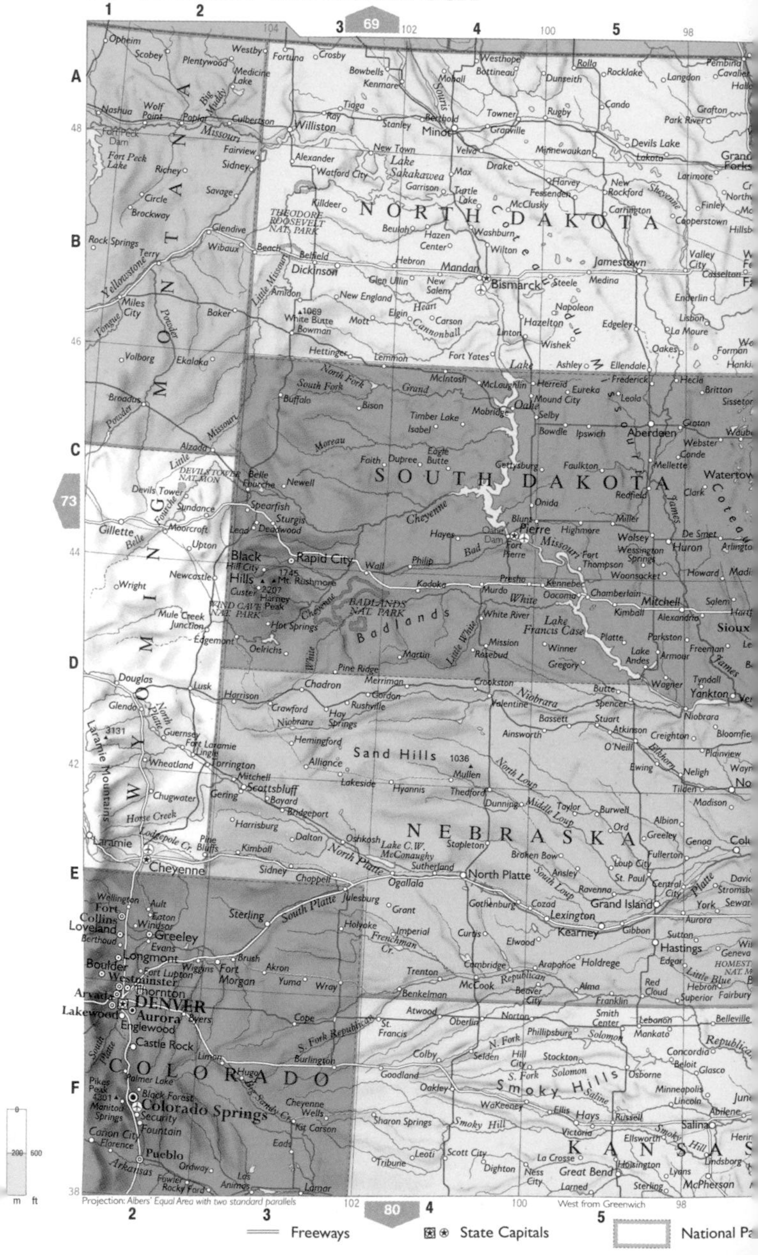

1
2
3
4
5
A
B
C
D
E
F
104
102
100
98
48
46
44
42
38
69
73
80
Opheim
Scobey
Plentywood
Westby
Fortuna
Crosby
Medicine Lake
Bowbells
Kenmare
Mohall
Westhope
Bottineau
Rolla
Dunseith
Rocklake
Langdon
Pembina
Cavalier
Nashua
Wolf Point
Poplar
Big Muddy
Culbertson
Missouri
Williston
Tioga
Ray
Stanley
Berthold
Minot
Towner
Rugby
Cando
Grafton
Park River
Fort Peck Dam
Fort Peck Lake
Fairview
Sidney
Richey
Savage
Alexander
Watford City
New Town
Lake Sakakawea
Garrison
Max
Velva
Granville
Minnewaukan
Devils Lake
Lakota
Drake
Harvey
Fessenden
New Rockford
Carrington
Sheyenne
Larimore
Finley
Cooperstown
Circle
Brockway
Killdeer
THEODORE ROOSEVELT NAT. PARK
NORTH DAKOTA
Turtle Lake
McClusky
Beulah
Hazen
Center
Washburn
Wilton
Coteau du Missouri
Jamestown
Valley City
Casselton
Glendive
Rock Springs
Terry
Wibaux
Beach
Belfield
Dickinson
Hebron
Glen Ullin
New Salem
Mandan
Bismarck
Steele
Medina
Yellowstone
Miles City
Tongue
Powder
Amidon
Little Missouri
New England
Heart
Napoleon
Enderlin
Baker
1069
White Butte
Bowman
Mott
Elgin
Carson
Cannonball
Hazelton
Linton
Wishek
Edgeley
Lisbon
La Moure
Hettinger
Lemmon
Fort Yates
Oakes
Forman
Volborg
Ekalaka
MONTANA
Ashley
Ellendale
Hankinson
North Fork
South Fork
Grand
McIntosh
McLaughlin
Herreid
Eureka
Frederick
Hecla
Britton
Sisseton
Broadus
Buffalo
Bison
Timber Lake
Isabel
Mobridge
Oahe
Mound City
Selby
Leola
Bowdle
Ipswich
Aberdeen
Groton
Webster
Conde
Alzada
Missouri
Moreau
Faith
Dupree
Eagle Butte
Gettysburg
Faulkton
Mellette
Little
DEVILS TOWER NAT. MON.
Belle Fourche
Newell
SOUTH DAKOTA
Watertown
Clark
Devils Tower
Sundance
Spearfish
Sturgis
Deadwood
Lead
Cheyenne
Onida
Redfield
James
Miller
Gillette
Belle Fourche
Moorcroft
Hayes
Blunt
Pierre
Oahe Dam
Fort Pierre
Highmore
Wolsey
Wessington Springs
De Smet
Huron
Arlington
Upton
Black Hills
Hill City
Rapid City
Wall
Philip
Bad
Missouri
Fort Thompson
Woonsocket
Howard
1745
Mt. Rushmore
Custer
2207
Harney Peak
Newcastle
Wright
Kadoka
Presho
Kennebec
Murdo
Oacoma
Chamberlain
Mitchell
Salem
White
Kimball
Alexandria
WIND CAVE NAT. PARK
BADLANDS NAT. PARK
Badlands
Mule Creek Junction
White River
Lake Francis Case
Hot Springs
Edgemont
Oelrichs
Mission
Rosebud
Winner
Platte
Parkston
Freeman
Sioux
Little White
Martin
Gregory
Lake Andes
Armour
Pine Ridge
Wagner
Tyndall
Yankton
Douglas
Lusk
Chadron
Merriman
Crookston
Niobrara
Butte
Harrison
Gordon
Rushville
Valentine
Spencer
Niobrara
Glendo
North Platte
Crawford
Niobrara
Hay Springs
Bassett
Stuart
Atkinson
Creighton
3131
Guernsey
Fort Laramie
Lingle
Hemingford
Ainsworth
O'Neill
Elkhorn
Plainview
Laramie Mountains
Wheatland
Torrington
Mitchell
Alliance
Sand Hills
1036
Mullen
North Loup
Ewing
Neligh
Lakeside
Hyannis
Thedford
Tilden
Scottsbluff
Gering
Bayard
Bridgeport
Chugwater
WYOMING
Dunning
Middle Loup
Taylor
Burwell
Madison
Horse Creek
Harrisburg
Ord
Albion
NEBRASKA
Laramie
Lodgepole Cr.
Pine Bluffs
Dalton
Oshkosh
Lake C.W. McConaughy
Stapleton
Greeley
Genoa
Kimball
Broken Bow
Loup City
Fullerton
Cheyenne
Sidney
Chappell
North Platte
Sutherland
North Platte
Ansley
St. Paul
South Loup
Central City
Platte
Ravenna
Ogallala
Wellington
Ault
Fort Collins
Eaton
Windsor
Loveland
Berthoud
Greeley
Evans
Longmont
Boulder
Westminster
Arvada
Thornton
Lakewood
DENVER
Aurora
Englewood
Sterling
South Platte
Julesburg
Grant
Gothenburg
Cozad
Lexington
Grand Island
York
Holyoke
Imperial
Frenchman Cr.
Curtis
Kearney
Gibbon
Aurora
Sutton
Elwood
Hastings
Brush
Wiggins
Fort Lupton
Fort Morgan
Akron
Yuma
Wray
Trenton
Cambridge
Arapahoe
Holdrege
Edgar
HOMESTEAD NAT. MON.
Little Blue
Benkelman
McCook
Republican
Beaver City
Alma
Red Cloud
Franklin
Hebron
Superior
Fairbury
Byers
Cope
Atwood
Oberlin
Norton
Smith Center
Lebanon
Mankato
Belleville
Castle Rock
S. Fork Republican
St. Francis
Phillipsburg
Solomon
N. Fork
Republican
South Platte
Limon
Burlington
Colby
Selden
Hill City
Stockton
Concordia
Beloit
Glasco
COLORADO
Palmer Lake
Hugo
Goodland
S. Fork
Solomon
Osborne
Smoky Hills
Pikes Peak
4301
Black Forest
Oakley
Minneapolis
Lincoln
Manitou Springs
Colorado Springs
Security
Big Sandy Cr.
Cheyenne Wells
Saline
WaKeeney
Ellis
Hays
Russell
Abilene
Fountain
Kit Carson
Sharon Springs
Smoky Hill
Victoria
Salina
Canon City
Florence
Ellsworth
Smoky Hill
Pueblo
Eads
Tribune
Leoti
Scott City
Dighton
Ness City
La Crosse
Great Bend
Hoisington
Lyons
Lindsborg
KANSAS
Arkansas
Ordway
Fowler
Rocky Ford
Las Animas
Lamar
Larned
Sterling
McPherson
Projection: Albers' Equal Area with two standard parallels
West from Greenwich
0
200
600
m
ft
Freeways
State Capitals
National Pa

50 0 50 100 150 200 km
50 0 50 100 150 miles
7
71
8
9
10
94
92
90
CANADA
Lake of the Woods
Rainy Lake
Warroad
Rainy River
Baudette
Emo
Fort Frances
International Falls
VOYAGEURS NAT. PARK
Kabetogama
Atikokan
Thunder Bay
Northern Light L.
Cloud Bay
Isle Royale
ISLE ROYALE NAT. PARK
Grand Portage
Grand Marais
Saganaga L.
Vermilion L.
Ely
Tower
Upper Red L.
Lower Red L.
Big Falls
Northome
Little Fork
Big Fork
Thief River Falls
L. Winnibigoshish
Erskine
Bagley
Bemidji
Cass Lake
Mahnomen
Leech L.
Deer River
Grand Rapids
Chisholm
Hibbing
Mountain Iron
Virginia
Biwabik
Eveleth
Cook
St. Louis
Hill City
Floodwood
Walker
Park Rapids
Detroit Lakes
Duluth
Superior
Cloquet
Two Harbors
APOSTLE ISLANDS NAT. LAKESHORE
Apostle Is.
Chequamegon Bay
Bayfield
Washburn
Ashland
LAKE SUPERIOR
Eagle River
Copper Harbor
Keweenaw Pt.
Keweenaw Pen.
Keweenaw B.
Pt. Abbaye
Laurium
Hancock
Houghton
Baraga
Ontonagon
L'Anse
Ishpeming
Marquette
Negaunee
Gwinn
Rockland
L. Gogebic
Wakefield
Bessemer
Ironwood
Hurley
Mellen
MICHIGAN
MINNESOTA
Pine River
Aitkin
Perham
Wadena
Staples
Brainerd
Mille Lacs L.
Baxter
Bottle Lake
Fergus Falls
Moose Lake
Solon Springs
Hayward
Hinckley
Little Falls
Long Prairie
Mora
Pine City
Milaca
Sauk Centre
Melrose
Sauk Rapids
Alexandria
Glenwood
St. Cloud
Paynesville
Morris
Benson
Cambridge
St. Croix Falls
Elk River
Monticello
Blaine
Coon Rapids
Brooklyn Park
Willmar
Litchfield
Montevideo
MINNEAPOLIS
ST. PAUL
Hutchinson
Bloomington
Glencoe
Burnsville
Lakeville
Hastings
Red Wing
Granite Falls
Redwood Falls
Minnesota
Marshall
New Ulm
Sleepy Eye
Le Sueur
St. Peter
Northfield
Faribault
Mankato
N. Mankato
Tracy
Owatonna
Waseca
Kasson
Stewartville
Rochester
Winona
Lake City
St. James
Windom
Worthington
Jackson
Fairmont
Blue Earth
Albert Lea
Austin
Preston
La Crescent
Holmen
Onalaska
La Crosse
Sparta
Tomah
Siren
Spooner
Rice Lake
Barron
Chippewa
Flambeau
Ladysmith
Phillips
Park Falls
Prentice
Rhinelander
Eagle River
Iron River
Watersmeet
Crystal Falls
Iron Mountain
Norway
Kingsford
Menominee
Powers
Crandon
Laona
Tomahawk
Merrill
Antigo
Wausau
Medford
Bloomer
New Richmond
Hudson
Menomonie
Chippewa Falls
WISCONSIN
Eau Claire
Durand
Neillsville
Marshfield
Stevens Point
Wisconsin Rapids
Whitehall
Alma
Black River Falls
Necedah
Mauston
Reedsburg
Baraboo
Viroqua
Richland Center
Prairie du Chien
Wisconsin
Madison
Portage
Adams
Montello
Berlin
Ripon
Waupaca
Wautoma
Clintonville
New London
Oshkosh
Neenah
Appleton
Kaukauna
De Pere
Green Bay
Shawano
Oconto Falls
Menominee
Peshtigo
Marinette
Oconto
Sturgeon Bay
Algoma
Kewaunee
Two Rivers
Manitowoc
Chilton
L. Winnebago
Sheboygan
Fond du Lac
Waupun
Beaver Dam
Plymouth
West Bend
Port Washington
Hartford
LAKE MICHIGAN
Watertown
Oconomowoc
Waukesha
Wauwatosa
MILWAUKEE
West Allis
S. Milwaukee
Racine
Kenosha
Waukegan
North Chicago
Highland Park
Wilmette
Evanston
Fitchburg
Whitewater
Delavan
Janesville
Beloit
Burlington
Lake Geneva
Dodgeville
Platteville
Lancaster
Monroe
Dubuque
Rockford
Loves Park
Woodstock
Freeport
Belvidere
Arlington Hts.
Elgin
St. Charles
Elmhurst
CHICAGO
Cicero
Aurora
Joliet
Oregon
Rochelle
De Kalb
Dixon
Sterling
Rock Falls
Mendota
Morris
La Salle
Peru
Ottawa
Princeton
Kankakee
Dwight
Streator
Pontiac
Clinton
Bettendorf
Moline
Rock Island
Davenport
Geneseo
Kewanee
Galva
Aledo
Henry
Galesburg
Chillicothe
Monmouth
Peoria
Washington
Pekin
Normal
Bloomington
Lexington
Paxton
Rantoul
Champaign
Urbana
ILLINOIS
Canton
Macomb
Carthage
Havana
Lincoln
Clinton
Rushville
Beardstown
Mount Sterling
Springfield
Decatur
Tuscola
Sullivan
Mattoon
Shelbyville
Taylorville
Pana
Jacksonville
Quincy
Hannibal
Pittsfield
White Hall
Carrollton
Carlinville
Litchfield
Effingham
Newton
Little Wabash
Jerseyville
Staunton
Vandalia
Alton
Granite City
E. St. Louis
Salem
Flora
Centralia
Kaskaskia
Belleville
Fairfield
Waterloo
Mount Vernon
McLeansboro
Benton
West Frankfort
Pinckneyville
Du Quoin
Illinois
Mississippi
Northwood
Decorah
Waukon
EFFIGY MOUNDS NAT. MON.
McGregor
Osage
Charles City
Cedar
New Hampton
Guttenberg
Oelwein
Sumner
Waverly
Hampton
Cedar Falls
Waterloo
Independence
Manchester
Wapsipinicon
Monticello
Maquoketa
Anamosa
Marion
Cedar Rapids
Vinton
Grundy Center
Estherville
Lake Mills
Forest City
Mason City
Clear Lake
Garner
Algona
Emmetsburg
Spencer
Humboldt
Clarion
Eagle Grove
Iowa Falls
Eldora
Fort Dodge
Webster City
Pocahontas
Storm Lake
Sac City
Rockwell City
Cherokee
Sheldon
Sibley
Sioux Center
Le Mars
Sioux City
Ida Grove
IOWA
Boone
Nevada
Marshalltown
Ames
Tama
Belle Plaine
Marengo
Tipton
Denison
Carroll
Jefferson
Perry
Ankeny
Newton
Grinnell
Iowa City
Audubon
Harlan
Urbandale
West Des Moines
Des Moines
L. Red Rock
Montezuma
Muscatine
Washington
Iowa
Norwalk
Indianola
Pella
Oskaloosa
Ottumwa
Knoxville
Des Moines
Skunk
Fairfield
Mount Pleasant
Burlington
Missouri Valley
Logan
Atlantic
Winterset
Greenfield
Council Bluffs
Glenwood
Red Oak
Creston
Osceola
Albia
Chariton
Corning
Shenandoah
Clarinda
Bedford
Corydon
Leon
Centerville
Bloomfield
Fort Madison
Keokuk
Kahoka
Rock Port
Grant City
Princeton
Unionville
Kirksville
Edina
Chariton
Thompson
Maryville
Bethany
Milan
Mound City
Trenton
Falls City
Savannah
Chillicothe
Palmyra
Canton
Hiawatha
Cameron
Grand
Macon
Monroe City
Horton
Troy
St. Joseph
Atchison
Holton
Excelsior Springs
Brunswick
Moberly
Louisiana
Vandalia
Leavenworth
Liberty
Richmond
Carrollton
Centralia
Mexico
Montgomery City
Kansas City
Lexington
Fayette
Troy
Independence
Marshall
Columbia
Florissant
Topeka
Overland Park
KANSAS CITY
Boonville
Fulton
St. Charles
ST. LOUIS
Lawrence
Olathe
Leawood
Warrensburg
California
Missouri
Hermann
Washington
Ottawa
Sedalia
Jefferson City
Union
Mehlville
Paola
Harrisonville
Windsor
MISSOURI
Festus
Emporia
Osawatomie
Clinton
Eldon
Sullivan
De Soto
Butler
Harry S. Truman Res.
Lake of the Ozarks
Osage
Vienna
Ste. Genevieve
Garnett
Burlington
Missouri
B
C
E
F
76
46
44
40
38
96
7
94
8
92
81
9
90
10
COPYRIGHT PHILIP'S

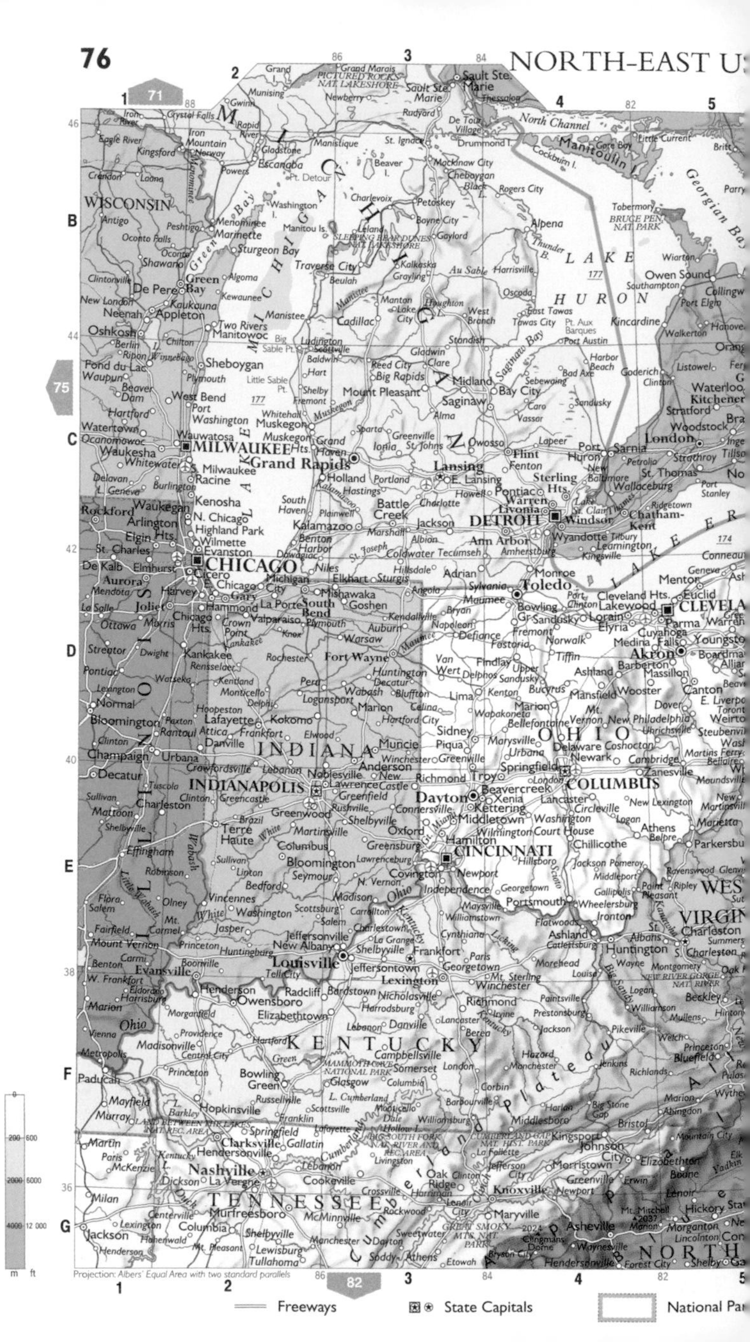
71
75
82
Projection: Albers' Equal Area with two standard parallels
Freeways
State Capitals
National Pa
m ft
200 600
2000 6000
4000 12 000
WISCONSIN
MICHIGAN
LAKE MICHIGAN
LAKE HURON
LAKE ERIE
ILLINOIS
INDIANA
OHIO
KENTUCKY
TENNESSEE
WEST VIRGINIA
Cumberland Plateau
APPALACHIAN
Georgian Bay
North Channel
Manitoulin I.
Green Bay
Saginaw Bay
Thunder B.
PICTURED ROCKS NAT. LAKESHORE
SLEEPING BEAR DUNES NAT. LAKESHORE
BRUCE PEN. NAT. PARK
MAMMOTH CAVE NATIONAL PARK
LAND BETWEEN THE LAKES NAT. REC. AREA
BIG SOUTH FORK NAT. RIVER AND REC. AREA
CUMBERLAND GAP NAT. HIST. PARK
GREAT SMOKY MTS. NAT. PARK
NEW RIVER GORGE NAT. RIVER
Sault Ste. Marie
Grand Marais
Munising
Newberry
Escanaba
Manistique
St. Ignace
Mackinaw City
Cheboygan
Petoskey
Charlevoix
Alpena
Traverse City
Gaylord
Cadillac
Ludington
Muskegon
Grand Rapids
Lansing
Flint
Saginaw
Bay City
Midland
Mount Pleasant
Kalamazoo
Battle Creek
Jackson
Ann Arbor
DETROIT
Windsor
Pontiac
Toledo
Green Bay
Appleton
Oshkosh
Sheboygan
Fond du Lac
Manitowoc
MILWAUKEE
Racine
Kenosha
Waukegan
Rockford
CHICAGO
Aurora
Joliet
Gary
South Bend
Elkhart
Fort Wayne
Kokomo
Lafayette
Muncie
Anderson
INDIANAPOLIS
Terre Haute
Bloomington
Champaign
Decatur
Evansville
Louisville
Lexington
Frankfort
Dayton
Springfield
COLUMBUS
CINCINNATI
Lima
Mansfield
Akron
CLEVELAND
Youngstown
Canton
Zanesville
Parkersburg
Charleston
Huntington
Ashland
Portsmouth
Owensboro
Bowling Green
Paducah
Clarksville
Nashville
Murfreesboro
Knoxville
Johnson City
Kingsport
Bristol
Asheville
Jackson
London
Sarnia
Kitchener
Waterloo
Stratford
Owen Sound
Chatham-Kent
Kincardine
Goderich
St. Thomas
Woodstock
Mt. Mitchell 2037
Clingmans Dome 2024

50 0 50 100 150 200 km
50 0 50 100 150 miles
7
8
9
10
76
74
72
CANADA
ONTARIO
OTTAWA
MONTREAL
Laval
Longueuil
St-Hyacinthe
Sherbrooke
Granby
Magog
Coaticook
Cowansville
Gatineau
Hull
Buckingham
Hawkesbury
Lachute
Salaberry-de-Valleyfield
Cornwall
Pembroke
Renfrew
Arnprior
Carleton Place
Smiths Falls
Perth
Brockville
Prescott
Kingston
Napanee
Belleville
Quinte West
Picton
Peterborough
Lindsay
Tecumseth
Clarington
Oshawa
Cobourg
Port Hope
TORONTO
Huntsville
Bracebridge
Gravenhurst
Bancroft
Hamilton
Niagara Falls
Lockport
Medina
Brockport
Rochester
Fairport
Newark
N. Tonawanda
Amherst
Batavia
Buffalo
W. Seneca
Hamburg
Gowanda
Salamanca
Olean
Wellsville
Jamestown
Corry
Warren
Bradford
LAKE ONTARIO
NEW YORK
Oswego
Fulton
Pulaski
Watertown
Adams
Lowville
Boonville
Carthage
Clayton
Gouverneur
Alexandria Bay
Ogdensburg
Massena
Malone
Potsdam
Canton
Saranac Lake
Tupper Lake
Long Lake
Plattsburgh
Champlain
Dannemora
ADIRONDACK PARK
Adirondack Mts.
Rome
Utica
Little Falls
Oneida
Syracuse
Fairmount
Herkimer
Johnstown
Amsterdam
Schenectady
Albany
Troy
Saratoga Sps.
Glens Falls
Hudson Falls
Granville
Whitehall
Ticonderoga
Port Henry
Cobleskill
Cooperstown
Hamilton
Norwich
Oneonta
Sidney
Catskill Mts.
Catskill
Saugerties
Kingston
Cortland
Ithaca
Auburn
Geneva
Seneca Falls
Canandaigua
Geneseo
Penn Yan
Dansville
Watkins Glen
Bath
Corning
Hornell
Elmira
Endicott
Binghamton
Sayre
Waverly
Towanda
Ellenville
Liberty
Poughkeepsie
Newburgh
Beacon
Middletown
Peekskill
Danbury
Port Chester
Yonkers
Stamford
Norwalk
Bridgeport
New Haven
Long Island Sound
Long Island
Riverhead
Southampton
Montauk Pt.
Port Jefferson
Patchogue
Levittown
Freeport
NEW YORK
Jersey City
Paterson
E. Orange
Newark
Elizabeth
Plainfield
Perth Amboy
New Brunswick
Long Branch
Asbury Park
Princeton
Trenton
NEW JERSEY
ATLANTIC OCEAN
VERMONT
NEW HAMPSHIRE
MASS.
CONN.
R.I.
Burlington
Winooski
St. Albans
Newport
Montpelier
Barre
St. Johnsbury
Lyndonville
Middlebury
Randolph
Rutland
Fair Haven
Bellows Falls
Springfield
Windsor
Claremont
Brattleboro
Bennington
Hanover
Lebanon
Laconia
Franklin
Concord
Rochester
Dover
Manchester
Nashua
Keene
Berlin
Mt. Washington
Conway
Littleton
Colebrook
Rangeley
Lawrence
Lowell
Haverhill
Salem
Lynn
Cambridge
Newton
BOSTON
Quincy
Brockton
Taunton
Attleboro
Fall River
New Bedford
Pawtucket
PROVIDENCE
Warwick
Woonsocket
Worcester
Fitchburg
Leominster
Greenfield
Pittsfield
N. Adams
Northampton
Holyoke
Chicopee
Springfield
Hartford
New Britain
Bristol
Waterbury
Meriden
Norwich
New London
Newport
Martha's Vineyard
Nantucket I.
Block I.
Cape Cod
C. Ann
S. Yarmouth
PENNSYLVANIA
Allegheny Plateau
Appalachian Mountains
Kane
Coudersport
Wellsboro
Emporium
St. Marys
Ridgway
Oil City
Clarion
Brookville
Dubois
Clearfield
Bellefonte
State College
Indiana
Altoona
Lewistown
Huntingdon
Hollidaysburg
PITTSBURGH
Penn Hills
Johnstown
Greensburg
Somerset
Monessen
Connellsville
Uniontown
Williamsport
Jersey Shore
Lock Haven
Milton
Sunbury
Shamokin
Bloomsburg
Berwick
Nanticoke
Kingston
Scranton
Wilkes-Barre
Hazleton
Dunmore
Carbondale
E. Stroudsburg
Easton
Bethlehem
Allentown
Pottsville
Reading
Pottstown
Norristown
Lebanon
Harrisburg
Camp Hill
Carlisle
Shippensburg
Chambersburg
Gettysburg
York
Lancaster
Columbia
Coatesville
PHILADELPHIA
Camden
Upper Darby
Chester
Wilmington
Newark
Willingboro
Hammonton
Vineland
Millville
Bridgeton
Salem
Pleasantville
Atlantic City
Ocean City
North Wildwood
Cape May
C. May
Waynesboro
Hanover
Hagerstown
Westminster
Frederick
Towson
BALTIMORE
Dundalk
MARYLAND
DELAWARE
Dover
Milford
Lewes
C. Henlopen
Delaware Bay
Smyrna
Aberdeen
Annapolis
Rockville
Wheaton
Arlington
Alexandria
WASHINGTON D.C.
Cumberland
Frostburg
Martinsburg
Brunswick
Charles Town
Winchester
Front Royal
Luray
Morgantown
Westernport
Keyser
Romney
Moorefield
Petersburg
SPRUCE KNOB-SENECA ROCKS NAT. REC. AREA
1482
Franklin
Harrisonburg
Shenandoah
Culpeper
Fredericksburg
Dale City
St. Charles
Chesapeake Bay
Easton
Seaford
Cambridge
Salisbury
Berlin
Ocean City
Snow Hill
Pocomoke City
Chincoteague
ASSATEAGUE ISLAND NAT. SEASHORE
Colonial Beach
Lexington Park
Potomac
Leonardtown
SHENANDOAH NAT. PARK
Orange
Staunton
Waynesboro
Charlottesville
Lexington
Buena Vista
Covington
Ashland
Accomac
VIRGINIA
Richmond
Lynchburg
Madison Heights
Bedford
Farmville
Hopewell
Petersburg
Williamsburg
West Point
Gloucester Point
Cape Charles
C. Charles
Hampton
Newport News
NORFOLK
Virginia Beach
Portsmouth
Suffolk
Chesapeake
Roanoke
Altavista
Blackstone
Nottoway
South Boston
John H. Kerr Res.
Danville
Franklin
Emporia
Murfreesboro
Ahoskie
Roanoke Rapids
Elizabeth City
Roxboro
Oxford
Henderson
Eden
Greensboro
Burlington
Enfield
Edenton
Albemarle Sd.
Manteo
Roanoke I.
Wake Forest
Rocky Mount
Tarboro
Plymouth
Williamston
CAPE HATTERAS NAT. SEASHORE
Belhaven
Pamlico Sound
Thomasville
Chapel Hill
Siler City
Cary
Smithfield
Asheboro
Greenville
Goldsboro
Kinston
New Bern
Sanford
Dunn
CAROLINA
Hatteras
Edmundston
St-Leonard
Grand Falls
Fort Kent
Van Buren
Eagle Lake
Caribou
Fort Fairfield
Presque Isle
Ashland
Mars Hill
Perth-Andover
Hartland
Eagle L.
Chamberlain L.
Houlton
Woodstock
Chesuncook L.
BAXTER STATE PARK
1605
Mt. Katahdin
Chamberlain
Chesuncook
Patten
Chiputneticook Lakes
Millinocket
Rockwood
Moosehead L.
Jackman
Greenville
Flagstaff L.
Milo
Dover-Foxcroft
Lincoln
Bingham
Dexter
W. Grand L.
Calais
Woodland
MAINE
Rangeley
Colebrook
Mooselookmeguntic L.
Skowhegan
Pittsfield
Bangor
Old Town
Orono
Brewer
Eastport
Machias
Groveton
Rumford
Farmington
Waterville
Ellsworth
Bar Harbor
Mt. Desert I.
ACADIA NAT. PARK
Berlin
Mt. Washington
1917
Norway
Augusta
Gardiner
Belfast
Camden
Rockland
Penobscot B.
Auburn
Lewiston
Conway
Lisbon Falls
Brunswick
Bath
Westbrook
Portland
S. Portland
Casco B.
Saco
Biddeford
Laconia
Sanford
Rochester
Dover
Kittery
Portsmouth
Gulf of Maine
HAMPSHIRE
12
68
44
continuation eastwards on same scale
A
B
C
D
E
F
G
80
78
6
West from Greenwich
COPYRIGHT PHILIP'S

83

1 2 3 4 5
122 120 118 116
72

SAN FRANCISCO
Oakland
Stockton
Manteca
Tracy
Hayward
San Mateo
Redwood City
Fremont
Modesto
Sunnyvale
SAN JOSE
Patterson
Turlock
Atwater
Merced
Gustine
Gilroy
Santa Cruz
Watsonville
Los Banos
Chowchilla
Mariposa
Madera
Hollister
Salinas
Pacific Grove
Monterey
Seaside
Gonzales
Soledad
Mendota
Fresno
Clovis
Sanger
Selma
Kingsburg
Reedley
Dinuba
Hanford
Visalia
Lemoore
Tulare
Exeter
Lindsay
Porterville
Corcoran
King City
Coalinga
Pt. Sur
Pinos Pt.
Angels Camp
Sonora
Bridgeport
YOSEMITE NAT. PARK
Mono Lake
Sierra Nevada
White Mountain Pk. 4341
Bishop
Big Pine
White Mts.
Inyo Mts.
KINGS CANYON NAT. PARK
North Palisade 4341
Independence
Mt. Whitney 4418
SEQUOIA NAT. PARK
Lone Pine
Owens L.
Olancha
DEATH VALLEY NAT. PARK
Death Valley
Panamint Ra.
-86
Telescope Pk. 3366
Death Valley Junc.
Pahrump
Spring Mts. 3633
NEVADA
Tonopah
Goldfield
Warm Springs
Grant Ra.
Beatty
Indian Springs
Pioche
Panaca
Caliente
Hiko
Alamo
Meadow Valley
Mesquite
LAS VEGAS
North Las Vegas
Sunrise Manor
Paradise
Henderson
Boulder City
Jean
Hoover Dam
LAKE MEAD NAT. REC. AREA
Searchlight
L. Mohave
Laughlin
Davis Dam
Kingman
Bullhead City
Needles
Topock
Lake Havasu City
Parker
Santa Lucia Range
L. Nacimiento
San Miguel
Paso Robles
Tulare Lake Bed
Cambria
Morro Bay
Atascadero
San Luis Obispo
CARRIZO PLAIN NAT. MON.
Arroyo Grande
Nipomo
Guadalupe
Santa Maria
Lompoc
Pt. Arguello
Pt. Conception
Solvang
Santa Barbara
Ojai
Carpinteria
Ventura
Oxnard
Delano
Earlimart
Wasco
Shafter
GIANT SEQUOIA NAT. MON.
Oildale
Bakersfield
Kern
Taft
Buena Vista Lake Bed
Maricopa
Lebec
Tehachapi
Tehachapi Mts.
Los Angeles Aqueduct
Mojave
Inyokern
Searles L.
Ridgecrest
Lancaster
Palmdale
Victorville
Santa Clarita
Simi Valley
Mojave Desert
Yermo
Barstow
Ludlow
Baker
MOJAVE NAT. PRESERVE
Soda L.
New York Mts.
CHANNEL IS. NAT. PARK
San Miguel I.
Santa Rosa I.
Santa Cruz I.
Channel Is.
Burbank
Glendale
Pasadena
Beverly Hills
Pomona
Santa Monica
LOS ANGELES
Ontario
Inglewood
Long Beach
Anaheim
Huntington Beach
Newport Beach
Santa Catalina I.
San Nicolas I.
SAN BERNARDINO
Apple Valley
Hesperia
San Gorgonio Mt. 3506
Riverside
Corona
Santa Ana
Banning
Hemet
Mission Viejo
Palm Springs
Indio
Coachella
JOSHUA TREE NAT. PARK
Twentynine Palms
Amboy
Bristol L.
Cadiz L.
Danby L.
Colorado River Aqueduct
L. Havasu
San Clemente
Oceanside
Vista
Temecula
Escondido
Carlsbad
Julian
SANTA ROSA AND SAN JACINTO MTS. NAT. MON.
Salton Sea
-72
Chocolate Mts.
Coachella Canal
Desert Center
Blythe
Colorado
Quartzsite
Sonoran Desert
Gulf of Santa Catalina
San Clemente I.
La Mesa
Ramona
SAN DIEGO
El Cajon
Chula Vista
National City
TIJUANA
Tecate
Westmorland
Calipatria
Brawley
Holtville
El Centro
Calexico
All American Canal
Imperial Dam
Yuma
Wellton
Somerton
San Luis
Mexicali
San Luis Río Colorado
Rosarito
PARQUE NACIONAL CONSTITUCIÓN DE 1857
Laguna Salada
Sierra de Juárez
Ensenada
Desierto de Altar
Pta. Santo Tomas
Santo Tomás
BAJA CALIFORNIA
C. Colonet
San Telmo
Cerro de la Encantada 3078
Sierra de San Pedro Mártir
PARQUE NACIONAL SAN PEDRO MÁRTIR
San Felipe
Puerto Peñasco
B. San Jorge
Golfo de California (Mar de Cortés)
C. San Quintín
El Rosario
Pta. Baja
Pta. San Antonio
I. San Luis
I. Ángel de la Guarda
Canal de las Ballenas
Punta Prieta
Isla Cedros
B. Sebastián Vizcaíno
PACIFIC OCEAN

HAWAI'I
Kapaa
Kaua'i
Lihue
Ni'ihau
Kauai Channel
O'ahu
Wahiawa
Kāne'ohe
Pearl City
Honolulu
Pearl Harbor
Kaunakakai
Moloka'i
Lāna'i
Kahului
Wailuku
Maui
Kaho'olawe
PACIFIC OCEAN
Hawaiian Islands
'Alenuihāhā Channel
Waimea (Kamuela)
Mauna Kea 4205
Hilo
Hawai'i
Mauna Loa 4169
Kailua
Kilauea
Mountain View
Pāhala
50 0 100 km
50 0 50 100 miles

m ft
0
200 600
2000 6000
4000 12 000

Projection: Albers Equal Area with two standard parallels

Freeways
State Capitals
National Parks

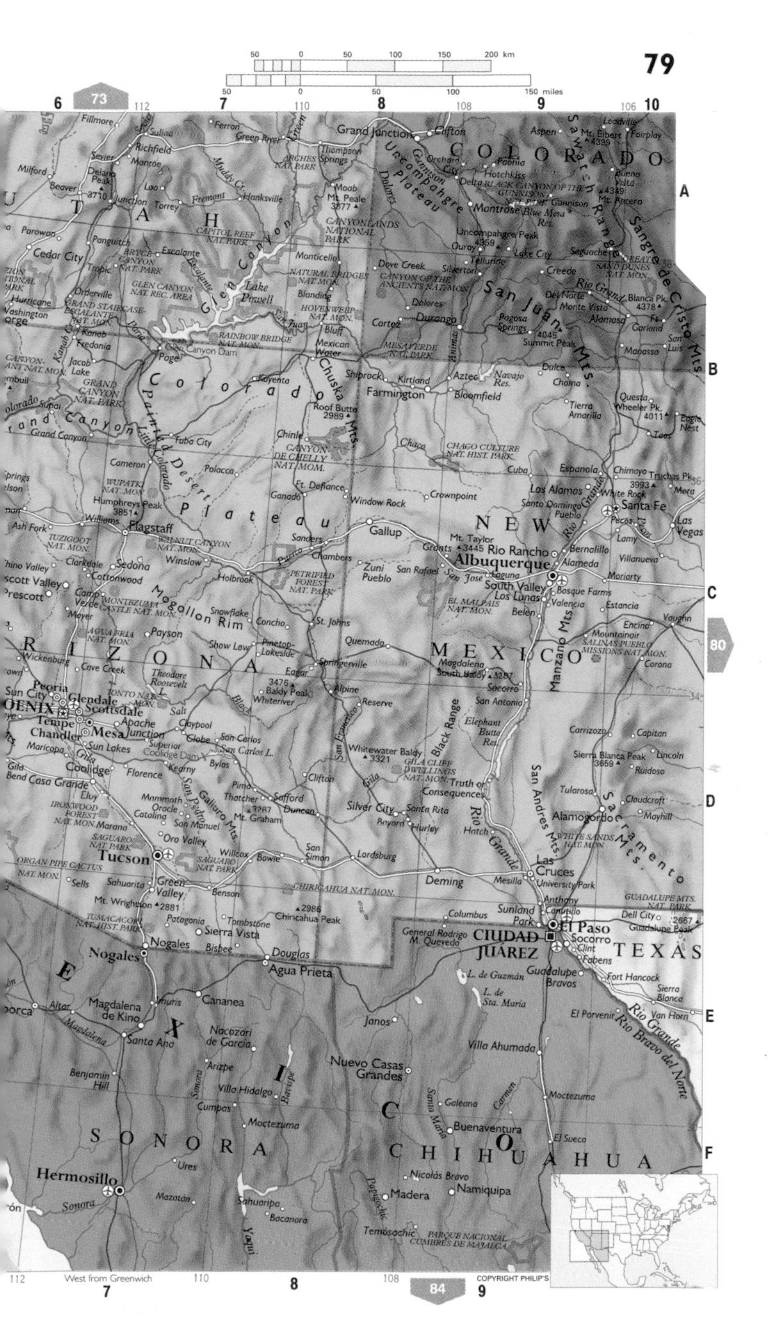
79
50 0 50 100 150 200 km
50 0 50 100 150 miles
UTAH
COLORADO
ARIZONA
NEW MEXICO
TEXAS
MEXICO
SONORA
CHIHUAHUA
Colorado Plateau
Painted Desert
Mogollon Rim
Grand Canyon
Glen Canyon
Lake Powell
San Juan Mts.
Sawatch Range
Sangre de Cristo Mts.
Uncompahgre Plateau
Chuska Mts.
Sacramento Mts.
San Andres Mts.
Manzano Mts.
Black Range
Rio Grande
Rio Bravo del Norte
Grand Junction
Moab
Durango
Farmington
Gallup
Flagstaff
Albuquerque
Santa Fe
Los Alamos
Rio Rancho
Phoenix
Glendale
Scottsdale
Tempe
Mesa
Chandler
Tucson
Nogales
Las Cruces
El Paso
CIUDAD JUÁREZ
Alamogordo
Deming
Silver City
Agua Prieta
Douglas
Hermosillo
Nuevo Casas Grandes
Villa Ahumada
Madera
Namiquipa
Cedar City
Page
Kayenta
Chinle
Window Rock
Sedona
Prescott
Payson
Socorro
Truth or Consequences
Roswell
West from Greenwich
COPYRIGHT PHILIP'S
73
80
84

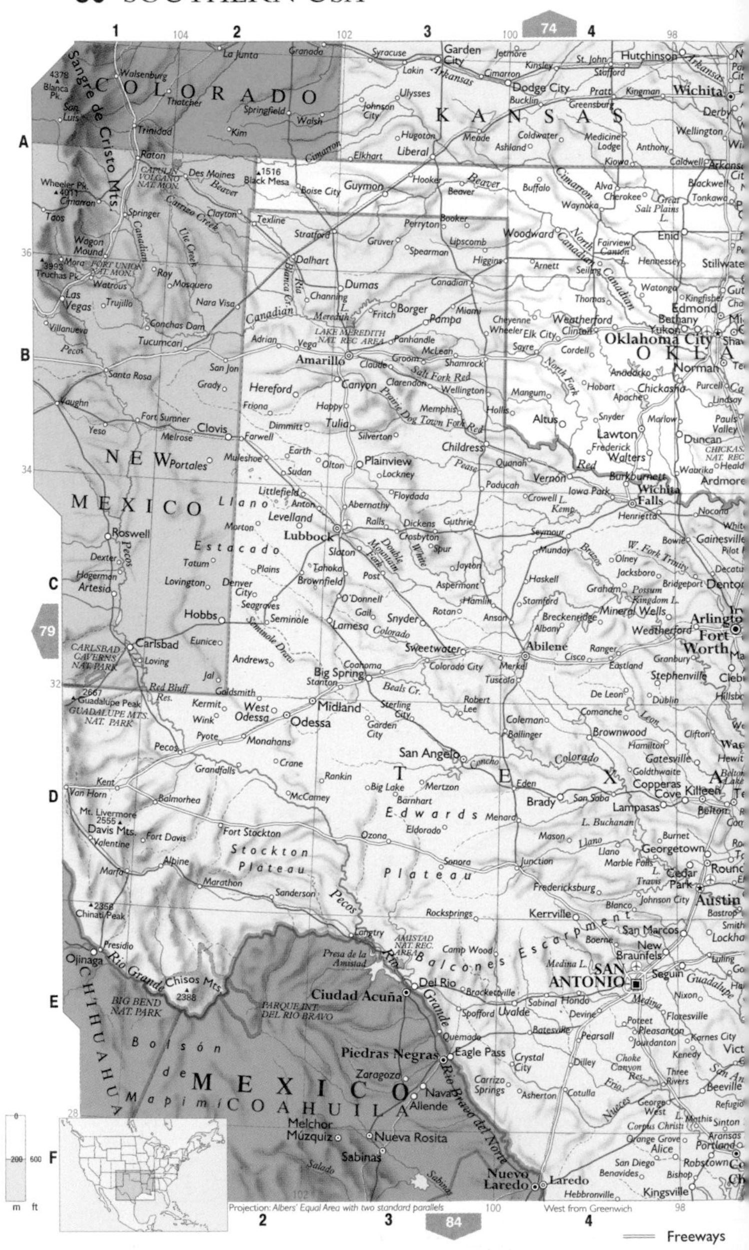
74
79
84
COLORADO
KANSAS
NEW MEXICO
TEXAS
OKLA
MEXICO
CHIHUAHUA
COAHUILA
Sangre de Cristo Mts.
Llano Estacado
Edwards Plateau
Stockton Plateau
Balcones Escarpment
Bolsón de Mapimí
Wichita
Dodge City
Garden City
Hutchinson
Liberal
Guymon
Dalhart
Dumas
Borger
Pampa
Amarillo
Canyon
Hereford
Clovis
Portales
Tucumcari
Santa Rosa
Las Vegas
Raton
Trinidad
Roswell
Artesia
Carlsbad
Hobbs
Lubbock
Plainview
Childress
Vernon
Wichita Falls
Lawton
Altus
Oklahoma City
Norman
Enid
Woodward
Abilene
Sweetwater
Snyder
Big Spring
Midland
Odessa
San Angelo
Pecos
Fort Stockton
Alpine
Marfa
Brownwood
Killeen
Georgetown
Austin
Kerrville
San Marcos
New Braunfels
SAN ANTONIO
Seguin
Uvalde
Del Rio
Ciudad Acuña
Eagle Pass
Piedras Negras
Nuevo Laredo
Laredo
Corpus Christi
Kingsville
Alice
Arlington
Fort Worth
Denton
CARLSBAD CAVERNS NAT. PARK
GUADALUPE MTS. NAT. PARK
BIG BEND NAT. PARK
Rio Grande
Pecos
Colorado
Red
Canadian
Brazos
Projection: Albers' Equal Area with two standard parallels
West from Greenwich
Freeways
m ft

81
50 0 50 100 150 200 km
50 0 50 100 150 miles
75
82
6 7 8 9
A B C D E F
96 94 92 90
MISSOURI
ARKANSAS
LOUISIANA
MISSISSIPPI
TENNESSEE
Ozark Plateau
Boston Mts.
Ouachita Mts.
Springfield
Joplin
Rolla
Cape Girardeau
Tulsa
Broken Arrow
Muskogee
Fayetteville
Fort Smith
Jonesboro
Little Rock
North Little Rock
Hot Springs
Pine Bluff
Texarkana
El Dorado
Memphis
Jackson
Shreveport
Monroe
Alexandria
Lafayette
Baton Rouge
NEW ORLEANS
Gulfport
Biloxi
Hattiesburg
Meridian
Tupelo
Beaumont
Port Arthur
HOUSTON
Pasadena
Galveston
Tyler
Longview
DALLAS
Lake Charles
Vicksburg
Natchez
Greenville
Paducah
Ohio
Mississippi
Arkansas
Red
White
Ouachita
GULF OF MEXICO
Mississippi River Delta
Chandeleur Is.
Kingsville
TEXAS
MEXICO
Rio Grande
McAllen
Harlingen
Brownsville
Edinburg
Padre I.
Laguna Madre
PADRE ISLAND NAT. SEASHORE
continuation southwards on same scale
COPYRIGHT PHILIP'S
State Capitals
National Parks

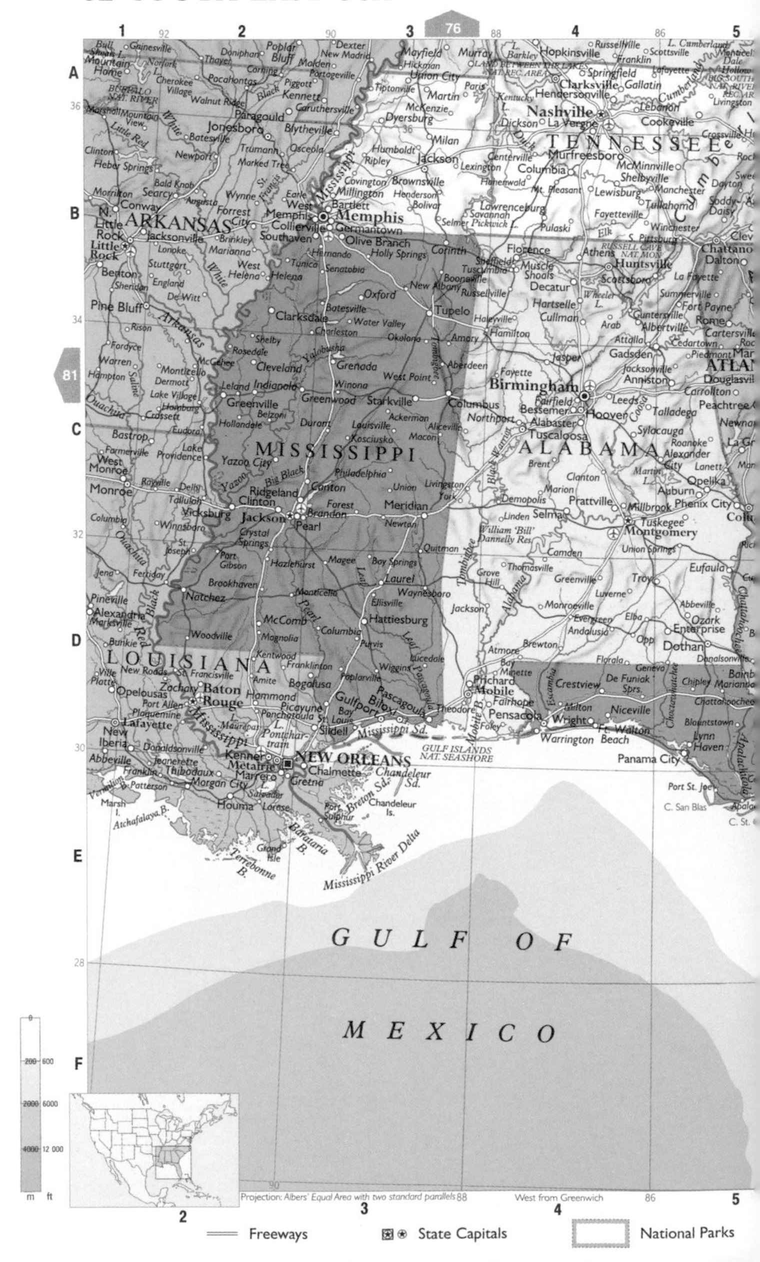
76
81
ARKANSAS
MISSISSIPPI
ALABAMA
TENNESSEE
LOUISIANA
GULF OF MEXICO
Memphis
Nashville
Birmingham
Jackson
Montgomery
Baton Rouge
NEW ORLEANS
Little Rock
Mobile
Pensacola
Huntsville
Tuscaloosa
Hattiesburg
Meridian
Tupelo
Gulfport
Biloxi
Pascagoula
Vicksburg
Natchez
Greenville
Columbus
Clarksville
Murfreesboro
Jonesboro
Pine Bluff
Monroe
Alexandria
Lafayette
Houma
Panama City
Dothan
Florence
Decatur
Gadsden
Anniston
Selma
Chattanooga
Mississippi River Delta
GULF ISLANDS NAT. SEASHORE
Mississippi Sd.
Chandeleur Sd.
Breton Sd.
L. Pontchartrain
Projection: Albers' Equal Area with two standard parallels
West from Greenwich
Freeways
State Capitals
National Parks

ATLANTIC OCEAN
NORTH CAROLINA
SOUTH CAROLINA
GEORGIA
FLORIDA
BAHAMAS
Raleigh
Charlotte
Greensboro
Durham
Winston-Salem
Fayetteville
Wilmington
Columbia
Charleston
Myrtle Beach
Augusta
Savannah
Jacksonville
ORLANDO
TAMPA
St. Petersburg
MIAMI
Daytona Beach
Gainesville
Sarasota
Fort Lauderdale
West Palm Beach
Hollywood
Hialeah
Grand Bahama
Freeport
Abaco I.
Little Abaco I.
Long Bay
Onslow Bay
Pamlico Sound
Albemarle Sd.
C. Hatteras
C. Lookout
C. Fear
C. Romain
C. Canaveral
Lake Okeechobee
Okefenokee Swamp
COPYRIGHT PHILIP'S

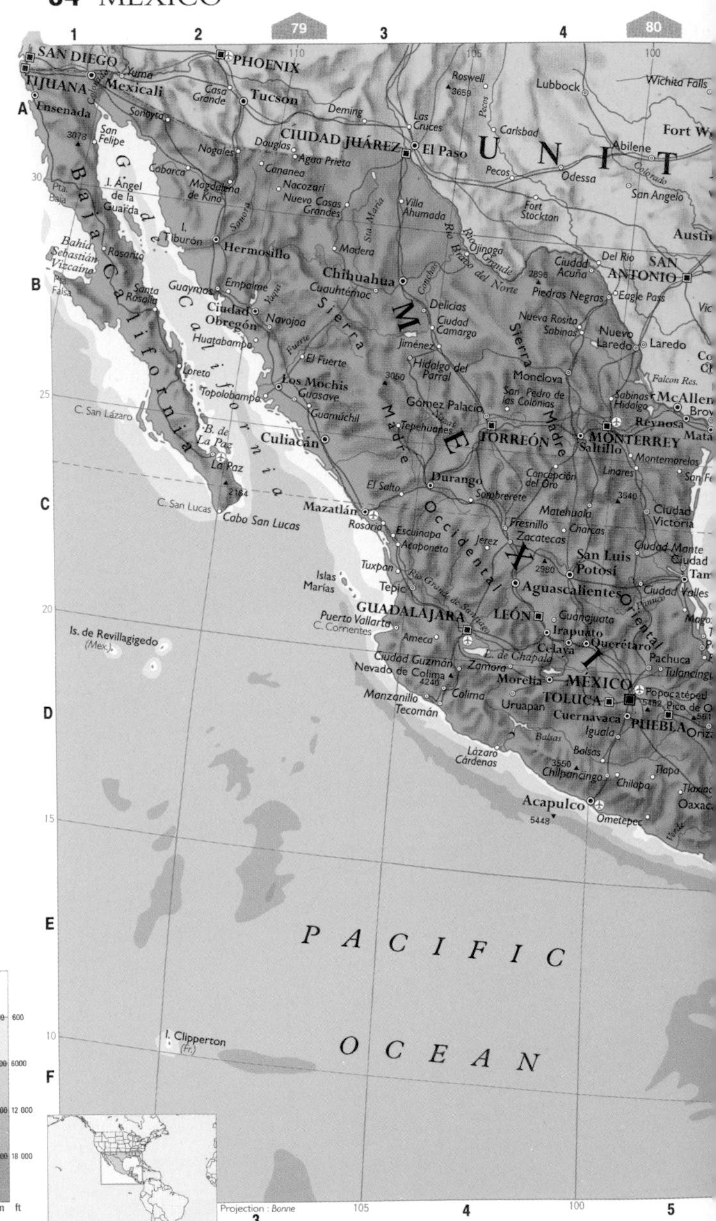

SAN DIEGO
TIJUANA
Mexicali
Ensenada
PHOENIX
Tucson
CIUDAD JUÁREZ
El Paso
Lubbock
Wichita Falls
Abilene
Odessa
San Angelo
UNITED
Baja California
Golfo de California
Hermosillo
Chihuahua
SAN ANTONIO
Piedras Negras
Nuevo Laredo
Laredo
McAllen
Reynosa
MONTERREY
Saltillo
TORREÓN
Culiacán
Los Mochis
La Paz
Cabo San Lucas
Mazatlán
Durango
Sierra Madre Occidental
Sierra Madre Oriental
MEXICO
Zacatecas
San Luis Potosí
Aguascalientes
GUADALAJARA
LEÓN
Irapuato
Querétaro
Celaya
Morelia
MÉXICO
TOLUCA
PUEBLA
Cuernavaca
Acapulco
Puerto Vallarta
Islas Marías
Is. de Revillagigedo (Mex.)
I. Clipperton (Fr.)
PACIFIC OCEAN
Projection : Bonne

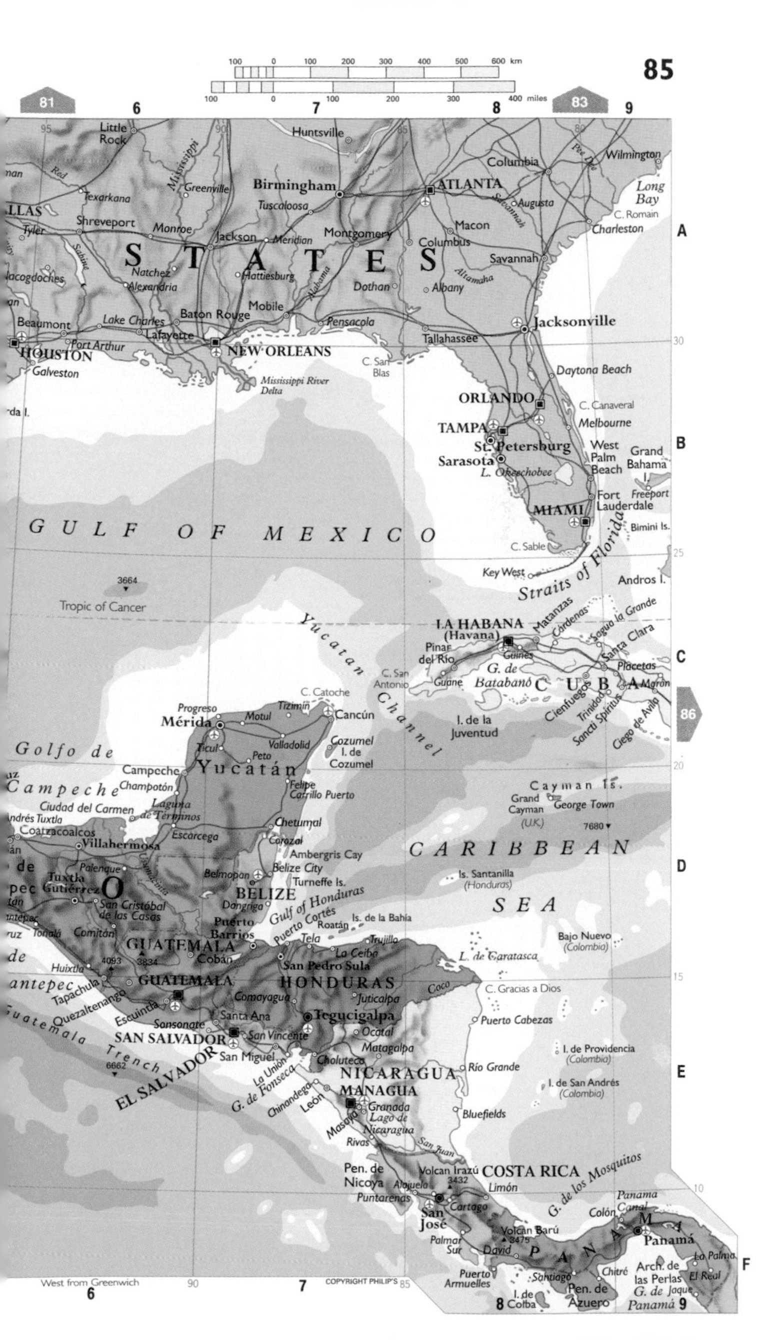
GULF OF MEXICO
CARIBBEAN SEA
STATES
Straits of Florida
Yucatan Channel
Golfo de Campeche
Gulf of Honduras
Tropic of Cancer
Little Rock
Huntsville
Birmingham
ATLANTA
Columbia
Wilmington
Long Bay
C. Romain
Charleston
Augusta
Macon
Columbus
Montgomery
Tuscaloosa
Greenville
Texarkana
Shreveport
Monroe
Jackson
Meridian
Tyler
Natchez
Alexandria
Hattiesburg
Dothan
Albany
Savannah
Mobile
Baton Rouge
Pensacola
Tallahassee
Jacksonville
Beaumont
Lake Charles
Lafayette
Port Arthur
HOUSTON
Galveston
NEW ORLEANS
Mississippi River Delta
C. San Blas
Daytona Beach
ORLANDO
C. Canaveral
Melbourne
TAMPA
St. Petersburg
Sarasota
L. Okeechobee
West Palm Beach
Grand Bahama I.
Freeport
Fort Lauderdale
MIAMI
Bimini Is.
C. Sable
Key West
Andros I.
LA HABANA (Havana)
Matanzas
Cárdenas
Sagua la Grande
Santa Clara
Placetas
Morón
Pinar del Río
Güines
G. de Batabanó
CUBA
Guane
C. San Antonio
Cienfuegos
Trinidad
Sancti Spíritus
Ciego de Avila
I. de la Juventud
C. Catoche
Progreso
Tizimín
Mérida
Motul
Cancún
Valladolid
Ticul
Peto
Cozumel
I. de Cozumel
Yucatán
Campeche
Champotón
Felipe Carrillo Puerto
Laguna de Términos
Ciudad del Carmen
Escárcega
Chetumal
Corozal
Ambergris Cay
Coatzacoalcos
Villahermosa
Palenque
Tuxtla Gutiérrez
Belmopan
Belize City
Turneffe Is.
BELIZE
Dangriga
San Cristóbal de las Casas
Comitán
Tonalá
Puerto Barrios
Puerto Cortés
Roatán
Is. de la Bahía
Tela
Trujillo
La Ceiba
GUATEMALA
Cobán
San Pedro Sula
HONDURAS
Huixtla
Tapachula
Quezaltenango
Escuintla
Comayagua
Juticalpa
Coco
Tegucigalpa
Santa Ana
Sonsonate
SAN SALVADOR
San Vicente
San Miguel
Ocotal
Matagalpa
Choluteca
La Unión
G. de Fonseca
EL SALVADOR
Guatemala Trench
NICARAGUA
MANAGUA
Chinandega
León
Granada
Masaya
Lago de Nicaragua
Rivas
San Juan
Bluefields
Río Grande
Puerto Cabezas
C. Gracias a Dios
L. de Caratasca
Bajo Nuevo (Colombia)
I. de Providencia (Colombia)
I. de San Andrés (Colombia)
Is. Santanilla (Honduras)
Cayman Is.
Grand Cayman (U.K.)
George Town
Pen. de Nicoya
Puntarenas
Alajuela
Volcan Irazú
COSTA RICA
Limón
San José
Cartago
G. de los Mosquitos
Panama Canal
Colón
PANAMA
Panamá
Volcan Barú
Palmar Sur
David
Puerto Armuelles
I. de Coiba
Santiago
Chitré
Pen. de Azuero
Arch. de las Perlas
G. de Panamá
La Palma
El Real
Jaque
3664
7680
6662
4093
3834
3432
3475
West from Greenwich
COPYRIGHT PHILIP'S
81
83
86

GULF OF MEXICO
U.S.A.
ORLANDO
TAMPA
St. Petersburg
Sarasota
L. Okeechobee
Daytona Beach
C. Canaveral
Melbourne
West Palm Beach
Fort Lauderdale
MIAMI
C. Sable
Key West
Straits of Florida
Grand Bahama I.
Freeport
Abaco I.
Bimini Is.
New Providence I.
Nassau
Eleuthera I.
Andros I.
BAHAMAS
Cat I.
Great Exuma I.
Long I.
Mississippi River Delta
Tropic of Cancer
Yucatan Channel
LA HABANA (Havana)
Matanzas
Cárdenas
Sagua la Grande
Santa Clara
Pinar del Río
Güines
G. de Batabanó
C. San Antonio
Guane
CUBA
Placetas
Morón
Camagüey
Nuevitas
Cienfuegos
Trinidad
Sancti Spíritus
Ciego de Avila
Holguín
Banes
Las Tunas
I. de la Juventud
Manzanillo
1972
Bayamo
Santiago de Cuba
Guantánamo
Greater
Cayman Is.
Grand Cayman (U.K.)
George Town
7680
Montego Bay
Mandeville
Spanish Town
Kingston
JAMAICA
Is. Santanilla (Honduras)
Pedro Cays (Jamaica)
Bajo Nuevo (Colombia)
Jérém
Les Ca
C. Catoche
Progreso
Tizimín
Cancún
Motul
Mérida
Valladolid
Ticul
Peto
Cozumel
I. de Cozumel
Yucatán
Campeche
Champotón
Felipe Carrillo Puerto
MEXICO
Chetumal
Escárcega
Corozal
Ambergris Cay
Belmopan
Belize City
Turneffe Is.
BELIZE
Dangriga
Gulf of Honduras
Puerto Cortés
Roatán
Is. de la Bahía
Puerto Barrios
Tela
Trujillo
La Ceiba
Cobán
GUATEMALA
San Pedro Sula
HONDURAS
L. de Caratasca
C. Gracias a Dios
Coco
Comayagua
Juticalpa
Santa Ana
SAN SALVADOR
Tegucigalpa
Sonsonate
San Vincente
Ocotal
Puerto Cabezas
EL SALVADOR
San Miguel
La Unión
Choluteca
Matagalpa
I. de Providencia (Colombia)
G. de Fonseca
NICARAGUA
Río Grande
MANAGUA
Chinandega
León
Granada
I. de San Andrés (Colombia)
Masaya
Lago de Nicaragua
Bluefields
Rivas
San Juan
CARI
Pen. de Nicoya
Alajuela
Volcan Irazú
3432
COSTA RICA
Limón
G. de los Mosquitos
Puntarenas
Cartago
San José
Palmar Sur
Volcán Barú
3475
David
Panama Canal
Colón
PANAMA
Panamá
Puerto Armuelles
Santiago
Chitré
Arch. de las Perlas
Pen. de Azuero
I. de Coiba
G. de Panamá
La Palma
El Real
Jaqué
Riosucio
Santa Ma
BARRANQUILLA
Cartagena
G. del Darién
Sincelejo
Montería
Barrancab
3960
Antioquia
Bello
G. de Cupica
Quibdó
C. Corrientes
Manizales
Pereira
Armenia
Buenaventura
CALI
Palmira
Huila
5750
Neiva
Popayán
Volcan Puracé
4646
Magdalena
PACIFIC OCEAN
I. del Coco (C. Rica)
I. de Malpelo (Colombia)
Projection : Bonne
West from Greenwich
m
ft
0
200
600
2000
6000
4000
12 000
6000
18 000

SARGASSO SEA
ATLANTIC OCEAN
Tropic of Cancer
Turks & Caicos Is. (U.K.)
Cockburn Town
Puerto Rico Trench
Mona Passage
SAN JUAN
DOMINICAN REP.
SANTO DOMINGO
PUERTO RICO (U.S.A.)
Virgin Is. (U.S.A.) (U.K.)
ST. KITTS & NEVIS
ANTIGUA & BARBUDA
GUADELOUPE (Fr.)
DOMINICA
MARTINIQUE (Fr.)
ST. LUCIA
BARBADOS
ST. VINCENT & THE GRENADINES
GRENADA
Leeward Islands
Windward Islands
Lesser Antilles
Hispaniola
TRINIDAD & TOBAGO
NETH. ANTILLES
CARACAS
MARACAIBO
VALENCIA
VENEZUELA
GUYANA
SURINAME
COLOMBIA
BRAZIL
Sierra Pacaraima
Mt. Roraima 2772
Equator
COPYRIGHT PHILIP'S

90
92

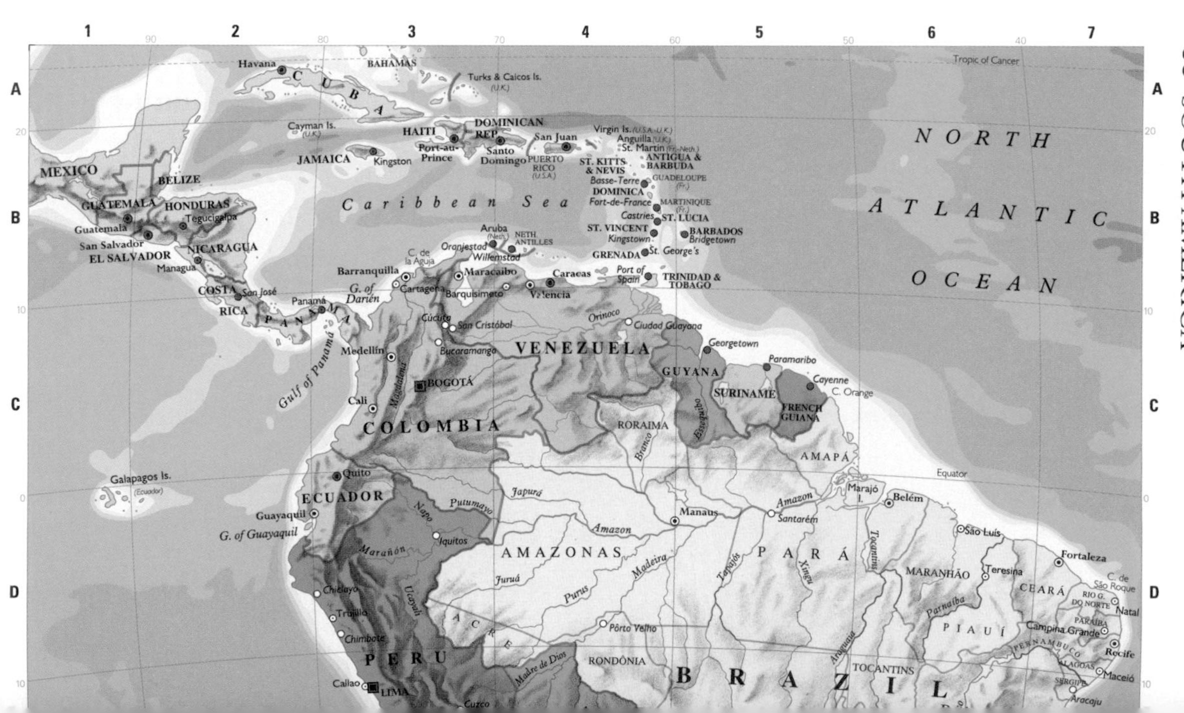
NORTH ATLANTIC OCEAN
Caribbean Sea
Tropic of Cancer
Equator
Gulf of Panama
G. of Guayaquil
G. of Darién
MEXICO
BELIZE
GUATEMALA
HONDURAS
EL SALVADOR
NICARAGUA
COSTA RICA
PANAMA
CUBA
BAHAMAS
JAMAICA
HAITI
DOMINICAN REP.
PUERTO RICO (U.S.A.)
Turks & Caicos Is. (U.K.)
Cayman Is. (U.K.)
Virgin Is. (U.S.A.-U.K.)
Anguilla (U.K.)
St. Martin (Fr.-Neth.)
ST. KITTS & NEVIS
ANTIGUA & BARBUDA
GUADELOUPE (Fr.)
DOMINICA
MARTINIQUE (Fr.)
ST. LUCIA
ST. VINCENT
GRENADA
BARBADOS
TRINIDAD & TOBAGO
Aruba (Neth.)
NETH. ANTILLES
VENEZUELA
COLOMBIA
ECUADOR
PERU
GUYANA
SURINAME
FRENCH GUIANA
BRAZIL
AMAZONAS
PARÁ
AMAPÁ
RORAIMA
ACRE
RONDÔNIA
MARANHÃO
PIAUÍ
CEARÁ
TOCANTINS
RIO G. DO NORTE
PARAÍBA
PERNAMBUCO
ALAGOAS
SERGIPE
Galapagos Is. (Ecuador)
Havana
Kingston
Port-au-Prince
Santo Domingo
San Juan
Basse-Terre
Fort-de-France
Castries
Kingstown
St. George's
Bridgetown
Port of Spain
Oranjestad
Willemstad
C. de la Aguja
Guatemala
San Salvador
Tegucigalpa
Managua
San José
Panamá
Barranquilla
Cartagena
Medellín
BOGOTÁ
Cali
Cúcuta
San Cristóbal
Bucaramanga
Quito
Guayaquil
LIMA
Callao
Cuzco
Maracaibo
Barquisimeto
Valencia
Caracas
Ciudad Guayana
Georgetown
Paramaribo
Cayenne
C. Orange
Marajó I.
Manaus
Belém
Santarém
São Luís
Teresina
Fortaleza
C. de São Roque
Natal
Campina Grande
Recife
Maceió
Aracaju
Iquitos
Chiclayo
Trujillo
Chimbote
Pôrto Velho
Amazon
Orinoco
Magdalena
Essequibo
Branco
Japurá
Putumayo
Napo
Marañón
Ucayali
Juruá
Purus
Madeira
Madre de Dios
Tapajós
Xingu
Tocantins
Araguaia
Parnaíba

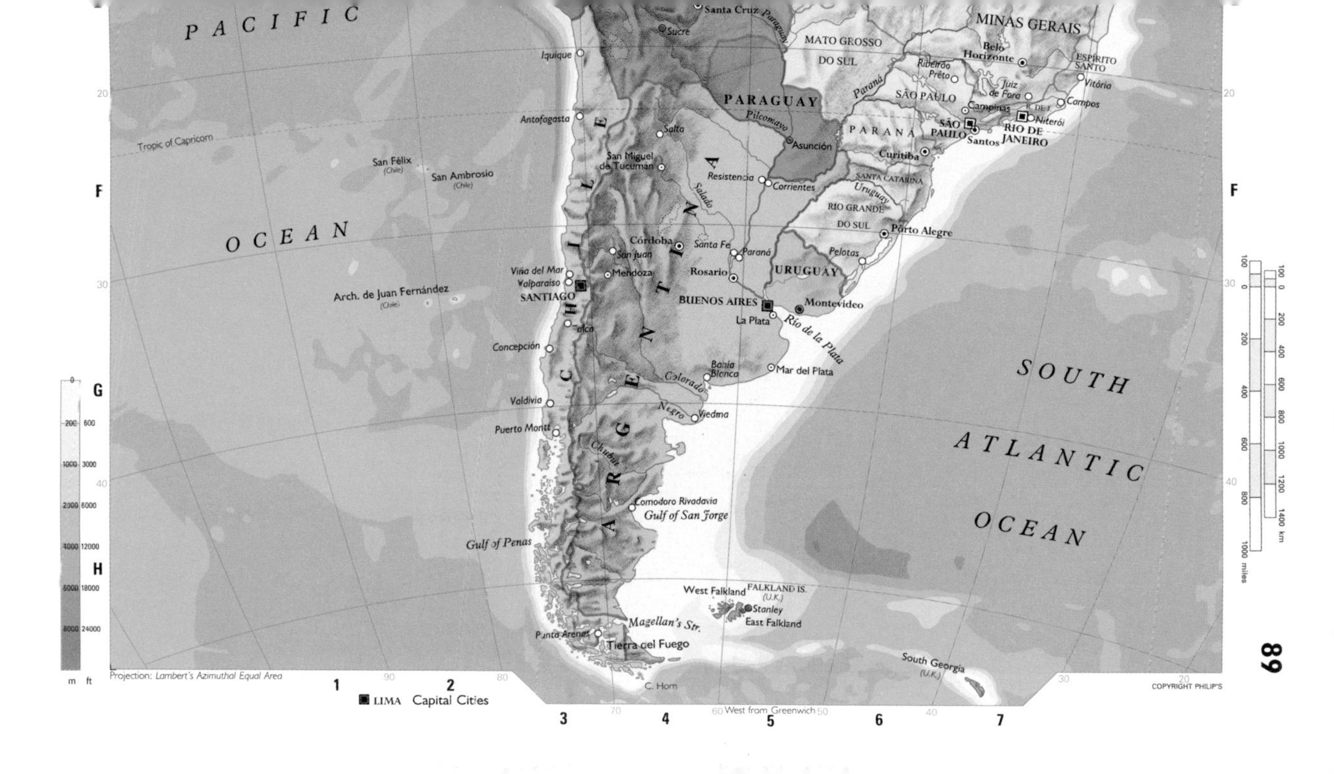
PACIFIC OCEAN
SOUTH ATLANTIC OCEAN
ARGENTINA
CHILE
PARAGUAY
URUGUAY
MATO GROSSO DO SUL
MINAS GERAIS
ESPÍRITO SANTO
SÃO PAULO
PARANÁ
SANTA CATARINA
RIO GRANDE DO SUL
Santa Cruz
Sucre
Paraguay
Iquique
Antofagasta
Salta
San Miguel de Tucumán
Pilcomayo
Asunción
Resistencia
Corrientes
Salado
Córdoba
San Juan
Mendoza
Santa Fe
Paraná
Rosario
Viña del Mar
Valparaíso
SANTIAGO
BUENOS AIRES
Montevideo
La Plata
Río de la Plata
Concepción
Bahía Blanca
Mar del Plata
Colorado
Valdivia
Negro
Viedma
Puerto Montt
Chubut
Comodoro Rivadavia
Gulf of San Jorge
Gulf of Penas
West Falkland
FALKLAND IS. (U.K.)
Stanley
East Falkland
Magellan's Str.
Punta Arenas
Tierra del Fuego
C. Horn
South Georgia (U.K.)
Belo Horizonte
Ribeirão Prêto
Juiz de Fora
Vitória
Campos
Campinas
SÃO PAULO
Santos
RIO DE JANEIRO
Niterói
Curitiba
Uruguay
Pôrto Alegre
Pelotas
Tropic of Capricorn
San Félix (Chile)
San Ambrosio (Chile)
Arch. de Juan Fernández (Chile)
LIMA Capital Cities
Projection: Lambert's Azimuthal Equal Area
West from Greenwich
m ft
0
200 600
1000 3000
2000 6000
4000 12000
6000 18000
8000 24000
100 0 200 400 600 800 1000 1200 1400 km
100 0 200 400 600 800 1000 miles
F
G
H
1 2 3 4 5 6 7
COPYRIGHT PHILIP'S

CARIBBEAN SEA
ATLANTIC OCEAN
PACIFIC
NICARAGUA
COSTA RICA
PANAMA
COLOMBIA
VENEZUELA
GUYANA
SURINAME
ECUADOR
RORAIMA
TRINIDAD & TOBAGO
GRENADA
MANAGUA
San José
BARRANQUILLA
Cartagena
MARACAIBO
CARACAS
VALENCIA
Barquisimeto
Ciudad Guayana
Georgetown
MEDELLÍN
BOGOTÁ
CALI
QUITO
GUAYAQUIL
MANAUS
Iquitos
Sierra Pacaraima
Serra Parima
Equator
85
87
92

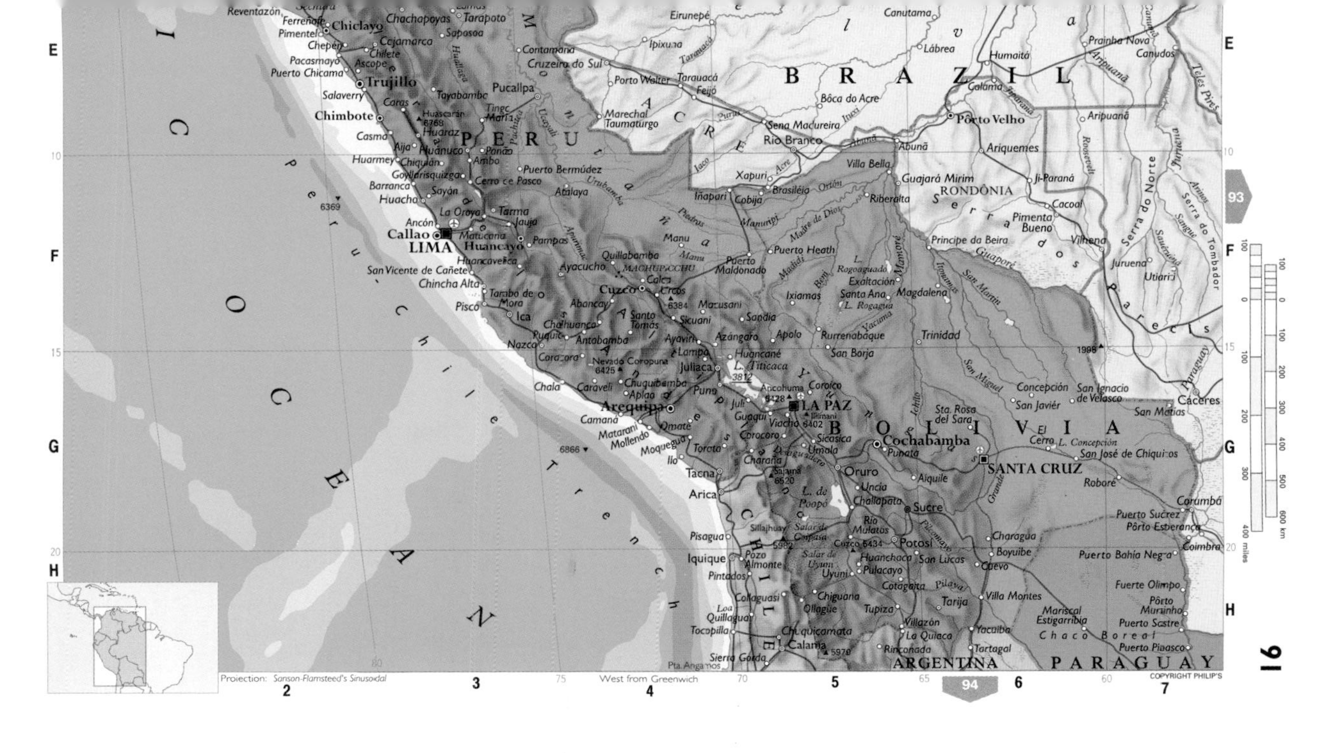

B R A Z I L
P E R U
B O L I V I A
C H I L E
ARGENTINA
P A R A G U A Y
A C R E
RONDÔNIA
LIMA
LA PAZ
SANTA CRUZ
Callao
Cochabamba
Arequipa
Cuzco
Huancayo
Trujillo
Chiclayo
Chimbote
Oruro
Sucre
Potosí
Iquique
Arica
Tacna
Pôrto Velho
Rio Branco
Pucallpa
Ica
Pisco
Juliaca
Puno
L. Titicaca
Serra do Norte
Serra do Tombador
Serra dos Parecis
Chaco Boreal
Peru-Chile Trench
93
94
E
F
G
H
2
3
4
5
6
7
100 0 100 200 300 400 500 600 km
100 0 100 200 300 400 miles
Projection: Sanson-Flamsteed's Sinusoidal
West from Greenwich
COPYRIGHT PHILIP'S

SOUTH AMERICA-NORTH-EAST

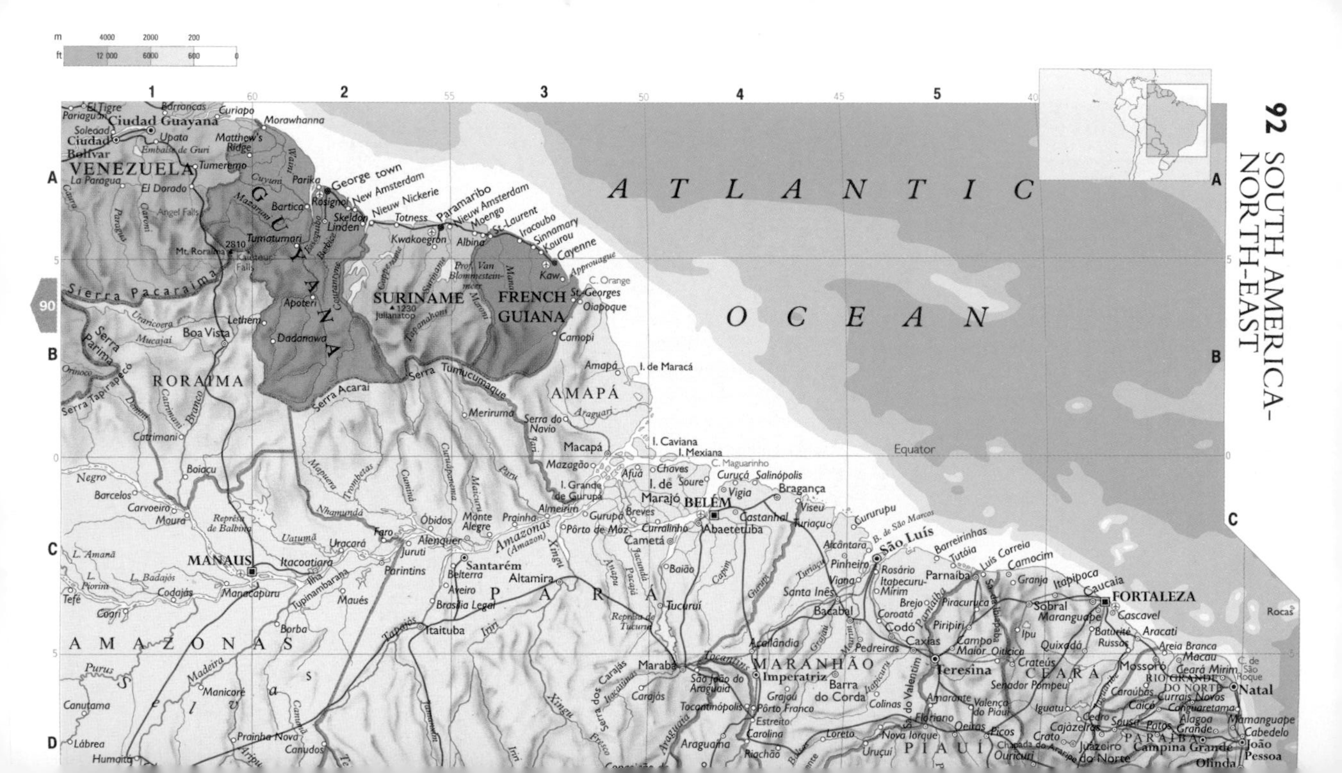

90

BRAZIL
BOLIVIA
PARAGUAY
ARGENTINA
RONDÔNIA
MATO GROSSO
TOCANTINS
BAHIA
GOIÁS
MATO GROSSO DO SUL
MINAS GERAIS
SÃO PAULO
PARANÁ
RIO DE JANEIRO
ESPÍRITO SANTO
SERGIPE
ALAGOAS
DIST. FED.
SALVADOR
BRASÍLIA
GOIÂNIA
BELO HORIZONTE
RIO DE JANEIRO
SÃO PAULO
CAMPINAS
SANTOS
CURITIBA
ASUNCIÓN
SANTA CRUZ
Cuiabá
Campo Grande
Vitória
Aracaju
Uberlândia
Ribeirão Prêto
Londrina
Joinville
Corrientes
Resistencia
Planalto do Mato Grosso
Serra do Roncador
Serra do Tombador
Pantanal
Chaco Boreal
Chaco Central
Tropic of Capricorn
West from Greenwich
Projection: Sanson-Flamsteed's Sinusoidal
COPYRIGHT PHILIP'S
100 0 100 200 300 400 500 600 km
100 0 100 200 300 400 miles
91
94

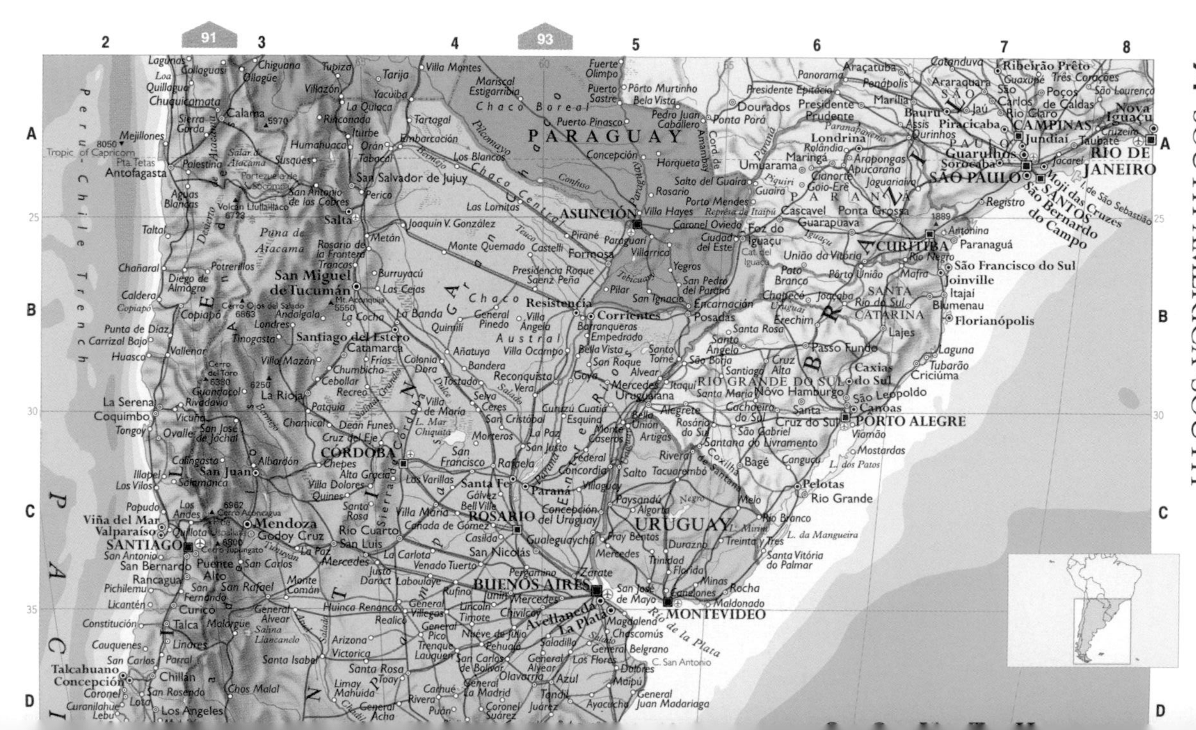
PARAGUAY
URUGUAY
ASUNCIÓN
MONTEVIDEO
BUENOS AIRES
SANTIAGO
RIO DE JANEIRO
SÃO PAULO
PÔRTO ALEGRE
CURITIBA
CÓRDOBA
ROSARIO
CAMPINAS
SANTOS
Mendoza
San Miguel de Tucumán
Salta
Antofagasta
Valparaíso
Viña del Mar
Concepción
La Plata
Corrientes
Resistencia
Santa Fe
Paraná
Florianópolis
São Francisco do Sul
Peru-Chile Trench
Chaco Boreal
Chaco Central
Chaco Austral
Río de la Plata
Tropic of Capricorn
RIO GRANDE DO SUL
SANTA CATARINA
PARANÁ
PACIFIC
91
93

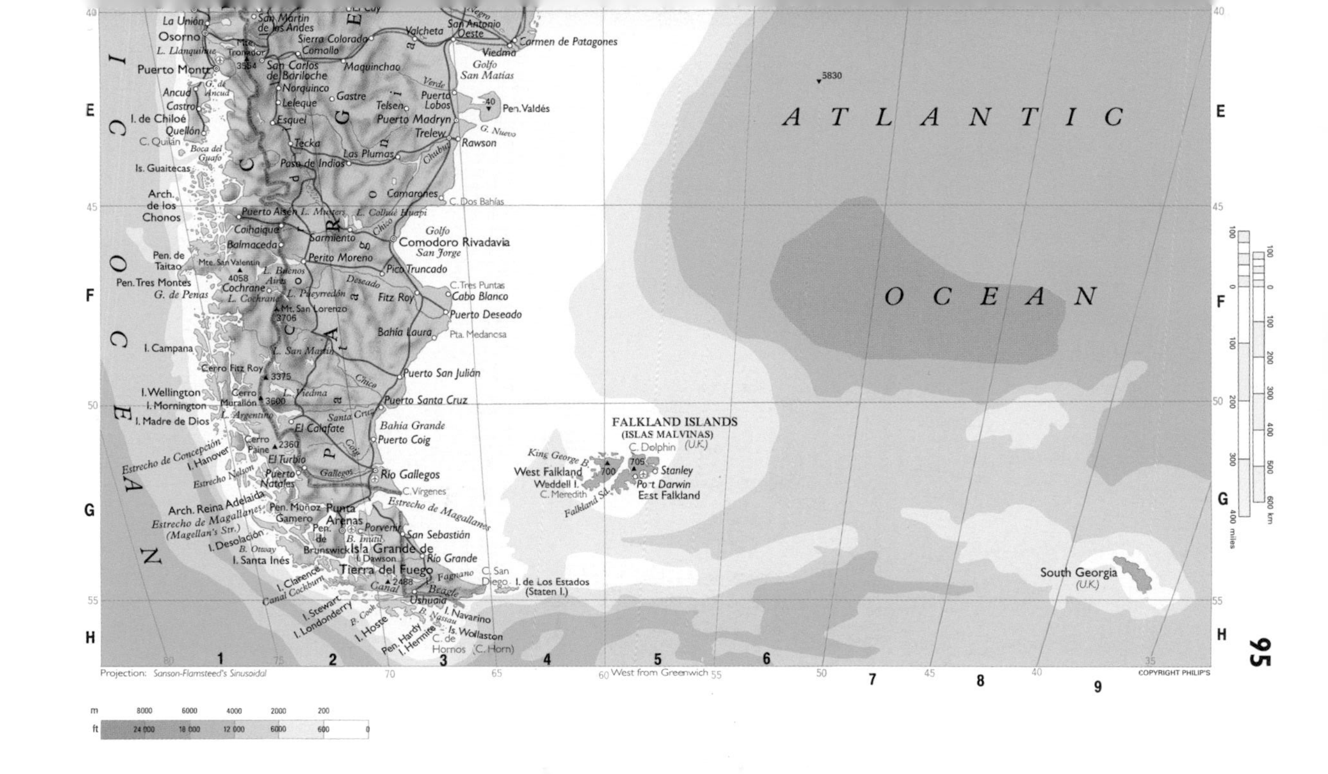
ATLANTIC OCEAN
FALKLAND ISLANDS (ISLAS MALVINAS) (U.K.)
West Falkland
East Falkland
Stanley
Port Darwin
King George B.
Weddell I.
C. Meredith
C. Dolphin
Falkland Sd.
South Georgia (U.K.)
La Unión
Osorno
L. Llanquihue
Puerto Montt
Ancud
Castro
I. de Chiloé
Quellón
C. Quilán
Boca del Guafo
Is. Guaitecas
Arch. de los Chonos
Pen. de Taitao
Pen. Tres Montes
G. de Penas
I. Campana
I. Wellington
I. Mornington
I. Madre de Dios
Estrecho de Concepción
I. Hanover
Estrecho Nelson
Arch. Reina Adelaida
Estrecho de Magallanes (Magellan's Str.)
I. Desolación
B. Otway
I. Santa Inés
I. Clarence
Canal Cockburn
I. Stewart
I. Londonderry
I. Hoste
Pen. Hardy
I. Hermite
C. de Hornos (C. Horn)
Is. Wollaston
I. Navarino
Ushuaia
Isla Grande de Tierra del Fuego
I. de Los Estados (Staten I.)
C. San Diego
Río Grande
San Sebastián
Porvenir
Punta Arenas
Pen. Muñoz Gamero
Pen. de Brunswick
I. Dawson
B. Inútil
Estrecho de Magallanes
C. Vírgenes
Río Gallegos
Puerto Natales
El Turbio
Cerro Paine
El Calafate
L. Argentino
Cerro Murallón
Cerro Fitz Roy
L. Viedma
Puerto Coig
Bahía Grande
Puerto Santa Cruz
Puerto San Julián
Bahía Laura
Pta. Medanosa
Puerto Deseado
Cabo Blanco
C. Tres Puntas
Fitz Roy
Pico Truncado
Comodoro Rivadavia
Golfo San Jorge
Perito Moreno
Sarmiento
Coihaique
Puerto Aisén
Balmaceda
Cochrane
L. Cochrane
L. Pueyrredón
L. Buenos Aires
Mte. San Valentín
Mt. San Lorenzo
Camarones
C. Dos Bahías
Rawson
Trelew
Puerto Madryn
Telsen
Puerto Lobos
Pen. Valdés
G. Nuevo
Golfo San Matías
Viedma
Carmen de Patagones
San Antonio Oeste
Valcheta
Sierra Colorada
Comallo
Maquinchao
San Carlos de Bariloche
Norquinco
Leleque
Gastre
Esquel
Tecka
Paso de Indios
Las Plumas
San Martín de los Andes
Mte. Tronador
L. Musters
L. Colhué Huapi
Deseado
Chico
Chubut
Santa Cruz
Coig
Gallegos
Canal Beagle
L. Fagnano
B. Nassau
B. Cook
PATAGONIA
PACIFIC OCEAN
West from Greenwich
Projection: Sanson-Flamsteed's Sinusoidal
m 8000 6000 4000 2000 200
ft 24 000 18 000 12 000 6000 600 0
100 0 100 200 300 400 500 600 km
100 0 100 200 300 400 miles

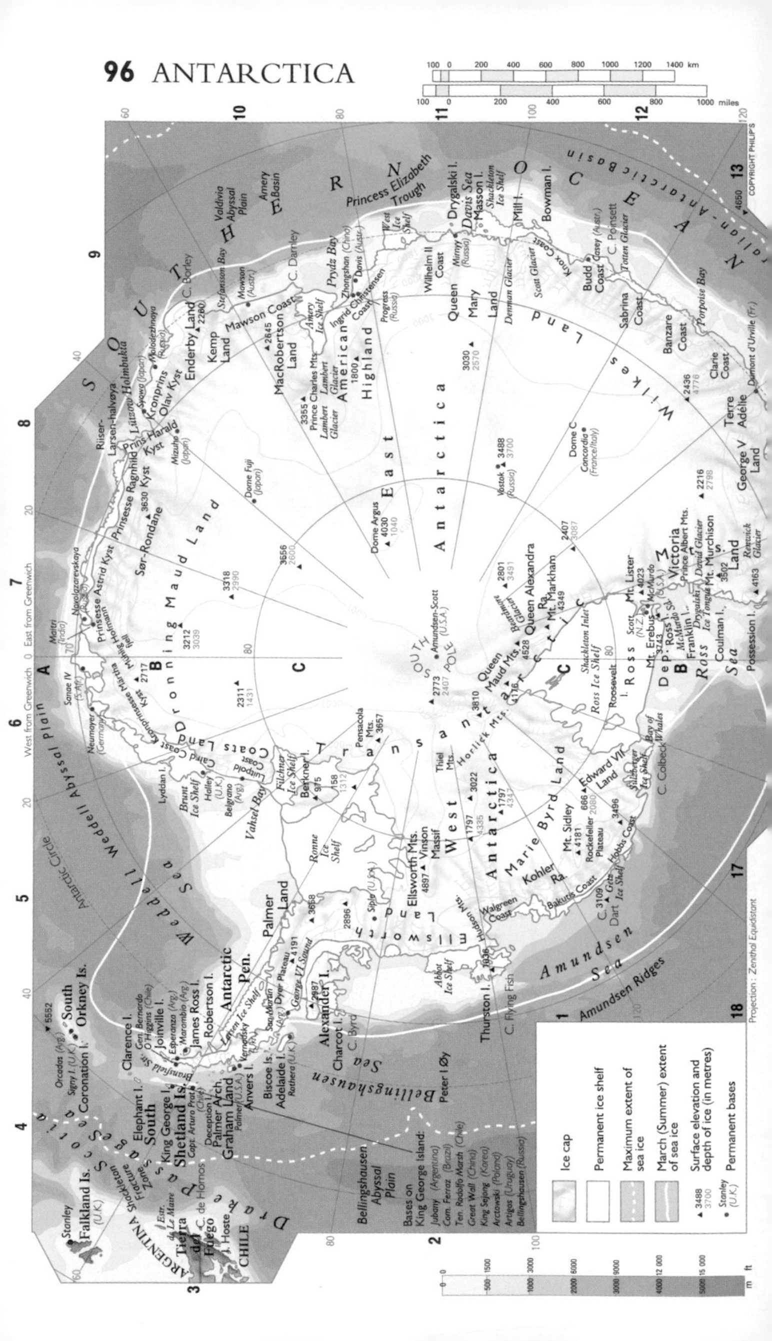

S O U T H E R N O C E A N
Weddell Abyssal plain
Weddell Sea
Antarctic Circle
Drake Passage
Scotia Sea
Bellingshausen Sea
Amundsen Sea
Amundsen Ridges
Ross Sea
Davis Sea
Indian - Antarctic Basin
East Antarctica
West Antarctica
Transantarctic Mts.
Ellsworth Land
Marie Byrd Land
Dronning Maud Land
Wilkes Land
American Highland
Queen Mary Land
Coats Land
Palmer Land
Graham Land
Antarctic Pen.
Victoria Land
George V Land
Terre Adélie
Enderby Land
Kemp Land
MacRobertson Land
Mawson Coast
Prinsesse Ragnhild Kyst
Prinsesse Astrid Kyst
Prins Harald Kyst
Kronprins Olav Kyst
Princess Elizabeth Trough
Amery Basin
Valdivia Abyssal Plain
Bellingshausen Abyssal Plain
Ronne Ice Shelf
Filchner Ice Shelf
Ross Ice Shelf
Amery Ice Shelf
Larsen Ice Shelf
Brunt Ice Shelf
Shackleton Ice Shelf
West Ice Shelf
Abbot Ice Shelf
Getz Ice Shelf
Sulzberger Ice Shelf
Ellsworth Mts.
Vinson Massif 4897
Queen Maud Mts.
Queen Alexandra Ra.
Horlick Mts.
Thiel Mts.
Pensacola Mts.
Prince Charles Mts.
Sør-Rondane
Lambert Glacier
Beardmore Glacier
Denman Glacier
Scott Glacier
Totten Glacier
Mt. Erebus 3743
Mt. Markham 4349
Mt. Lister 4023
Mt. Sidley 4181
Mt. Murchison
Dome Argus 4030
Dome Fuji (Japan)
Dome C
Vostok (Russia)
Concordia (France/Italy)
Amundsen-Scott (U.S.A.)
SOUTH POLE
McMurdo (U.S.A.)
Scott (N.Z.)
Mawson (Austr.)
Davis (Austr.)
Casey (Austr.)
Mirnyy (Russia)
Progress (Russia)
Zhongshan (China)
Dumont d'Urville (Fr.)
Syowa (Japan)
Mizuho (Japan)
Molodezhnaya (Russia)
Novolazarevskaya (Russia)
Maitri (India)
Sanae IV (S.Afr.)
Neumayer (Germany)
Halley (U.K.)
Belgrano (Arg.)
Rothera (U.K.)
Palmer (U.S.A.)
Vernadsky (Ukr.)
Esperanza (Arg.)
Marambio (Arg.)
Orcadas (Arg.)
Signy I. (U.K.)
South Orkney Is.
South Shetland Is.
Falkland Is. (U.K.)
Stanley
Tierra del Fuego
ARGENTINA
CHILE
Alexander I.
Charcot I.
Adelaide I.
Thurston I.
Roosevelt I.
Berkner I.
Ross I.
Peter I Øy
Bases on King George Island:
Jubany (Argentina)
Com. Ferraz (Brazil)
Ten. Rodolfo Marsh (Chile)
Great Wall (China)
King Sejong (Korea)
Arctowski (Poland)
Artigas (Uruguay)
Bellingshausen (Russia)
Ice cap
Permanent ice shelf
Maximum extent of sea ice
March (Summer) extent of sea ice
Surface elevation and depth of ice (in metres)
Permanent bases
West from Greenwich
East from Greenwich
Projection : Zenithal Equidistant
COPYRIGHT PHILIP'S

INDEX TO MAP PAGES

The index contains the names of all the principal places and features shown on the world maps. Physical features composed of a proper name (Erie) and a description (Lake) are positioned alphabetically by the proper name. The description is positioned after the proper name and is usually abbreviated:

Erie, L. **76 C5**

Where a description forms part of a settlement or administrative name, however, it is always written in full and put in its true alphabetical position:

Lake Charles **81 D7**

Names beginning St. are alphabetized under Saint, but Sankt, Sant, Santa and San are all spelt in full and are alphabetized accordingly.

The number in bold type which follows each name in the index refers to the number of the map page where that feature or place will be found. This is usually the largest scale at which the place or feature appears.

The letter and figure which are in bold type immediately after the page number give the grid square on the map page, within which the feature is situated.

Rivers are indexed to their mouths or confluences, and carry the symbol → after their names. The following symbols are also used in the index: ■ country, ▨ overseas territory or dependency, □ first order administrative area, △ national park.

A

B

D

H

I

L

O

P